Everywhere and Nowhere

Everywhere and Nowhere

Anonymity and Mediation in
Eighteenth-Century Britain

MARK VARESCHI

University of Minnesota Press
Minneapolis
London

The University of Minnesota Press gratefully acknowledges the work of Richard Grusin, editorial consultant, on this project.

An earlier version of chapter 3 was originally published as "Attribution and Repetition: The Case of Defoe and the Circulating Library" in *Eighteenth-Century Life* (2012) 36(2): 36–59. An earlier version of part of chapter 4 was previously published as "Motive, Intention, Anonymity, and *Evelina*," *ELH* 82, no. 4 (2015): 1135–58; copyright 2015 The Johns Hopkins University Press.

Published by the University of Minnesota Press
111 Third Avenue South, Suite 290
Minneapolis, MN 55401-2520
http://www.upress.umn.edu

ISBN 978-1-5179-0406-7 (hc)
ISBN 978-1-5179-0407-4 (pb)

A Cataloging-in-Publication record for this book is available from the Library of Congress.

Printed in the United States of America on acid-free paper

The University of Minnesota is an equal-opportunity educator and employer.

For my father, Richard

Contents

Introduction

Everywhere and Nowhere

This book considers the ubiquity and near-invisibility of anonymity and mediation in the publication and circulation of literature. Anonymous authorship was typical and therefore everywhere: from pamphlets to prose fiction to poems to pantomimes, attributed authorship was far from the norm. However, because anonymity is largely characterized as absence—that is, the absence of the author's name on the page—it was also nowhere.[1] My title reverses a formulation offered by Susan Lanser in her discussion of implied authorship and anonymity as "nowhere and everywhere" to signal both the pervasiveness of anonymity and the broadness of my study.[2]

Just as anonymity is often "nowhere" on the page, it has likewise been consigned to "nowhere" in literary studies. Literary critics and literary historians have been generally unable to account for anonymity as anything more than a footnote or curiosity.[3] I take the opposite tack and attend to the widespread phenomenon of authorial anonymity in the long eighteenth century. Focusing on anonymity allows the relationship between mediation and literariness to come to the fore. The literary is a complex of human, material, and verbal action whose ontological and epistemological status shifts over time through processes of circulation. Anonymity is the condition under which these multiple forms of action become most evident. When presented with the name of the author, we typically come to characterize and know the text through the figure of the author: we have a named agent ostensibly responsible for the text; we have a name under which to catalog the text. The absence of the authorial name complicates the whole.

What that complication makes palpable is the multiple agents and actions—human and nonhuman—involved in the production, circulation, and reception of a text. Mediation names these processes and the intertwining of human and nonhuman action in the production of meaning, yet, like anonymity, that mediation is taken to be invisible. In the absence of the authorial name, putatively transparent media and processes of mediation finally become visible. What is revealed when mediation comes to the fore is not simply media as passive intervening substances but media as active agents. Part of why literature "works," and continues to work over time, this book shows, is because it is inherently a complex of agents and actions.

My study is undergirded by quantitative analyses of both eighteenth-century and contemporary catalogs—from William Rufus Chetwood's *The British Theatre* (1750) to English Short Title Catalog (ESTC)—to establish the ubiquity of anonymity in the period and the ways it has been made to disappear. For example, roughly 21 percent of the texts in ESTC remain anonymous; yet, because anonymity has typically been consigned to nowhere, searching for those texts through the online user interface is an impossibility. I thus offer a history of cataloging and show the limits of recent mass digitization and cataloging efforts and chart a method for exploring their absences and exclusions.

I bring together fields that have been largely removed from each other—book history and media theory—to show the entangled and mutually revealing relationship between mediation and anonymity. The work of D. F. McKenzie, and that of other book historians, has greatly expanded our notion of what constitutes the literary text. But despite their groundbreaking attention to the material "stuff" of the book—from typography to graphic design to book binding—these studies inevitably have to locate action and intention in known human actors. This results in a delicate, and often unsatisfactory, balance being struck between the interpretive richness offered by their attention to the material text and the desire to justify such interpretations through recourse to the choices of authors, printers, publishers, apprentices, and others. Recent work in media theory, however, has offered expanded notions of agential action that allow for a fuller account of the literary artifact without necessarily attributing that action to humans alone.

I extend the insights of media theory further by asking how a theory of mediation renews questions about agency and intention. Such questions have been, of course, at the heart of literary criticism since its inception. I seek to understand the material instantiation of the literary artifact and the multilayered complex of agencies and intentions that both bring about and inhere in the artifact. I do not reduce the objects of my analysis to textuality. Rather, I bring a media-specific analysis to my archive and take up debates about the place of intention in the analysis of cultural artifacts to offer an attenuated account of the nature and place of intention in literary interpretation. My account offers an alternate genealogy of the concept of intention that follows from analytic philosophy and understands intention as a description of action, not as a mental state. Crucially, this formulation of intention is still largely observed by those in textual studies.[4] Given the ubiquity of anonymity in the period, this book asks how the absence and presence of authorial names compels us to reimagine the place of action and intention in literary interpretation and the production of meaning.

Counting Anonymous

Establishing just how typical anonymous publication was over the course of the eighteenth century is, however, no easy task. The tendency toward making anonymity disappear through retroactive authorial attribution in databases and on modern editions puts the scholar in the position of recovering a phenomenon that has been made to disappear. This book offers analyses of quantitative data of publication, cataloging, and attribution to reveal patterns of thought and networks of textual circulation. These methods have been invaluable in allowing me to move beyond the organizing categories within literary studies, of which the named authorship is central, to see a phenomenon that is primarily only known through a blank space on the title page.

That blank space, however, poses yet another challenge. While we may identify and count all the woman authors in a given decade or count all the novels and novel-like books published in a given year, how do we count those blank spaces? I mean this question very literally. To quantify anonymous texts in a given period or in a certain location requires identifying those texts without a named author in or on a text. James Raven's work to count anonymous novels proceeds in just such a manner; he has examined eighteenth- and nineteenth-century novels in libraries around the world to identify their bibliographic features and verify their anonymity or named authorship.[5]

Online databases, such as Eighteenth-Century Collections Online (ECCO) and ESTC, have undoubtedly revolutionized the research process of scholars by providing access to hundreds of thousands of texts as highly remediated digital images available through keyword searching, in the case of ECCO, or allowed rapid apprehension of the output of a given publisher in a given year, as in the case of ESTC.[6] Research questions that once required travel across thousands of miles to answer can, in many cases, be answered in mere minutes by the scholar adept at searching and navigating these databases. Questions about anonymous publication, however, are not so easily answered. One of the consequences of the emphasis on attribution as a means of dealing with anonymity is the near-invisibility of both once- and still-anonymous texts in many current online resources of eighteenth-century texts. Though searching for "Anon." in Early English Books Online yields those documents with nothing in the author field, there is no way to perform a similar search in ECCO or ESTC.

What this means is that for the typical user of ECCO or ESTC, for whom the databases are accessed through her web browser, anonymous texts are mostly invisible unless a user is looking for a specific title. There is no way to perform an author query with nothing in the author field of either database. Moreover, retroactive attribution has filled in the author field for countless texts and thus obscured their initial anonymity. Although one of the promises of quantitative approaches to literary history has been access to, and consideration of, what Franco Moretti has called the "great unread," thousands of eighteenth-century texts remain doubly disappeared: unread and largely ignored because of their anonymity and inaccessible because of cataloging methods and database design.[7]

I have worked to develop a method that, albeit imperfectly, and necessarily so, given the current state of databases and digitized archives, is a key support for my claim in this book—that anonymity was ubiquitous in the long eighteenth century—and the arguments of each chapter. I move between high-level analyses of massive metadata files to looking at each instance of "anonymous" in ECCO. I consider the ways in which anonymous texts historically have been cataloged, or not. I also draw extensively on the work of other scholars whose near-heroic efforts in cataloging and counting have provided us with a fuller account of literary history.

Working around the constraints of searching both ESTC and ECCO required gaining access to the metadata of the collections' holdings.[8] Rather than relying on the ability (or inability) to search a given field, the metadata reveal immediately those texts with nothing in the author field. Though it is an imperfect indicator of the ubiquity of anonymous publication in the period due both to the problem of retroactive attribution and its effacement of initially anonymous texts and to the incomplete nature of the database itself, it can serve as a proxy for estimating the prevalence of anonymous publication in the period.

Even with these caveats, my findings immediately challenge the dominant narrative that anonymous publication was a rarity and that it declined over the course of the long eighteenth century. For example, 337,043 texts in ESTC have dates from 1700 to 1799.[9] Of those, 72,795 remain anonymous (21.59 percent).[10] Nearly one-quarter of the texts in ESTC from this period are still anonymous; despite their prevalence, there is no way in using the browser-based interface to find these texts based on the criteria of their anonymity.

Decade-by-decade and year-by-year analyses further illuminate trends in anonymous publication. What they show is not a decline in anonymous authorship but a steady pulse of anonymous publication with periods of marked increase. Figure 1 is suggestive but ultimately misleading. The graph suggests a sharp spike in the number of titles from 1780 to 1799 amid a relatively low prevalence of anonymous titles from 1700 to 1779. A graph of the same data visualizing yearly trends (Figure 2) is far more informative.

Figure 2 offers a more granular picture of what is going on with the titles cataloged in ESTC and, by proxy, publication trends in the period. Rather than the sharp upward trend at the end of the period we see in Figure 1, Figure 2 shows an upward trend in the number of anonymous texts, with marked spikes in the years surrounding the American and French Revolutions and a decline thereafter. One might therefore intuit that the total number of anonymous titles tracks along with total number of attributed titles. Figure 3 illustrates just this relationship.

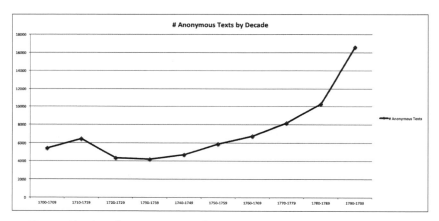

Figure 1. Number of anonymous texts in ESTC, 1700–1799, by decade.

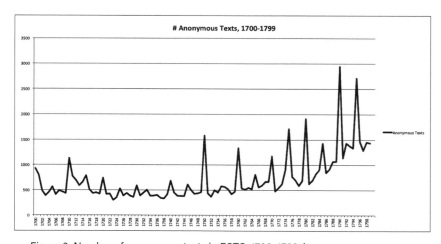

Figure 2. Number of anonymous texts in ESTC, 1700–1799, by year.

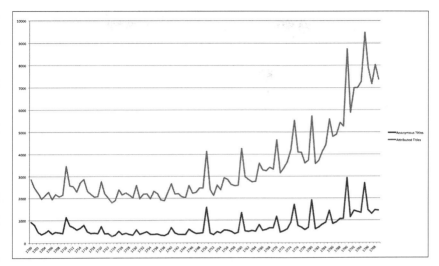

Figure 3. Number of anonymous titles versus attributed titles in ESTC, 1700–1799, by year.

A final graph, Figure 4, visualizes the trends of anonymous and attributed titles alongside all titles, from 1700 to 1799, in the corpus. This graph best visualizes the steady pulse of anonymous textual production throughout the period. The peaks and valleys of the stacked graphs indicate that in the years where there are more texts as a whole, anonymous texts maintain a similar proportion to attributed texts. That proportion, represented as a percentage of the total corpus, ranges from a low of 15.1 percent (1771) to a high of 33.4 percent (1780), with an average from 1700 to 1799 of 21.1 percent.[11]

This analysis of ESTC is necessarily blunt and imperfect. It is subject to the vagaries of textual survival, collection, and curation. I have relied on the dates of publication indicated in the metadata; such dates are not entirely reliable. Furthermore, the analysis does not distinguish between new titles and those that are reprinted or between multivolume versus single-volume works. Every row of the spreadsheet in which the metadata exist counts as a single "text." Michael J. Suarez has estimated that at least two hundred thousand different works were printed over the course of the eighteenth century in Britain.[12] The 337,043 titles in ESTC, which includes titles published in both Britain and America, though not an

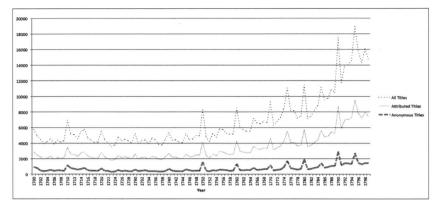

Figure 4. Number of anonymous titles, attributed titles, and all titles in ESTC, 1700–1799, by year.

absolute indicator of publication numbers, nor an exact picture of anonymous publication in the period, offers perhaps the closest surrogate available.

Despite all these caveats, it is clear that anonymity does not decline in the eighteenth century; moreover, we can safely assume that more than 21 percent of all texts published in a given year were anonymous. James Raven, for example, has shown that 80 percent of new novels between 1750 and 1800 were published anonymously.[13] Leah Orr has further estimated that 50 percent of the fiction published between 1660 and 1750 was anonymous.[14] Taken as a whole, these findings offer a richer context in which to consider the nature of anonymous literary texts in the period—a context in which anonymity is far from an outlier.

Mediation and the Literary

Scholars have however, approached authorial anonymity as an outlier in need of explanation, and as such they have often sought that explanation in discussions of authorial liability and copyright. Robert Griffin's work on anonymity in the British eighteenth century has challenged narratives about the relationship between copyright and named authorship.[15] He has shown repeatedly that there has never been, with a few brief exceptions, a requirement that an author's name be printed on a book or pamphlet for reasons of either authorial liability or copyright protection.[16] That literary property and liability are linked to the absence or presence of an author's name is a retrospective construction that is informed by modern concepts of authorship and property and projected into the period.[17] These claims about authorial liability and literary property warrant further notice, for they invite reflection on our own reluctance to acknowledge the relationship of mediation and remediation to authorship in the twenty-first century.

What the emphasis on liability narratives and property in discussions of anonymity does highlight is the central problem of agency that anonymity makes evident. Typically, the problem of agency is understood as the difficulty in naming the agent who wrote the text. This is indeed *one* problem of agency raised by anonymity, but it is one among many. The varying ways in which we describe the anonymous status of a text give some indication of the complexities inherent in attributions of agency. We may speak of an anonymous text as having a name "left off" or of there being "an absent name" or "no name," or, in Samuel Johnson's formulation, "[w]anting a name."[18] In each of these instances, the subject and object of the description may vary. Johnson's definition, for example, indicates that the text is lacking a name but does not imply agency on the part of those involved with its creation. When we consider the broader contexts in which that anonymity occurs, it may be more fully understood as possibly an act—sometimes voluntary, not necessarily intentional or motivated. Anonymous publication, though it may seem like a choice or like an action on the part of an author, may be no choice or action at all.

It may be that eighteenth-century authors consciously acted to withhold their names from texts. It may also be that publishers acted to withhold those names instead. We may consider the latter on that part of authors as "voluntary anonymity." G. E. M. Anscombe separates the voluntary from the involuntary and from the intentional. She writes, "Things may be voluntary which are not one's own doing at all, but which happen to one's delight, so that one consents and does not protest or take steps against them."[19] That is, an author may simply sell her manuscript outright to a publisher, as so many did in the eighteenth century, with no expectation or strong desire that her name be attached to the published text. In this case, there is no action on the part of the author to publish anonymously, only inaction in not protesting or taking steps against it.

Importantly, anonymous publication may be neither the choice nor the action of author or publisher; I argue throughout that we cannot know what passed in the minds of authors or publishers or the actions they did or did not take in not attaching a name to a text, except in very rare cases. Rather, by looking to what was published in the period, we find instead anonymity as a typical feature of a given medium and genre of a text. Raven's astonishing finding that the majority of new novels from the mid- to late eighteenth century were published anonymously is suggestive of the broader tendencies toward anonymous publication within the period. These tendencies vary across different media—the typicality of anonymity in written fictional prose is different from that of staged drama—and genres within those media: pantomime, for example, tends to be a more anonymous genre than other staged drama.

Reconceiving anonymity not only as an absence of a name but as a possible absence of action on the part of the author poses new questions about agency. Chief among them is how to characterize the mode of being of a text and understand its work in the world without the named author or its surrogate: the figure of the author motivated to choose anonymity over named authorship. This is, of course, a question not limited solely to anonymous texts; the ontological nature of literary artifacts is invariably complex. Long ago, F. W. Bateson asked, "What is the literary equivalent of a picture that is not being looked at? When *Hamlet,* say, is not being acted or recited or read, what are the physical constituents which are its potential cause of future aesthetic pleasure? And where are they located?"[20] This question of where literature is has, then, this corollary: what is literature? Bateson answered that the literary artifact was an unfolding of the utterance in the past or the future.[21] The verbal is but one aspect of literary artifacts, however. We must consider the materials from which these artifacts are composed, the multiple hands involved in the making, the networks through which they circulate, and the historically sedimented and collective action that produces features as diverse as genre and book size.

In the absence of a known or knowable agent, I shift from asking what an author *did* to what a text *is doing*. By emphasizing the text composed of human, material, and verbal action, I am giving priority neither to humans—authors, editors, compilers, publishers, printers, and so on—nor to "text." Rather, the text emerges as a radically mediated complex of multiple, and sometimes competing, actions and actors. Radical mediation is the process in which human and nonhuman action is intertwined and through which meaning is made, yet, like anonymity, that mediation is typically taken to be intermediate and invisible. Richard Grusin, however, has argued that

> mediation should be understood not as standing between preformed subjects, objects, actants, or entities but as the process, action, or event that generates or provides the conditions for the emergence of subjects and objects, for the individuation of entities within the world. Mediation is not opposed to immediacy but rather is itself immediate.[22]

The immediacy of mediation is never more apparent than in the absence of the authorial name. Without the ready ability to tether the literary artifact to its ostensible agent and creator, one turns to other ways of categorizing the artifact and understanding its mode of being in the world; chief among these modes is the artifact's medium and hence its mediation. It is through this categorical instability and process of recategorization that putatively transparent media and processes of mediation finally become visible.

Like anonymity, mediation is both everywhere and nowhere, and it invites divergent accounts of agency.[23] What is revealed when mediation comes to the fore is not simply media as passive intervening substances but media as active agents. Sarah Kember and Joanna Zylinska have dubbed this the *"lifeness* of media"—"the possibility of the emergence of forms always new, or its potentiality to generate unprecedented connections and unexpected events."[24] A radically mediated account of the literary expands the nature of the literary artifact from purely verbal to a complex of agents and actions to explore this "lifeness" and the sometimes unexpected lives of texts and the work they do in the world.

As John Guillory has shown, the concept of mediation has a long history within Hegelian and Marxist thought, most fruitfully in the writing of Theodor Adorno and Raymond Williams.[25] Adorno's clarification of mediation in "Theses on the Sociology of Art" denies the sense of the term as being concerned with the intermediate, or in between. It is, rather, "as to how social structural moments, positions, ideologies, and whatever else assert themselves in the works of art themselves."[26] In his discussion of mediation in *Marxism and Literature*, Williams argues that Adorno maintains the dualism between " 'reality' and 'speaking about reality' " as the passive (art) object finds itself the bearer of "positions, ideologies, and whatever else."[27] Thus, though Adorno claims to do away with mediation as intermediate, it nonetheless persists in a middle position. Mediation, as metaphor, serves as a "hindrance" (Williams's term) to recognizing "language and signification as indissoluble elements of the material social process itself, involved all the time in both production and reproduction" (99). In his insistence on human language and signification as "constituitive and constituting" of the social reality, Williams, like Adorno, overlooks the nonhuman, the objects, the media that are too "constituitive and constituting" of the social reality (100). We might, then, reverse and expand Adorno's formulation of the task of the sociology of music concerned with knowing "how society objectivates itself in works of art" to a sociology of cultural artifacts interested in knowing how objects and works of art act and are made to act in society.

Book History to Media Theory

Everywhere and Nowhere focuses on mediation and, in doing so, discovers a world of action with, very often, unknown human agents. It challenges the Derridean account of writing alone as action. For Jacques Derrida, the sole locus of agency and action is in the writing itself; "it must continue to 'act' and to be readable even when what is called the author of the writing no longer answers for what he has written."[28] What is absent is the mode and media of inscription that necessarily *also* act and are *also* readable independent of human agency. As Roger Chartier has argued, "texts are not deposited in books, whether handwritten or printed, as if in a mere recipient.

Readers only encounter texts within an object whose forms and layout guide and compel the production of meaning."[29]

Chartier comes closest among social historians of the book to recognizing the agency of the material text. Book history is concerned, as we have been told from its enunciation, with the production, circulation, and reception of books. D. F. McKenzie's work expanded this language by asking us to think broadly of "texts as recorded forms," not merely manuscripts and books.[30] Book history, then, takes as its object some material instantiation of "the text." A funny sleight of hand, though, happens in accounts of what book history shows through such analysis. Robert Darnton concludes his "What Is the History of Books?" by writing, "By unearthing those circuits [of communication], historians can show that books do not merely recount history; they make it."[31] Darnton, like Chartier, makes thinkable the agency of books, but recurs consistently to the authors, publishers, printers, shippers, and readers in the "communications circuit." Thus, though the object is the book, the concern is with the human action connected to the book; humans, it seems, make history through books as their intermediaries.[32]

From a rather different angle, McKenzie performs a similar sleight of hand. He compellingly and convincingly shows the importance of the material aspects of texts, such as typography, to the production of meaning but concludes that "[bibliography] can . . . show the human presence in any recorded text" (29). In distinct ways, the work of Darnton and McKenzie oscillates between texts seeming to take action and humans as decisive sources of action. In these accounts, human action wins out.[33]

By taking mediation as a starting point, I reimagine McKenzie's notion of the "sociology of texts" not as interested in the "truths of social development, structure and function" but as concerned with tracing a "trail of *associations* between heterogenous elements."[34] Central to my reimagining is the recognition that nonhuman actors might, too, share intention and agency. This formulation nudges the claims of McKenzie's method to their logical conclusion. It may seem absurd, but as we have seen in the recent work on It-Narratives, those in the eighteenth century were quite comfortable with imagining dislocated agencies and things bearing intention.[35]

While the period saw experiments in narrating agential objects, it also flirted with the idea as a source of humor. Consider how anonymity, mediation, and agency intertwine in Jonathan Swift's *The Battle of the Books*, a text that emerges out of debates about attribution, authenticity, and origin around the *Epistles* of Phalaris, in which we are told in the "Booksellers Note to the Reader,"

> I must warn the Reader, to beware of applying to Persons what is here meant, only of Books in the most literal Sense. So, when *Virgil* is mentioned, we are not to understand the Person of a famous Poet, call'd by that Name, but only certain Sheets of Paper, bound up in Leather, containing in Print, the Works of the said Poet, and so of the rest.[36]

The note gives this warning so that it operates in a manner typical of disavowals that fictional persons are not meant to refer to actual persons. The humor arises at the seeming absurdity that books could be mistaken for persons and that books could be animated by any other force than the author. The allegory, however, turns these "Books in the literal sense" into something resembling humans. The reader is told to attend to the minute features of the physical book—"certain Sheets of Paper, bound up in Leather"—but these features are easily forgotten, because the books share the name of humans, are animated like humans, and, in the frontispiece, are depicted as human figures with books on their heads (Figure 5).

The implied absurdity in the "Booksellers Note" that books could act on their own is resolved with image and text depicting booklike humans or humanlike books doing battle. *The Battle of the Books* demonstrates the double move of recognizing the potential agency of media while disavowing it through authorial attribution and personification. This move is pervasive in approaches to anonymity. *The Battle* thus allegorizes the battle of the ancients and the moderns and demonstrates the way in which naming and attribution occlude mediation. The practice of attribution as a primary mode of making anonymity disappear has resulted in a similar slide from agential media to human persons.[37]

The slide from agential media to human persons is perhaps best illustrated in Harold Love's account of the work of attribution

Before the Title of the Battle.

Figure 5. Frontispiece to *The Battle of the Books,* fifth edition (1710). Courtesy of the Department of Special Collections, Memorial Library, University of Wisconsin–Madison.

studies. For Love, "the subject of attribution studies is the uniqueness of each human being and how this is enacted in writing."[38] Love holds a vision of authorship, inflected by poststructuralism, that understands authorship not as isolated individuals writing works but as a series of functions in the work needed to produce text. To that end, his vision of attribution is to identify, as much as possible, the many hands involved in textual production. Such an approach is consistent with much of the work of book history. It, however, neglects other agencies and material forms. It is, for him, a validation of individual human agency, even if the work of authorship is inherently a collaboration among persons and things.

Donald Foster has gone further to suggest that anonymity poses an "impasse" to the critic constructing a reading.[39] His example is the particularly fraught case of the attribution problem posed by *Funerall Elegye* (1612), thought to be written by William Shakespeare. Foster's account, however, speaks more broadly to the unease with which literary scholars approach anonymous texts. Authorial attribution, it seems, is the necessary precondition for literary critical practice. Practices of attribution, of course, have a long history that well predates both the rise of the named, professional author and professional literary criticism. Archer Taylor and Fredric J. Mosher have traced the developments in dictionaries of anonyma and pseudonyma from their origins in the theological scholarship of pseudoepigrapha through the development of secular, vernacular dictionaries in the nineteenth century. One of the central shifts, they show, was the development of an increasingly taxonomic approach to distinguishing various forms of contested authorship, including plagiarism, pseudonymity, and anonymity, in the seventeenth century. Whereas earlier dictionaries of anonyma and pseudonyma often folded the two together and included plagiarisms, by the time of Vincent Placcius's posthumously completed *Theatrum Anonymorum et Pseudonymorum* (1708), anonymous texts and pseudonymous texts occupied separate volumes, and plagiarisms were omitted entirely.[40]

This taxonomy suggests the ways in which what Susan Stewart calls "crimes of writing" were being sifted out on the basis of the perceived agency of the author.[41] That is, both pseudonymity and plagiarism imply deliberate action: in the case of the former, it is "to hide the true name"; in the latter, it is to pass another's work off as one's own.[42] Anonymity bears a far more complex and less clear relationship to authorial agency. It is for this reason I follow Placcius and others in distinguishing between anonymity, pseudonymity, and plagiarism. This book is ultimately about the question of action or inaction posed by anonymity, which is different from that raised by either pseudonymity or plagiarism.

Pseudonymity, despite its long-standing association with anonymity—it is often understood as either interchangeable with anonymity or a subset of anonymity—when considered from the perspective of authorial action, is certainly of a different kind. The absence of a name implies typically inaction (that is, not acting to attach a name to a text). While things like "by a Lady" or "from the author of" both occupy an intermediary area between the authornym, pseudonym, and anonym, the presence of a false name, or quasi-authornym (as in "by a Lady"), implies only a form of action in attaching pseudonym or authornym to text. Moreover, the function of the pseudonym is very different from that of the anonym. The notion of the "false name" reveals the underlying logic of substitution that assumes some correspondence to its referent—the "flesh-and-blood author." One may group together the writings of Publius, for example, and, if not identify an actual individual in the world, identify a similar or consistent mode of discourse in the world. One would be hard-pressed to similarly group texts under the absence of any name.

Whereas the seventeenth century saw shifts in practices surrounding the organization of dictionaries of anonyma and pseudonyma, the eighteenth century saw a curious absence in efforts to compile similar dictionaries. Taylor and Mosher show that the Latinate dictionaries of anonyma and pseudonyma disappear in the eighteenth century. Instead, they find "only casual lists of cryptonyms in out-of-the-way places, special sections set apart in lists of books made by auctioneers or cataloguers of private libraries, and collections for reference use that were extracted from general lists of books" (134). Correspondence to *The Gentleman's Magazine* evinces a desire for such dictionaries in the period (135). It is, however, not until the nineteenth century that Samuel Halkett's efforts to compile the *Dictionary of Anonymous and Pseudonymous English Literature* offered a systematic attempt to collect and identify works by anonymous and pseudonymous authors.[43]

The absence of dictionaries of anonyma and pseudonyma in the period, despite the ubiquity of anonymity in the period and the apparent desire for such works, is connected to broader movements in bibliographic scholarship. Taylor has dubbed these movements the "three epochs" in bibliographic history.[44] Taylor describes the shifts from periods "in which men wrote primarily lists of authors" to "a new epoch in which men thought in terms of a subject" to an epoch in which scholars came to think of the book as physical object (46). This he finds toward the end of the eighteenth century: "since 1800—and for one class one might set the date 1700—examples of the third variety of bibliography have become numerous. This variety of bibliography includes lists of books chosen for the circumstances in which they were produced or for their physical peculiarities" (48).

These shifts—from individuals to subjects to books as physical objects—mesh with transformations in the scholarship of anonymity and its eventual, though temporary, disappearance in the eighteenth century. This disappearance is linked to the "third epoch" (to follow Taylor) in bibliographic sensibility, wherein books were acknowledged primarily as objects, each with its unique properties. Attending to the book as physical object decenters the author as locus of choice and action; the "third epoch" draws attention to the medium.

These shifts also echo a literary landscape in which objects and books, and particularly the components of books and pamphlets, as in sheets of paper, bore a particular intimate relationship to readers and other book users. As Joshua Calhoun and Jonathan Senchyne have shown of the early modern period and the nineteenth century, respectively, paper made from rag linen carried the traces of its former life first as flax, then as garments, then as pulp to make paper.[45] Readers in the hand press and rag paper era, which includes the long eighteenth century, could not forget the medium, for its traces were both in the page and all around them. Furthermore, the interest in and awareness of such mediation arises amid what William B. Warner has named a "media culture."[46] Unlike what has been named print culture, media culture recognizes the simultaneity and endurance of orality, performance, manuscript, and print within the culture.[47] This media culture is necessarily a culture of inter- and remediation wherein the interactions among different media forms reveal not only their unique representational logics but also their agential nature.[48]

Anonymity in Theory and Actuality

While the absence of the author's name on the page has generally been cause for "impasse" for critics, as a theoretical construct or critical precondition, anonymity has been central to many literary critical movements. I. A. Richards's *Practical Criticism* (1929), for example, begins with a description of an ongoing experiment in which Richards "issu[ed] printed sheets of poems . . . to audiences who were requested to comment freely in writing upon them. The authorship of the poems was not revealed, and with rare exceptions it was not recognized."[49] The absence of the author's name was essential to the experiment, because it reoriented his subjects from the habit of imagining "the *mental operations* of the person" to "consider[ing] *what seems to be said*" (6). For Richards, poetry was a mode of communication, and the aim of criticism was to understand what is being communicated, without regard to the mental state or biography of the author/communicator (10). The anonymity of the poems in such experiments, then, enabled such focus on "*what seems to be said*." Indeed, two anonymous pamphlets attributed sometimes to Daniel Defoe, considered in chapter 3, imply similar claims about the functional nature of anonymity to get one's message across.

To a very different end, Roland Barthes, too, espoused a theoretical anonymity as critical necessity. In his familiar "Death of the Author," Barthes writes that the conception of the author is "a limit" on the text that "suits criticism very well, the latter then allotting itself the important task of discovering the Author . . . beneath the work: when the Author has been found, the text is 'explained'—victory to the critic."[50] Naming and discovering authors and their meanings has been, Barthes claims, the central task of criticism such that "there is no surprise in the fact that, historically, the reign of the Author has also been that of the Critic." He imagines the death of the "Author-God" and instead the birth of the "modern scriptor . . . born simultaneously with the text" and "the reader" (146, 145, 147, respectively).

In advocating for a relationship between "scriptor," text, and reader, Barthes argues that the author must be rejected in favor of what Michel Foucault names a "transcendental anonymity."[51] This Barthesian notion of *écriture*—textuality in the wake of the author's death—Foucault claims

> has merely transposed the empirical characteristics of an author to a transcendental anonymity. The extremely visible signs of the author's empirical activity are effaced to allow the play, in parallel or opposition, of religious and critical modes of characterization. (120)

This anonymization of the text, according to Foucault, bears with it the same Romantic notions with which Barthes wished to do away. In the opening afforded by such anonymity, Foucault offers a consideration of the nature of authorship and an account of authorial names.[52] The authorial name is "not a pure and simple reference, [it] . . . has other than indicative functions. It is more than a gesture, a finger pointed at someone; it is, to a certain extent, the equivalent of a description" (121). The name takes on the character of something closer to a metaphor, which may signify not only the actual writer but the totality of his or her works, and functions "as a means of classification" (123).

We move, then, from theoretical anonymization as critical precondition—as in Richards and Barthes—to an invitation to consider the function of the name and, by extension, its *actual* absence as part of the task of criticism. It is this invitation that *Everywhere and Nowhere* takes up. In this book, I seek to valorize neither the Romantic concept of authorship nor the equally Romantic concept of textuality in the absence of an author. Rather, if authorship is a function that extends beyond empirical human individuals to any aspect of the text—its editor, publisher, format, genre, style, typography, or medium (to name only a few aspects)—the task is to describe what those aspects do.[53]

Anonymous Bodies

Within the literary context, the name may not, to follow Foucault, take on "indicative" functions, but within legal discourse, the opposite is true, particularly in instances when the actors' names are unknown. As I show in my first chapter, Anonymous nearly never appears as an authorial name attached to those texts we consider literary until the 1770s; we only begin to see texts "by Anonymous" in the latter part of the eighteenth century. Anonymous as a kind of name is, however, ubiquitous in legal texts throughout the period. Take, for example, the report of a case from the High Court of Chancery, "*Anon. February* 18, 1742. *first seal after Hil. term.*":

> An attachment issued against a person out of this court, and the sheriff had the body in custody, and took a bail-bond for his appearance, which he delivered to the plaintiff, who moved at a former seal, that the sheriff might bring in the body; and the court made a rule upon him to shew cause why he did not bring in the body.[54]

Unlike like surrounding cases, *Lingood v. Eade* or *Emes v. Hancock*, Anon. has no plaintiff or defendant with a proper name.[55] "Anon." takes the place of the proper name, and it does so due to the legal custom by which cases are referenced by the names of the parties involved.

Anonymous has long been used as a name within printed accounts of legal proceedings. *Laws Relating to the Poor, from the Forty-Third of Queen Elizabeth to the Third of King George II. With Cases Adjudged in the Court of King's* (1739) collects case law relating to the poor and includes in its index of cases "Anonymous" for six cases. Likewise, *Reports of Cases Argued and Determined in the High Court of Chancery* regularly includes Anonymous within its "Table of the Names of Cases" and case reports in each of its volumes throughout the period. Within these texts, Anonymous serves a twofold purpose: it both describes a case as "nameless" while simultaneously naming the case. Anonymous becomes a name within these texts as it stands in for the absent or missing proper names necessary to refer to the cases. It is not, as in its literary usage, meant to describe the absence of an authorial name in these texts or make explicit the origin of the text. Within the legal discourse that these texts represent, the actors in the cases must be noted, even if their names are unknown or withheld. Anonymous thus functions to point to "flesh-and-blood" actors, or empirical individuals, whose presence must be marked as essential to the action of the cases.

Marking the absent proper name as "Anonymous" in these legal cases follows the same logic as the writ of habeas corpus, which coalesced over the course of the late seventeenth century. As it makes present what is absent, the explicit "Anonymous" in the cases cited presents the unnamed, but nonetheless accountable, actors in the cases. Of habeas corpus, Robert Searles Walker explains, "The writ is simply a judicial command directed to a jailer instructing him to produce a named prisoner together with the cause of his detention in order that the legal warrant of detention might be judicially examined."[56] Though he contends that we find evidence of habeas corpus in legal accounts as early as the thirteenth century, it is codified in the 1679 Act of Habeas Corpus and is noted as significant to the development of the modern legal and political subject (13).[57]

The Act's claimed connection to personal liberty has rendered it as a privileged site of the emergence of the autonomous modern subject. Giorgio Agamben points directly to the 1679 Act as the origin of this "new political subject":

> The first recording of bare life as the new political subject is already implicit in the document that is generally placed at the foundation of modern democracy: the 1679 writ of *habeas corpus*. Whatever the origin of this formula, used as early as the eighteenth century to assure the physical presence of a person before a court of justice, it is significant that at its center is neither the old subject of feudal relations and liberties nor the future *citoyen*, but rather a pure and simple *corpus*.[58]

Strikingly, Agamben connects the emphasis on "a pure and simple *corpus*" to the anonymity of the subject:

> The fact that, of the all various jurisdictional regulations concerned with the protection of individual freedom, it was *habeas*

corpus that assumed the form of law and thus became inseparable from the history of Western democracy is surely due to mere circumstance. It is just as certain, however, that nascent European democracy thereby placed at the center of its battle against absolutism not *bios*, the qualified life of the citizen, but *zoê*—the bare, anonymous life that is as such taken into the sovereign ban ("the body of being taken . . . ," as one still reads in one modern formulation of the writ, "by whatsoever name he may be called therein"). (124)

As Agamben suggests and case law demonstrates, no proper name was needed. The name works merely to indicate the body whose presence is requested. In this way, "Anon." can function just as well as the proper name. Indeed, we see the legacy of this logic in the contemporary American use of "John Doe" and "Jane Doe" to name litigants and cases. This "bare, anonymous life" is a "flesh-and-blood" body, not a name that indexes that body.

At the heart of the use of Anon. or Anonymous as a name within English law, rather than as only an adjective signaling its absence, is the difference between legal language and language in its literary uses. Walker connects the desire for the presence of the body to "the structure of legal language itself": "Literally habeas corpus means 'have the body,' and cast in the imperative mode by a court it is quite conceivable that natural usage could, in time, evolve into discrete process" (13). Walker, here, offers a way of distinguishing the nature and function of legal language from other uses of language and locates the roots of the discourse in the world that is eventually transformed into legal process. Through this legal process, long distanced from its "natural usage," habeas corpus gives rise to the political subject (if we follow Agamben), but that subject is a nameless, embodied subject that still harkens back to its translation, "have the body."

Anonymous in these collections of cases echoes the logic of habeas corpus wherein "the body" must be produced. Changes in 1640 and 1679 ensured that the king's proclamation alone was not sufficient for charges to stand, and so the bodies of those charged must be brought before a judge. So, too, does the name Anonymous evoke a presence on the page that fulfills the role of the (juridical) subject, though he is not named.

This "Anonymous" is, however, not the authorial subject within literary discourse. We see a marked delay in the use of Anonymous as a name within literary texts, because Anonymous within legal cases is meant to indicate a body—any body; Anonymous when used as a name within literary texts is meant to indicate the absence of a name—a particular name—to whom a text may be attributed. Both the former and the latter are subject to historical change over time; however, they operate on different timelines and are subject to different forces. While developments around the writ of habeas corpus may be most directly tied to the desire to place limits on monarchical power in the wake of the English Civil War and Restoration, developments toward the expected attribution of authorship or acknowledgment of anonymity on literary texts are shaped by myriad forces from legal prescription to generic expectations to typographical practice.

Such a difference between the legal and the literary points us to the manner in which the literary realm functions differently than the specialist discourses of law. The law offers a particular consolidation of the subject through legal responsibility. It is, as Sandra Macpherson notes, a "formal person" "whose content as represented by the state of her interior (or mind) is irrelevant to the question of her responsibility and thus to the question of what or who she is."[59] The literary, on the other hand, contests such consolidation. The many hands and many things involved in the production, circulation, and reception of the literary text means necessarily that any single human actor can only be a single piece of a much larger assemblage.

Intention and Anonymity

My turn away from the unified, autonomous author figure and toward a dispersed literary assemblage echoes many of Barthes's insights; however, mine is not a typically semiotic account of the aspects of textual production. Whereas semiotics usually concerns itself with representation to the detriment of media specificity, starting with mediation means engaging with media qua media and describing their action, rather than converting them to a sign.[60] That description of action, to follow G. E. M. Anscombe, may be called intention. I accept the formulation offered by Walter Benn Michaels and Steven Knapp of intention as coterminous with meaning with one significant qualification—intention need not be the sole province of humans.[61]

I distinguish between intention and motive throughout this book and refuse the tendency to ascribe authorial motives *for* anonymous publication and instead prefer to examine intentions *in* the text and its contexts. This distinction is complicated because motive and intention are notoriously difficult to piece apart. However, piecing out that difference is crucial if we wish to understand the relationship between the individual and her actions in the world—or, for our purposes, the relationship between the individual and her writing.

Much of this confusion in literary studies can be traced back to Wimsatt and Beardsley's "The Intentional Fallacy." " 'Intention,' " Wimsatt and Beardsley write, "corresponds to *what he intended* in a formula which more or less explicitly has had wide acceptance. . . . Intention is design or plan in the author's mind."[62] As Joshua Gang has noted, "this definition of intention is at best nebulous (and at times tautological)."[63] Their usage of intention alludes to some mental state antecedent to the text and detached from action, which may be more associated with "motive."[64]

Central to Wimsatt and Beardsley's argument is the unavailability and undesirability of the "design or intention of the author."[65] The interchangeability of "design or intention" here signals their use of the term as a phenomenon that precedes action. They instead advocate evaluating a poem "like judging a pudding or a machine." In their view, the critic "demands that it work. It is only because an artifact works that we infer the intention of an artificer."[66] The text is thus rendered as an inanimate object apart from its author, and the critic is freed from attending to anything antecedent to, or outside of, it.[67] The individual agency and intention of the author (as they have defined it) in the creation of the text is, in Wimsatt and Beardsley's view, irrelevant.

The conception of intention offered by Wimsatt and Beardsley, in its conflation with motive, is largely inconsistent with philosophical accounts of action. Stanley Cavell, for example, describes their "concept of intention as relevant to art which does not exist elsewhere."[68] For Cavell, "intention is no more an efficient cause of an object of art than it is of human action; in both cases it is a way of understanding the thing done, of describing what happens."[69] This account of intention defines it as a description of action, not, as in Wimsatt and Beardsley, "design or plan in the author's mind." Such an account follows from the tradition in analytic philosophy that has sought to define and separate out intention and motive as distinct concepts. In her still influential 1957 treatise on the subject, Anscombe links intention to action as a means of distinguishing it from motive. She writes, "if you want to say at least some true things about a man's intentions, you will have a strong chance of success if you mention what he actually did or is doing."[70] While Anscombe is not interested in entirely disregarding interior states of mind, her theorization focuses on external action; intention describes that action.

Because it is a description of what happens in the world, intention in this account need not be the sole province of human action. Anscombe's explanation of the applicability of intention concepts to animal action elucidates her rather opaque formulation:

> Still, we certainly ascribe intention to animals. The reason is precisely that we describe what they do in a manner perfectly characteristic of the use of intention concepts: we describe what *further* they are doing *in* doing something (the latter description being *more* immediate, nearer to the merely physical): the cat is stalking a bird *in* crouching and slinking along with its eye fixed on the bird and its whiskers twitching.[71]

In this instance, we may ask why the cat is "crouching and slinking along with its eye fixed on the bird." By asking this question, we are seeking an answer that articulates the cat's intention. The answer, "the cat is stalking the bird," describes the present action and implies its end: catching and (perhaps) eating the bird. This example models the approach to intention my argument adopts; in interpreting the cat's intention, we do so without recourse to her prior mental states (motive). In describing what the cat is doing, we are not interested in what the cat was thinking. Indeed, motive is not relevant to an account of what this cat is doing, nor need it be relevant in many of our accounts of what happens in the world.[72]

I follow historian Quentin Skinner in disregarding motive as "antecedent" to the work; however, intention, he argues, is embodied in the work and is therefore relevant to interpretation.[73] Skinner dismisses Wimsatt and Beardsley's central claim that a given author's intention is unavailable to the critic. As it is with Anscombe, Skinner claims that intention, and therefore meaning, is manifest externally and may be read from actions or texts. Motive in his account (and mine) remains outside the text and largely inaccessible and irrelevant to the critic.

While the ascription of intention is sometimes straightforward when considering direct observation of what a human (or cat) "did or is doing," it is much less clear when dealing with processes of inscription by unknown agents upon supposedly inanimate media. Consider Knapp and Michaels's much-discussed thought experiment of the appearance, written in the sand on a beach, of the first stanza of William Wordsworth's "A Slumber Did My Spirit Seal."[74] Initially, the encounter with the "squiggles in the sand" suggests that they may have been inscribed by a human passerby with a stick, but then "a wave washes up and recedes, leaving in its wake (written below what you now realize was only the first stanza)" what appears to be the second stanza of the poem (727).

For Knapp and Michaels, the presence of the second stanza throws into doubt the intentional character of the first and therefore its meaning. They argue that without even being conscious of it, the reader, upon encountering the first stanza, posits a human author as intentional agent. The presence of the second renders implausible human agency, and one is left to "either . . . ascrib[e] these marks to some agent capable of intentions (the living sea, the haunting Wordsworth, etc.), or . . . count them as nonintentional effects of mechanical processes (erosion, percolation, etc.)" (728). It is clear here that Knapp and Michaels are working with a notion of intention that understands it in some way to be related to mental states. Intention, however, as it is concerned with describing what happens in the world, need not depend on inner mental states. My robust account of intentionalism runs counter to the long critical history of disavowing its critical relevance. In my expanded account of agency and action, which includes humans, nonhumans, and objects, the description of those actions or expressions of agency is an identification of intention—an identification made without reference to mental states.[75]

While Knapp and Michaels consider the idea of the ocean as intentional agent "farfetched," I want to argue that in this case, the action of the ocean may be described with an intentional character without imputing sentience to the ocean. So, too, may we speak of the action of the sand into which the words of "A Slumber Did My Spirit Seal" are inscribed. That they act in such a way that is legible to the human observer conveys their intention and therefore their meaning.

Rather than understand this moment as one of an absence of intention entirely, it is instead a moment of a likely absence of human intention, which does not negate the meaning of the stanza. In contrast to Knapp and Michaels's insistence on human intention as the prerequisite for meaning, Latour has argued that "existence and meaning are synonymous. *As long as they act, agents have meaning.*"[76] What Latour offers is an account of the production of meaning that greatly expands the province of who and what can make meaning. The robust intentionalism I offer provides a means of describing action, and therefore meaning, without requiring a known or knowable agent as precondition for interpretation.

Let us consider another paradigmatic moment of inscription upon a beach—Robinson Crusoe's discovery of a single footprint upon the island he has come to inhabit:

> It happen'd one Day about Noon going towards my Boat, I was exceedingly surpriz'd with the Print of a Man's naked Foot on the Shore, which was very plain to be seen in the Sand: I stood like one Thunder-struck, or as if I had seen an Apparition; I listen'd, I look'd round me, I could hear nothing, nor see any Thing, I went up to a rising Ground to look farther, I went up the Shore and down the Shore, but it was all one, I could see no other Impression but that one; I went to it again to see if there were any more, and to observe if it might not be my Fancy; but there was no Room for that, for there was exactly the very Print of a Foot, Toes, Heel, and every Part of a Foot; how it came thither, I knew not, nor could in the least imagine.[77]

Crusoe is presented with evidence of action and likely, though not guaranteed, action by another human. His response, along with shock and terror, joins a search for other footprints, a search for their origin and their interpretation:

> Sometimes I fancy'd it must be the Devil; and Reason joyn'd in with me upon this Supposition: For how should any other Thing in human Shape come into the Place? Where was the Vessel that brought them? What Marks was there of any other Footsteps? And how was it possible a Man should come there? (171)

He seeks to understand what the single footprint means by understanding both what the maker of the footprint was doing—the Devil terrifying him, for example—and what the footprint is doing. The footprint is thus not simply evidence of an act; *it keeps acting*—as Crusoe notes, "the farther I was from the Occasion of my Fright, the greater my Apprehensions were, which is something contrary to the Nature of such Things" (171). The psychic weight that bears down on Crusoe in the wake of this incident evinces that continued action. The stories Crusoe tells himself about the print toggle between attribution (the Devil, Crusoe himself, "cannibals") and interpretation—what it means that this print appeared in this place on the island (a warning, punishment).

This episode in *Robinson Crusoe* is illustrative of Alfred Gell's notion of the abduction of agency. Borrowed from logic, abduction "covers the grey area where semiotic inference (of meanings from signs) merges with *hypothetical inferences* of a non-semiotic (or not conventionally semiotic) kind."[78] When faced with a phenomenon that offers evidence of action—an index—abduction names the inference of agency that brought that index about. Thus Crusoe's thoughts about the origin of the footprint are moments of abduction; Knapp and Michaels's thoughts about the stanzas from "A Slumber Did My Soul Seal" are a moment of abduction; every instance of authorial attribution is an instance of abduction.

The kinds of indices I have discussed—footprints, stanzas, texts—are deliberately of different kinds. Knapp and Michaels's suggestion that the first reaction to the stanza in the sand is to infer it as a product of a human mind and therefore an instance of what is typically understood as a sign is seemingly distinct from the fact of a footprint in the sand as encountered by Crusoe. Gell's concept of abduction, however, seeks to broaden accounts of agency and art objects beyond the purely linguistic. He writes, "The usefulness of the concept of abduction is that it designates a class of semiotic inferences which are, by definition, wholly distinct from the semiotic inferences we bring to bear on the understanding of language, whose 'literal' understanding is a matter of observing semiotic conventions, not entertaining hypotheses derived *ad hoc* from the 'case' under consideration" (14–15).[79] From the perspective of the flattened semiotics offered by Gell, we look to the specific case, the footprint or stanza in the sand, and, at least temporarily, equate them to think broadly about the agency that brought them about and their potential meanings.

Agency, Gell offers, "is a culturally prescribed framework for thinking about causation," and he is quick to link intention as an internal state as one of the qualities of agential action: "whenever an event is believed to happen because of an 'intention' lodged in the person or thing which initiates the causal sequence . . . [it] is an instance of 'agency'" (17). While intention may very well be "lodged" in a person or thing, it is only accessible to the observer through action. I revise Gell's formulation to argue that intention is not the *cause* of an action; it is the *description* of an action. Therefore we might say that whenever an event is believed to happen due to the initiation of a causal sequence and it may be described with an intentional character, it is an instance of agency.

Authorial anonymity offers instances par excellence for the abduction of agency. Like Crusoe's footprint, the anonymous text is an index without an obvious agent. As ought to be clear by now, abduction needn't require humans as agents or as primary actors. Rather, the inferences of agency one makes in the event of anonymous texts may well identify an assemblage of actions, agents, and actants that bring about the text and characterize the work they do in the world.[80] The process of identification and characterization of the literary assemblage is the work of literary history and criticism, respectively.

Such work aligns well with certain formulations of formalism, particularly those of R. S. Crane. In searching for first principles of both literary writing and criticism, Crane finds them in form. Form, for Crane, is "the shaping cause of any given literary work."[81] This account is profoundly impersonal, as it locates formal causation outside or beyond the writing subject; the writer "can know what he [or she] can do, in fact, only after he [or she] has done it" (144). This notion of form contests psychologized accounts of literary production that speak of, or wish to dismiss, the "design or plan in an author's mind." Form acts on and through the writing subject and the medium of inscription. More recently, Sandra Macpherson has offered a perhaps even more elemental account of form: she describes "form as nothing more—and nothing less—than the shape matter (whether a poem or a tree) takes."[82] These fundamental forms need human actors neither to produce nor to receive them to have meaning, as Jonathan Kramnick and Anahid Nersessian have noted of Macpherson's ontology.[83] Poems and trees happen; we may not be able, or wish, to attribute their being to a human actor. Such an absence of attribution does not negate their meaning.

Everywhere and Nowhere is inflected by such formalism in identifying and characterizing the actions and agents that bring about texts. At times, this means that the ever-porous boundary between description and interpretation is made even more so.[84] Describing the work of literary artifacts in the world is simultaneously descriptive and interpretive, for to describe the causal chain brought about by an artifact is to interpret its actions.

My central concern in this book is anonymity and its implications for agency and literary criticism. I am further concerned with the categories and methods used in the production of knowledge. Anonymity, in its lack of one of the primary pieces of information often required for categorization, lays bare the limits of these categories and methods. What my survey of cataloging practices reveals is not a presentist concern with a decentered form of authorship but a diverse history of practices, each attentive to the differences among the media of the objects they catalog and the primacy (or not) of the author's name or the text's anonymity.

The chapters of this book engage both with instances in which anonymity is an absence and when it is made an explicit presence. In chapter 1, I explore the appearance of "Anonymous" as an authorial name. This study takes the very typical work of the scholar of literature and culture—the hunt for a keyword and its close reading—and amplifies it via keyword search.[85] The result is an ability to make very fine distinctions in usage and explore those distinctions across a very large corpus. I turn my focus to the late eighteenth-century moment when "Anonymous" begins to be used as an authorial name in the reprinting of early eighteenth-century poems. Almost nonexistent on literary works prior to 1770, the figure of "Anonymous," still without name, but nonetheless the locus of choice and action, resolves the complex textual and medial lives of these poems. The poem "To Belinda," which bore no authorial attribution when first published in Richard Steele's *Poetical Miscellanies* (1714), was attributed to "Anonymous" when it was reprinted in John Nichols's *A Select Collection of Poems* (1780). Yet throughout the volume, Nichols insists that though he has noted the anonymity of poems included in Steele's *Poetical Miscellanies*, he is confident that Steele is himself the author. The acknowledgment of anonymity, then, confers its status as explicitly without name while at the same time undoing that anonymity through attribution. Thus "Anonymous" is neither merely signaling an already present yet tacit anonymity nor providing a name to fill an absence. Rather, it occupies an intermediate position between these two poles that takes the form of the authorial name without performing the name's function.

The second chapter pursues the practices of categorization, already raised in this introduction, among those who have sought to write histories and catalogs of the drama of the Restoration and eighteenth century. I arrived at the meta-analysis of seventeenth- and eighteenth-century dramatic catalogs and cataloging practices explored in chapter 2 through the serendipity of keyword search for the term "anonymous." This search yielded dramatic catalog after dramatic catalog that set aside anonymous plays as distinct from those with named authors. These catalogs—from Gerard Langbaine to John Egerton—narrate a prehistory of practices that still shape theater history. Allardyce Nicoll, for example, adopts the similar schema of setting anonymous plays as distinct in his multi-volume *A History of English Drama*. Moreover, these dramatic catalogs offer an alternate vision of how we might catalog, and therefore make available for study, anonymous texts. Rather than disappear anonymous texts as ECCO and ESTC do, earlier cataloging schemas made their anonymity explicit. These cataloging practices attended to the anonymity of the drama of this period due to the readily apprehended distinction in medium between the anonymity of the printed text and the anonymity of staged performance. Such a distinction simultaneously recognizes the complexities of mediation in both the theatrical milieu and the printed text and effaces them. In the second half of the chapter, I turn to the world of eighteenth-century theater to demonstrate the utter typicality of authorial anonymity in dramatic performance and the manner in which the complexity of the theatrical milieu disrupts any attempt to attribute dramatic action to a single agent. What this chapter shows is both how the differences in and among media reveal anonymity and how anonymity reveals those differences in and among media.

My third chapter emphasizes the competing strands and underlying collectives that are occluded by the retroactive attachment of the author's name to the (previously anonymous) text. I show that the practice of authorial attribution relies on the processes of circulation, mediation, and interpretation but that it disavows those processes in the naming of the author, which takes attribution to be a binary process. My focus in this chapter is on Defoe, whose work was almost entirely published anonymously. I first take up early anonymous political pamphlets regularly attributed to Defoe. While the pamphlets themselves consider anonymity essential to a work being read and interpreted, paradoxically, twentieth- and twenty-first-century critics insist on correct attribution as the starting point for interpretation. The chapter then turns to the late eighteenth-century attributions of the previously anonymous *Roxana* (1724) and *Moll Flanders* (1722) in 1775 and 1776, respectively. Their attributions to Defoe occurred through the iterative circulation practices of the circulating library over time, and yet the authorship of these novels is taken as obvious and self-evident without reference to their prior, extended histories as anonymous novels.

Chapter 4 returns to questions of intention and action to consider Frances Burney's anonymously published *Evelina* and Walter Scott's Waverley novels. Rather than resolve anonymity as a conscious choice or action of an individual human authorial agent, I consider anonymity as a typical and tacit feature of the novel that blurs the distinctions that can be drawn between human, material, and verbal action. In this chapter, I insist on broadening our horizons beyond Burney's and Scott's motives as reasons for the novels' anonymous publication. In *Evelina*, I find the creation of editorial personae whose intentions may well exceed those of the biographical person, Burney. In *Waverley* and the Waverley novels, I find an account of motive that dislocates it from the individual's psychology and instead locates it in the world; in this way, Scott's novels complicate any attempt to ascribe with positive knowledge the personal motives for his continued anonymity. These late eighteenth- and early nineteenth-century novels, then, offer a theory of the complex networks of human and nonhuman action that bring them into being and sustain them in the world in a manner that contests accounts of the autonomous, proprietary author with his motives for choosing anonymity.

The epilogue explores claims about the death of anonymity with the coming of print (as in Virginia Woolf and Lucien Febvre and Henri-Jean Martin) and the explosion of anonymity with the coming of the digital. Neither claim is true. Both claims depend, however, on the (sometimes) dramatic shift from one dominant medium to the other. Such shifts make evident the networked and agential nature of media and, in doing so, also draw out the persistent, yet unnoticed, current of anonymous cultural production.

In *Everywhere and Nowhere*, I identify the collectives that enable the historical shift in articulations of the figure of the singular "Anonymous" or the named individual author, while showing the simultaneous continued and steady flow of anonymous literary production. Although the eighteenth century has been pointed to as the age of the professional, named author, anonymity persists in and beyond the period. So, too, do the collective agencies that make up literary phenomena. Literary scholars depend on those collectives for the formations of the author and forget about them once there is some version of a single, knowable authorial subject. What this occludes is a whole history of textual engagement and interpretation that does not hinge on the known individual human. My book uncovers this history.

1

Anonymous as Author

What signifies a? A is privative, and signifies not; as,
anonymous, i.e. without, wanting, or not having a Name.
—*The British Grammar* (1762)

Anonymous (A.) a Book or Person without a Name,
or Title of Distinction.
—*A New General English Dictionary* (1737)

This chapter takes up the difference between texts that are tacitly
anonymous (those whose anonymity is not expressed) and those
that are explicitly anonymous (those that are by Anonymous).[1]
Anonymous is a curious sort of authorial name; it signifies a nega-
tion of the name, yet in certain contexts, it also appears as a name.[2]
Charting the course of the adjective *anonymous* from Greek to English, Anne Ferry notes, "It [*anonymous*] was almost always used to
describe a piece of writing or its author, and seems to have carried no
generally held associations beyond the translation of its Greek root:
'without name.' It stayed close to this lexical meaning until the first
half of the twentieth century."[3] As my epigrams suggest, the uses
of "anonymous" ranged far beyond describing writing or authors.
Sir Isaac Newton's *Opticks* (1704) describes "some faint anonymous
Colour."[4] From John Quincy's *Lexicon Physico-Medicum: or, a New
Medicinal Dictionary* (1722), anonymous "signifies without a Name,
for which Reason this hath been at first given to Parts newly taken
notice of, as once to the second Cartilage in the Throat now called
Cricoides or *Cartilago annuliformis*."[5] Most strangely comes a secondary definition from Nathan Bailey's *An Universal Etymological*

English Dictionary (1721): "Anonymous" "*Spirit*, (in *Chymistry*) a sort of Spirit that may be separated from Tartar, and several sorts of Wood."[6]

The definitions offered here suggest a variety of ways of thinking about the relationship between objects and naming. Anonymous may signal something indistinct or something as-of-yet unnamed. Or, as *The British Grammar* (1762) phrases it, while anonymous can mean "wanting" a name, it can also simply mean "without" or "not having" a name. These broad notions of what *anonymous* means, and to whom and what it may be applied, suggest how we might approach anonymity without inevitably recurring to an individual author. To assume that anonymity is a conscious withholding of a name is to assume intentionality in ways that distract us from more intriguing questions of media, agency, and autonomy. Newton had no name for that faint color; *Cartilago annuliformis* was once anonymous before it was named. In studies of literary anonymity, on the other hand, there is an almost universal tendency to regard anonymity as deliberate and self-evident. Anonymity is taken to be the product of conscious choice, and it is immediately obvious to readers. Given the widespread publication of anonymous texts in the period, however, it is not tenable to assume consciousness of either the decision to omit a name on the part of an author or the absence of that name for the reader.

Anonymous, as a kind of authorial name, *does* signal both deliberate action on the part of authors, publishers, or editors—to note a text is "without a name"—and it marks for readers the anonymous status of a text. I extend Marcy North's suggestion that anonymity may be "read through the spaces, expectations, and frames that other paratexts establish" to attend to those moments where anonymity is made visible *as text*.[7] I show the difference between anonymous texts that are attributed to Anonymous and those that are not. This difference is bound to a consciousness of the mediation of the text wherein its anonymity remains tacit or is made explicit.

Moreover, this difference has a particular historical dimension: somewhere around 1770, literary texts began, increasingly, to be attributed to Anonymous. In a study of Eighteenth-Century Collections Online (ECCO 1 and 2), there is a marked increase in the prevalence of "anonymous" from 1700 to 1799. The word goes from appearing in 2 percent of the documents in the period between 1700 and 1709 to appearing in 7 percent of the documents in the period between 1790 and 1799 (Table 1).[8] That particular study does not differentiate between *anonymous* in its adjectival form and Anonymous as a name. However, an examination of all instances of "anonymous" in documents reproduced in ECCO reveals a near-absence of Anonymous as a name on texts that we would consider literary prior to the 1770s.[9] This interest in making anonymity explicit emerges in the latter part of the eighteenth century and is connected to two intellectual developments both concerned implicitly with mediation: a shift in scholarly editing practices toward a bibliographic sensibility and the elocutionary movement.

Though analytical bibliography was not recognizable as a field until the nineteenth century, interest in scholarly editing methods that draw on bibliographic methods appear throughout the seventeenth and eighteenth centuries.[10] Most famously, Edmond Malone's edition of *The Plays and Poems of William Shakespeare* (1790) crystallizes a shift in scholarship in which new forms of evidence were brought to bear on the works of Shakespeare and there emerged an "investigation and explanation of a book as a material object."[11] Margreta de Grazia has argued that

> Malone's overwhelming preoccupation with objectivity marks a significant shift in the focus of Shakespeare studies from what might be termed the discursively acceptable to the factually verifiable, from accounts whose validity was assured by continued circulation to information whose accuracy was tested by documents and records.[12]

In its new interest in authenticity, this form of editing and criticism draws its focus on a biographical writing subject—an author, in this case, Shakespeare—in its object to discover the actual words that he or she wrote.[13] It necessarily recognizes the nature of mediation but disavows it as mere corruption and instead aims at the purification of the text. If there are to be authentic words to be recaptured, it follows that there must be a known or knowable author who wrote them. It is from this context of simultaneous recognition of mediation—the flip side of the aim of textual authenticity

Table 1. A decade by decade count of instances of "anonymous" from *Eighteenth Century Collections Online* (1 and 2)

Year range	Number of total documents with keyword
1700–1709	240 results (11500 total) 2%
1710–1719	382 results (15766 total) 2.4%
1720–1729	531 (13247 total) 4%
1730–1739	626 (13929 total) 4.49%
1740–1749	661 (15438 total) 4.28%
1750–1759	1005, 885 English (17722 total) 5.67%
1760–1769	1160 (21346 total) 5.4%
1770–1779	1626 (23723 total) 6.85%
1780–1789	2091 results (27198 total) 7.68%
1790–1799	2791 results (39391 total) 7.08%

is the recognition of the inherently mediated nature of the text—and its disavowal that Anonymous emerges as a kind of authorial name.[14] De Grazia links these developments to Enlightenment rationality and the emergence of the modern subject, particularly the Foucauldian "author-function." Anonymous is the converse of the author-function. It lacks both the presumed autonomy (and liability) of the authorial subject and the particular classificatory function of the authorial name. It is the form of the authorial name without its function.

Malone was, of course, not alone in adopting these new methods. John Nichols, whose *Select Collections of Poems* (1780) is explored in the second section of this chapter and who was a correspondent of Malone and James Boswell (whose son would publish the 1821 edition of Malone's *Plays and Poems of William Shakespeare*), was likewise interested in practices of collation and attribution in his work in editing Jonathan Swift and Richard Steele.[15] His work as an editor was undoubtedly shaped by his work as a printer. In particular, his notions surrounding authorial attribution and the explicitation of anonymity were bound to his intimate understanding of the materiality of the text and its mediation.

The development in editorial scholarship exemplified by Malone has been pointed to as evidence of the codification of the modern subject whose hallmark is its autonomy.[16] Yet, part and parcel of the emergence of the modern subject within this discourse is an awareness of the subject's entanglement with media and the agencies, both human and nonhuman, that question such claims to autonomy. Anonymous, as a name, occupies a special position between subject and medium; its explicitation makes evident this fundamental tension and entanglement.

This chapter moves across the publication, republication, and circulation of poetry to chart both the historical and epistemic movements in the explicitation of anonymity. I examine anonymous poems and their reprinting and circulation to consider the ways in which poems may be first published with no indication of their anonymity but in reprinting become by "Anonymous."

"Anonymous" as a kind of authorial name gestures at the fictive particularity of the authorial individual's interior life. Anonymous as a name works to signal anonymity as intentional. It turns what may be described as an indication of no action at all—the absence of a name—into the deliberate withholding of the name. In doing so, it gives shape to a fictive person whose motive and thereby interior life may be guessed at. Rather than ceding anonymity as the default and typical condition of publication or a feature of a genre, Anonymous marks anonymity as something extraordinary and in need of explanation.

However, given the expressly mediated and circulated nature of the literary, the marking of that absence may vary across instantiations of a given text, and that marking may only very rarely be attributed properly to an author's action. One edition of a text may appear with no name at all attached to it. Another may be attributed to Anonymous. A third may bear the proper name of an author, though it may be a misattribution. The materiality of the printed text may further ensure that all three (or more) editions circulate simultaneously, each edition casting the relationship, or not, between author and text in a different light. The movement toward consolidation through the explicitation of anonymity is then complicated by the mediation—circulation, materiality, and so on—of the text, most obviously in the variations of attribution present in different instantiations of the text.

Circulation fosters variation while simultaneously imparting a sense of stability in the literary artifact. It is the condition through which the conceptual, material, and agential aspects of the literary assemblage coalesce; it captures both the material movement of things and the conceptual movement of ideas among human and nonhuman agents.[17] Crucially, circulation provides shape and the sense of a structure in a world of movement. That is, an abstraction like the "text," despite the variability in its physical instantiations, may be understood and spoken of as a stable whole through its material and conceptual iteration. In what follows, I trace the circulation of poems across the eighteenth century and the manner in which they do or do not acknowledge their anonymity. What this analysis reveals is that "Anonymous" is neither merely signaling an already present yet tacit anonymity nor providing a name to fill an absence; rather, it occupies an intermediate position between these two poles that indexes the form of the authorial name. It is rather the circulation and iteration of the poems and the media context in which they appear that characterize their mode of being in the world.

Retroactively by Anonymous

This section examines the emergence of Anonymous as a name to whom authorship is explicitly attributed in literary texts. While reports of legal cases used Anonymous as a proper name throughout the period, literary texts only very rarely did so prior to 1770. I take the late eighteenth-century reprinting of several poems included in Richard Steele's 1714 *Poetical Miscellanies* by John Nichols as exemplary of this transformation in attribution practice. In his practice of attributing anonymous poems from the Steele volume to Anonymous, Nichols demonstrates the intermediate position the name Anonymous occupies. Nichols's attributions function not simply to name the absence of the author's name but also unsuccessfully to appease the uncertainty brought about by this absence by consistently attaching the name of an individual human to the words of an explicitly anonymous author.

"My Name," Richard Steele writes at the beginning of the epistle dedicatory to his *Poetical Miscellanies*, "as Publisher of the following Miscellanies, I am sensible, is but a slight Recommendation of them to the Publick; but the Town's Opinion of them will be raised, when it sees them address'd to Mr. *Congreve*."[18] William Congreve receives a laudatory poem and is appealed to as the patron of the volume by Steele through this epistle dedicatory.[19] Steele begins by noting the inadequacy of his own name on the volume to endorse the poems therein contained. Congreve's name when associated with *Poetical Miscellanies*, Steele asserts, "gives an hopeful Idea of the Work," because "He is an acknowledg'd Master of the Art He is desired to Favour." Through his poetry and plays, the name "Congreve" has been established as a kind of commodity upon which Steele hopes to trade in his epistle dedicatory.

For Steele, "Congreve" toggles between its role as a proper name indicating a man of the "most equal, amiable, and correct Behaviour, which can be observed only by [his] intimate Acquaintance" and its role in naming his "several Excellencies as a Writer." David Brewer has shown the way in which authorial names, because of their impersonality, were akin to objects.[20] They were types, means of reference, not indicators of actual humans. Steele, however, holds both uses of the name in mind in this epistle dedicatory; it can authorize, validate, and promote, and it can also name an acquaintance, one with whom Steele "has passed many Happy Hours."

While these uses of the name are central in the epistle dedicatory, it is unclear how important the authorial name is to the remainder of the volume. *Poetical Miscellanies* is filled with anonymous poems. More than half of the poems in the collection are without a named author.[21] The title page promises "original poems and translations" "By the best Hands." Indeed, the table of contents announces poems by Mr. Pope, Mr. Philips, Mr. Parnell, Mr. Tickell, Mr. Gay, Mr. Eusden, Mr. Steele, Mr. Budgell, and others. However, alongside poems and translations from these named authors sit poems that are attributed neither to a named author nor to the suggestive name—Anonymous.

Anonymous poems in the miscellanies, collections, and anthologies of the early eighteenth century were, as Barbara Benedict has suggested, hardly an anomaly.[22] Given this typicality, it is unsurprising that the anonymous status of the poems in this collection is utterly unremarkable despite it seeming otherwise so interested in the authorial name.

In the table of contents (Figure 6), a variety of attributions are given: to named authors, to "the author of," to "several hands," and to "the same hand." However, several poems sit in the table with no attribution at all. For example, "To Belinda" sits in same table of contents with "The Wife of Bath her Prologue from Chaucer By Mr. Pope." "To Belinda" has no attribution; it needs none. It is an anonymous verse in a collection predominated by anonymous verse. In the interior of the volume, on the poem itself, the authorship of "To Belinda" is similarly unattributed (Figure 7).

"To Belinda" remains an anonymous poem; though it has occasionally been attributed to Anne Finch on the basis of internal evidence, no manuscript exists and no external evidence supports such an attribution. The poem first appears in Steele's *Poetical Miscellanies* in 1714 and is reprinted throughout the period in thirteen other collections.[23] In these collections, "To Belinda" is unattributed, except in the fourth volume of John Nichols's 1780 *A Select Collection of Poems with Notes Bibliographical and Historical*, where it is by Anonymous.

A Select Collection of Poems reprints much of the content from Steele's *Poetical Miscellanies*, and whereas in the 1714 volume Steele discounts the ability of his name alone to recommend the poems, the 1780 *Select Collection* features an engraving of Steele as its frontispiece. It is Steele, it seems, who is to endorse this volume in both name and image. Indeed, Steele's name has such weight with Nichols that in lamenting the dearth of poetry by Steele in a note to "Horace, Book I. Ode VI. Applied to the Duke of Marlborough," Nichols writes, "It is rather surprizing that we have no more of his [Steele's] poems. I imagine, however, that some of the verses by anonymous authors in *this* volume, which are said to be from Mr. Steele's collection, are his own."[24] Nichols wishes to attribute to Steele poems of unknown authorship from the *Poetical Miscellanies* as a means of endorsing their inclusion within his own *Collection*, as the watchful engraving of Steele on the frontispiece seems to endorse the collection as a whole.

Nichols, in addition to his role in printing and editing *The Gentleman's Magazine* after 1778, was a noted printer and scholar who was significant in the editing of the works of Jonathan Swift, contributing to Boswell's *Life of Johnson* and editing, printing, and publishing *The Epistolary Correspondence of Richard Steele* (1787). It is

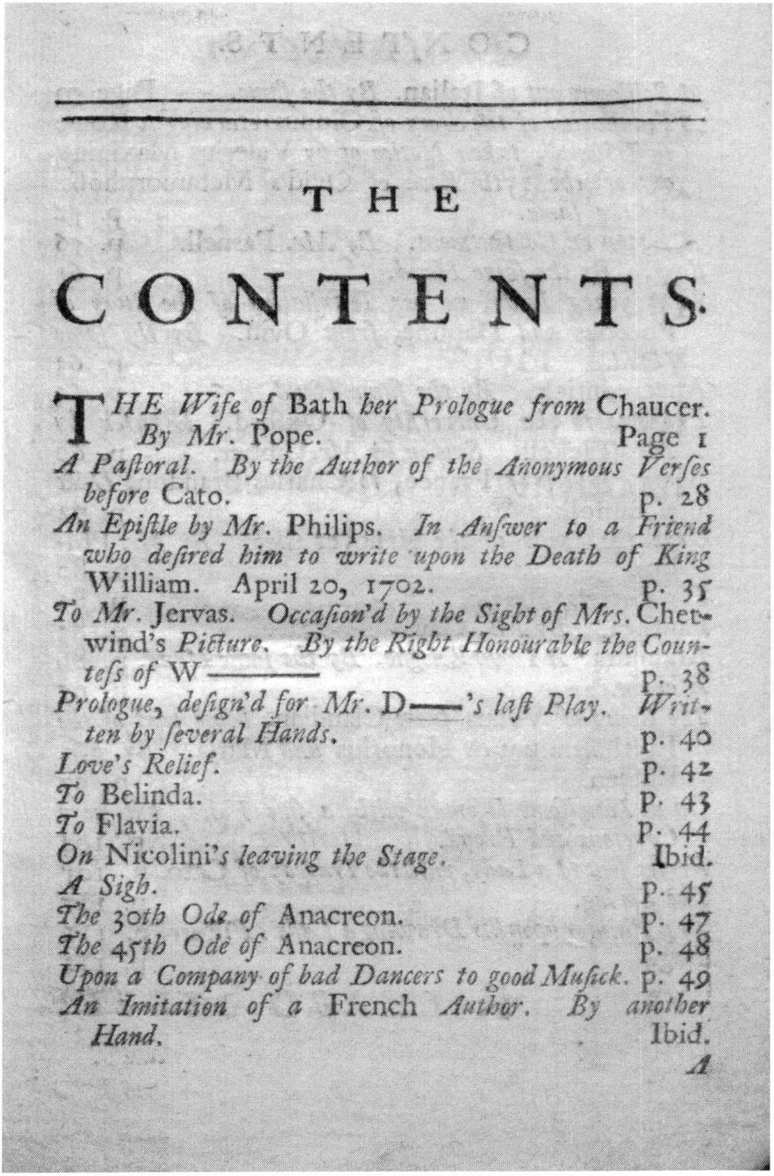

THE

CONTENTS.

A

Figure 6. Table of contents from *Poetical Miscellanies . . . Publish'd by Mr. Steele* (1714). Courtesy of the Department of Special Collections, Memorial Library, University of Wisconsin–Madison.

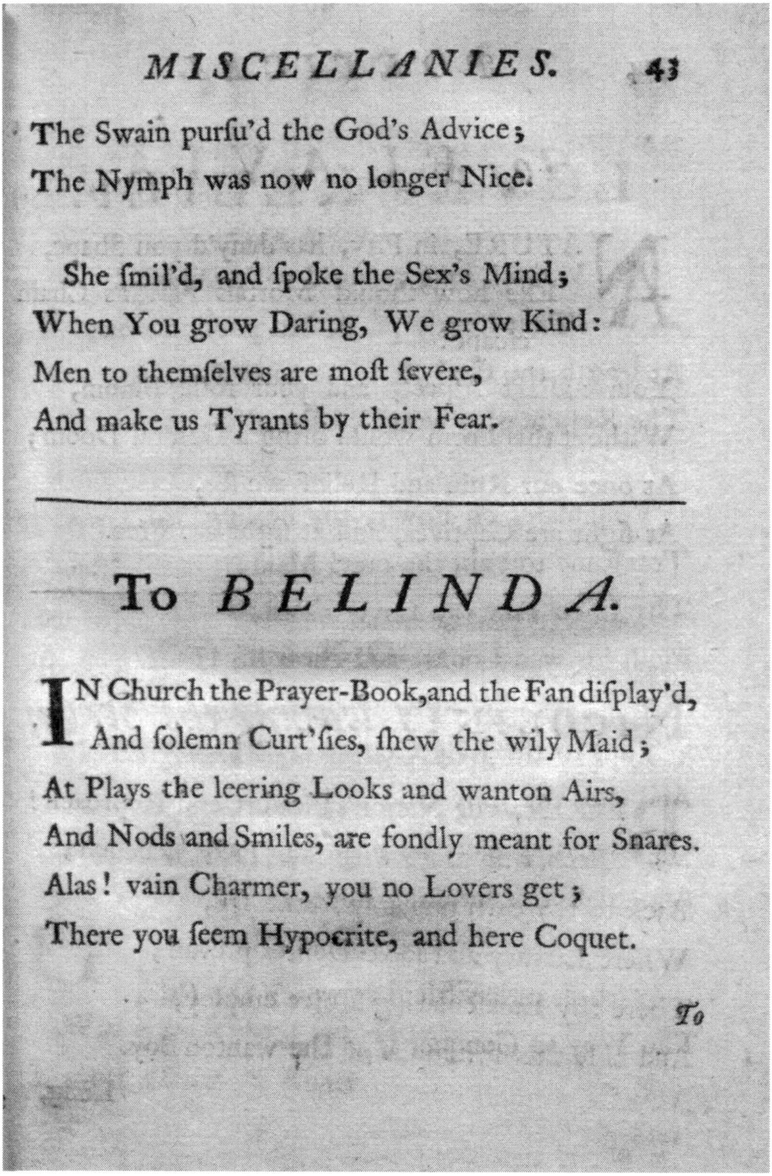
MISCELLANIES. 43

The Swain purſu'd the God's Advice;
The Nymph was now no longer Nice.

She ſmil'd, and ſpoke the Sex's Mind;
When You grow Daring, We grow Kind:
Men to themſelves are moſt ſevere,
And make us Tyrants by their Fear.

To *BELINDA.*

IN Church the Prayer-Book, and the Fan diſplay'd,
And ſolemn Curt'ſies, ſhew the wily Maid;
At Plays the leering Looks and wanton Airs,
And Nods and Smiles, are fondly meant for Snares.
Alas! vain Charmer, you no Lovers get;
There you ſeem Hypocrite, and here Coquet.

To

Figure 7. "To Belinda" from Steele's 1714 *Poetical Miscellanies.* Courtesy of the Department of Special Collections, Memorial Library, University of Wisconsin–Madison.

significant, if not crucial, that Nichols operated both as a printer, acutely attuned to the physical properties of the book, and as a scholarly editor, interested in authorial attribution and collation.[25] Martin W. Maner, for example, has written of Nichols that his "habits as a scholar were inextricably connected with his vocation as a printer. He seems to have thought of his own books less as physical objects than as temporal processes capable of infinite expansion and alteration."[26] While Maner considers books as physical objects in opposition to expansion and alteration, Nichols, as a printer, was keenly aware of the ways in which books, too, were "capable of infinite expansion and alteration." Indeed, Nichols's notions surrounding attribution and the explicitation of anonymity were bound to his intimate understanding of the materiality of the text and its mediated nature.

The most striking example of Nichols's desire to attach Steele's name and names in general to his collection is the reprinting of "To Belinda." "To Belinda" appears among many anonymous poems from *Poetical Miscellanies*. The source of the poems, "From Steele's Collection," is noted, and more importantly, the collection makes explicit their anonymous authorship. Anonymous occupies the position of the author's name on the page underneath the titles of the poems (Figure 8). In the case of "To Belinda," the anonymous status of the poem is further qualified by a note from Nichols that states, "Some of these poems, as I have already mentioned, I believe to be Mr. Steele's" (74).

In their original context from *Poetical Miscellanies*, the anonymous status of the many anonymous poems goes unremarked upon in both the table of contents and the poems themselves. In *Poetical Miscellanies* (1714), Anonymous has no authorial position on the page for "To Belinda." *A Select Collection* (1780) makes explicit the absence of a proper authorial name by placing Anonymous in the position of names like Mr. Prior and Mr. Steele elsewhere in the collection. The unremarkably anonymous poems of *Poetical Miscellanies* become remarkably anonymous in their reprinting in *A Select Collection*.

While Anonymous groups together otherwise disparate poems within the table of contents and the texts themselves under a shared absence of names, it is insufficient as either point of origin

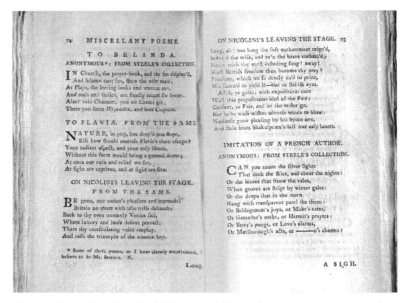

Figure 8. "To Belinda," "To Flavia," "On Nicolini's Leaving the Stage," and "Imitation of a French Author," reprinted in volume 4 of *A Select Collection* (1780). From the General Collection of John J. Burns Library, Boston College.

or classifier. Rather, *A Select Collection* groups "To Belinda," "To Flavia," and "On Nicolini's Leaving the Stage," all anonymous poems from the Steele volume, together in both the table of contents and on the page as "From the same" (74) (Figure 9). "From the same" seems deliberately vague; "from the same" suggests that they are all from the same volume—"Steele's Collection." "By the same" is the phrase used by the collection to signal pieces that share the same author. However, in the case of the poems from the Steele collection, "from the same" is collapsed by Nichols into "by the same." This is made evident in the attribution of "To Belinda": "Anonymous; From Steele's Collection" suggests not only Steele's collection as an original source but Steele himself as the originator. As noted previously, the attribution of Anonymous in "To Belinda" is footnoted, and Nichols suggests, "Some of these poems . . . I believe to be Mr. Steele's" (74). The three poems are, then, grouped as both from the same volume and from the same author, whom Nichols believes to be Steele.

Figure 9. Table of contents of volume 4 of *A Select Collection* (1780). From the General Collection of John J. Burns Library, Boston College.

I argue that for Nichols to note a text being "by the same" is the same as it being "from the same"; he thereby folds the source collection and (incorrectly) presumed author together. By attributing the poems to Anonymous and then twice linking the anonymous poems to Steele, Nichols is not using Anonymous as a means of classifying poems for which he has no authorial attribution. Nor in its explicit attribution, qualified with editorial textual apparati, does Anonymous become the originator of these poems. Rather, Anonymous points back to, and reminds us of, both the context of original publication of the poems *(Poetical Miscellanies)* and the current context of publication *(A Select Collection)*.

Given the manner in which Anonymous refracts notions of origin away from human authors, even as Nichols works to attribute poems to Steele, and toward texts and contexts of publication, the frontispiece depicting "Sir Richard Steele" takes on a different cast. There is a double move in the frontispiece that exceeds its obvious aim to represent Steele's visage; rather, in the same way that "from the same" and "by the same" are collapsed, it asserts the mediation of the poems and the materiality of these volumes, and all volumes.

Steele's image is most readily apprehended from the frontispiece. Under his image is the inscription "SIR RICHARD STEELE ÆT. 46." This is, then, an image of man and an attribution of his name and age. The inscription above the image, however, points away from Steele as a biographical individual and toward Steele as a name in a book among other names. The inscription reads "IMPROVING YOUTH, AND HOARY AGE, ARE BETTER'D BY THY MATCHLESS PAGE!" This line is taken from *Bibliotheca: A Poem Occasioned by the Sight of A Modern Library*. First published anonymously in 1712 and currently attributed to Thomas Newcomb on the basis of the initials "T. N.," which sign the epistle dedicatory, *Bibliotheca* is a lengthy poem that reflects on books, authors, and their collisions in the space of the library. It narrates the difficulty of choice for a reader whose "thoughts were fixt to read" but who is confronted with "the Sight of A Modern Library" wherein "the Treatise [to read] was not yet decreed."[27] Much like Swift's *Battle of the Books*, *Bibliotheca* slides from talking about books as objects on the shelf with reflections on binding, gilding, and, indeed, shelving to those books as metonyms for authorial persons.

The lines about Steele inscribed on the frontispiece of *A Select Collection* appear near the end of the poem where Steele's works are celebrated for banishing dullness:

> Still to proceed the Goddess try'd,
> 'Til S——le's Immortal Works espy'd,
> Trembling her dreaded Foe to view;
> She sunk and silently withdrew . . .
> Hail mighty Name! of all, they [sic] Pen
> Has drop't to charm both Gods and Men,
> Time nor Oblivion e'er shall boast
> One Line, or single Period lost!
> Improving Youth, and Hoary Age,
> Are better'd by thy matchless Page . . . (61)

Steele's "mighty Name" is here blanked out. This blank between letters invites the reader to fill in the name and in doing so also calls attention to the typography and the materiality of the page itself; the blank space ought to correlate to the missing letters. The name does not immediately refer to the person but rather routes the reader through the page and type before her. In the same way, the stanzas speak of the abstract "Immortal Works" but ground them in their instantiation, "One Line, or single Period" on the "matchless Page."

The inscription is drawn from the 1712 *Bibliotheca,* but it is more clearly quoting the poem as it is reprinted in the third volume of *A Select Collection.* This is the volume that directly precedes volume four, in which Steele's frontispiece and the reprinted poems from *Poetical Miscellanies* appear. In its reprinted state, the anonymous poem is attributed to William King, whose portrait serves as frontispiece for the volume in which it appears, but Nichols notes, "This is ascribed to Dr. King upon conjecture only. It was published in 1712, the winter before he died, by *his* bookseller, inscribed to *his* patron, and is very much in *his* manner" (emphasis in original).[28]

The attribution of the poem to King is not the only alteration or attribution that this instance of the poem attracts. "Still to proceed the Goddess try'd, / 'Til S——le's Immortal Works espy'd" in the 1712 edition becomes in the 1780 collection "Still to proceed the Goddess try'd, / Till Steele's Immortal Works espy'd;" (71). Nichols in his *Select Collection* has effectively "filled in the blank" in explicitly naming Steele. It is within this context that the inscription from the poem appears in the Steele frontispiece. Despite the presence of Steele's name in the reprinted poem, the inscription on the frontispiece works only to assert the bookishness of the volume and the visual and textual elements inscribed thereon.[29]

The frontispiece gestures at the previous volume in which the poem appears and to *Bibliotheca,* a poem explicitly about the materiality of books. This produces a recursive loop where the reader moves from image to poem in the prior volume back to image, where she is reminded of the "matchless page" that indicates Steele's oeuvre but nonetheless is a reminder that an actual page lay before her. The frontispiece does the work of reminding one of that book (Steele's *Poetical Miscellanies*), this book (Nichols's *Select Collection,* vol. 4), the prior volume (Nichols's *Select Collection,* vol. 3), and books as material objects writ large.[30]

"Steele" in *A Select Collection* toggles between mediation and name as type and means of reference; this is different than Steele's deployment of "Congreve" in his *Poetical Miscellanies*.[31] While "Congreve" could work to name both type and the biographical person with whom Steele had a personal acquaintance in 1714, "Steele" never recurs to an actual person in 1780. This is not simply a consequence of Steele's death in 1729. Rather, it is connected with the explicit presence of "Anonymous" as an authorial name—Anonymous in this volume is, of course, meant to point toward "Steele." Anonymous, however, signals and enables the shift away from persons and toward media. Anonymous undoes the fiction that one could, within the mediated literary context, ever get to the named, human author.

The explicitation of the anonymous status of the poems from Steele's volume is not an isolated decision made by a printer publisher of reprinted poems. Rather, it represents a larger historical movement in which the anonymous status of literary texts is marked and made explicit by attributing them to "Anonymous." This transformation is not complete within the period, nor does it hold true for all printed texts; however, within the period from 1770 to 1800, there is a remarkable increase in the number of anonymous literary texts that are marked or attributed explicitly to "Anonymous." Attributed anonymity appears to assuage the uncertainty engendered by anonymity by placing a name of an author, Anonymous, where there is none. In the case of *A Select Collection*, Anonymous brings with it further attributions; however, those attributions, rather than pointing toward a biographical personage, or even an authorial personage, point primarily toward the mediated text itself. In what follows, I show just how anonymity and the explicit attribution to Anonymous further work to call attention to the medium across the broader historical circulation of one of the period's most well-known poems.

"Anonymous" in Circulation

Near the very beginning of Jane Austen's *Northanger Abbey*, amid the description of unlikely heroine Catherine Morland, the reader is told,

Her mother was three months in teaching her only to repeat the "Beggar's Petition;" and after all, her next sister, Sally, could say it better than she did. Not that Catherine was always stupid—by no means; she learnt the fable of "The Hare and Many Friends" as quickly as any girl in England.[32]

Nearly forgotten in our own period, "The Beggar's Petition," or "The Beggar" (1769), as it was originally titled, was one of the most well-known poems of the late eighteenth and nineteenth centuries. As Romantic-era essayist Charles Lamb remarks, "who cannot say by heart the 'Beggar's Petition?'"[33] In *Northanger Abbey*, "The Beggar's Petition" is set alongside "The Hare and Many Friends" as two op-posing texts for oral recitation and performance. Catherine's diffi-culty in memorizing the piece, as Claire Grogan suggests, "indicates her refreshingly independent spirit," while her ready ability to memorize and repeat "The Hare and Many Friends" "foreshadows Catherine's own predicament" in Northanger Abbey (n. 1 and 2).

Despite the current sense of "The Beggar's Petition" as a "tawdry piece," in its adaptation and circulation as the anonymous "The Beggar's Petition," "The Beggar" became one of the most popu-lar poems of the late eighteenth century. "The Beggar's Petition," correspondent Salopiensis writes to *The Gentleman's Magazine* in 1790,

> has, by the force of intrinsic merit, found its way into almost every collection which has been made for several years past; but, what I think a great injustice to the author, has always been in-serted without a name. Whilst every admirer of genuine poetry is delighted with its beauties, the author's name is only known in the circle of his friends.[34]

Salopiensis identifies three key features of the poem and its circula-tion: its "intrinsic merit," its presence in "almost every collection," and its anonymity. While he finds a tension between the popular-ity and anonymity of the poem, I contend that its popularity in fact enabled its continued anonymity because of its sustained existence and circulation across multiple genres and media forms.

To illustrate this counterintuitive dynamic between popularity and anonymity wherein the anonymity of a piece is sustained through its popularity and continued circulation, consider that though Salopiensis acknowledges the anonymity of "The Beggar's Petition" and writes to give the author his due by identifying "Rev. Thomas Moss" as the writer of the poem, this attribution did not seem to matter or stick. Even with the 1790 letter to *The Gentleman's Magazine* attributing "The Beggar's Petition" to Moss, when the magazine reprinted the poem in 1791, it appeared with no authorial attribution.[35] In short, the circulation of the poem outran its authorial attributions; it continued to circulate anonymously and with false attributions well into the nineteenth and twentieth centuries.[36]

"Rev. T. Moss A. M. Minister of Brierley Hill Staffordshire" is indeed the accepted author of the poem "The Beggar."[37] "The Beggar" appeared in 1769 as part of the anonymous *Poems on Several Occasions*, which was "published at the Request of a few Friends who were pleas'd to honour them with their Approbation,"[38] with its author supposedly "stipulating that his name should be affixed to no more than twenty copies."[39] "The Beggar," despite its inclusion in twentieth-century collections of eighteenth-century verse and the attribution of the 1783 poem *The Imperfection of Human Enjoyments* to "The Reverend Thomas Moss . . . Author of the Poem Entitled 'The Beggar,'" is rarely considered in the canon of eighteenth-century poetry.[40]

As the examples from Austen, Lamb, and *The Gentleman's Magazine* suggest, however, "The Beggar's Petition" had saturated the culture as both a print and oral phenomenon by the late eighteenth century and taken its place within a canon of popular literature. It had done so as a primarily anonymous poem, despite attributions to Moss throughout the period. The reason for this is simple: Thomas Moss did not author "The Beggar's Petition." "The Beggar" is a source for "The Beggar's Petition" and Moss most likely the writer of that source. However, one can point neither to Moss as origin for the poem nor to a single instance of the poem as *the text* of the "The Beggar's Petition." Rather, it is in its circulation through which the conceptual, material, and agential aspects of the text coalesce, such that Lamb or Austen could invoke the poem by its accepted title and be apprehended by a reader, that the poem appears as a consistent whole. Thus the discrete instance of the text, the seemingly solid "thing in the hand," or the name of an author, matters less than the poem's continued movement across time and space.[41]

One of the primary vectors for movement across time and space of "The Beggar's Petition" was through anthologies.[42] Between 1769 and 1901, "The Beggar's Petition" appears in at least eighty-six different collections (and likely many more) printed in Britain, Ireland, Vienna, New York, Boston, and Philadelphia. Barbara Benedict has argued that the anthology, in recontextualizing texts, works to universalize them by removing their historical specificity (17). Such recontextualization does not, however, stop at the anthology in its book form. Rather, as a medium, the anthology enables further instantiations of poetry across new and different media forms and contexts.[43] Appearing in elocution manuals, magazines, primers, reading manuals, and poetry collections, this "pathetic" poem, as several collections classified its genre, reached an amazingly wide reading, and listening, public.[44]

Both Austen and Lamb indicate that one of the other primary modes of transmission of "The Beggar's Petition" was rote memorization and recitation. Indeed, in her biography of James Fenimore Cooper, Mary E. Phillips describes a young Cooper performing "The Beggar's Petition" at a school exhibition:

> These "Academy boys" were ambitious; each annual exhibition was crowded, to listen to the speeches "of Coriolanus, Iago, Brutus, and Cassius" by "raw lads from the village and adjoining farms," all in the bravery of local militia uniform—blue coats "faced with red, matross swords, and hats of '76." On such an occasion James Cooper . . . became the pride and admiration of Master Cory for his moving recitation of the "Beggar's Petition"—acting the part of an old man wrapped in a faded cloak and leaning over his staff.[45]

In this scene of oral performance, Cooper does not simply recite "The Beggar's Petition"; he becomes the petitioning beggar, acting the part with costume to match. Tellingly, "The Beggar's Petition" is set alongside "speeches 'of Coriolanus, Iago, Brutus, and Cassius,'" each texts frequently reprinted in elocution manuals, to represent its place in a canon of texts for oral performance.[46]

This process of canonization began with the first print appearance of the retitled "The Beggar's Petition" in William Enfield's *The Speaker* (1774).[47] This elocution manual was the likely source of the poem for Austen.[48] The title page of *The Speaker* announces that its purpose is "to facilitate the improvement of youth in reading and speaking," and "The Beggar's Petition" appears in the volume without any authorial attribution; it is not attributed to Moss, and it is not attributed to Anonymous.[49] Enfield is credited with making the changes from "The Beggar" to "The Beggar's Petition," and it is these changes at the level of textual representation that are the most significant to the poem in its circulation.[50] Take, for example, the stanza that opens and concludes "The Beggar":

> PITY the Sorrows of a poor old Man!
> Whose trembling Limbs have borne him to your Door,
> Whose Days are dwindled to the shortest Span,
> Oh! give Relief—-and Heav'n will bless your Store.
> (1–4, 41–44)[51]

This stanza represents the address of the poor old man to the petitionee at the door of the home. Here, the dashes in the final line serve as a means of representing a pause in speech. The fourth stanza makes similar use of textual effect to represent emphasis in speech as the beggar narrates his experience begging at a neighboring home:

> (Hard is the Fate of the infirm, and poor!)
> *Here* craving for a Morsel of their Bread,
> A pamper'd Menial forc'd me from the Door,
> To seek a Shelter in an humbler Shed. (13–16)

The opening line of the stanza, with its use of parentheses, marks both a contrast with the previous lines, "For Plenty there a Residence has found, / And Grandeur a magnificent Abode" (11–12), where they textually mark the meagerness of the beggar and a change in tone of his speech. Likewise, the italicized *"Here"* emphasizes both the deictic to indicate the beggar's situation and the emphatic tone that ought to be placed on it. These textual effects work to shape the reception of the poem by marking emphasis for private reading or reading aloud.[52] In its representation of the address of the beggar, the poem invites one to imagine and enact its oral performance. The textual presentation of the poem follows on the rhetorical situation of the petitioning beggar by marking how one ought to read and speak its content.

So, too, the epigraph that precedes the first stanza, "— — — inopemque paterni Et Laris, et Fundi — — —" (lacking paternal land and estate), anticipates the story of the poem in which the beggar tells of having lost his father's land. The epigraph, however, elides the full line from Horace's *Epistles*: "inopemque paterni et laris et fundi paupertas impulit audax, ut versus facerem"[53] (without support / from the family farm, the insolence of poverty / drove me to verse).[54] Preceded by the epigraph, the textual presentation of "The Beggar" on the page replaces the claim for a poet compelled by poverty to write verses with the actual verses on the page and the beggar as the poet who composes and recites those verses. While the Steele frontispiece from *A Select Collection* invites recursive looping and reflection on the books in and on which the frontispiece and the poetry appear, here the relationship between the title of the poem, the epigraph, and the text of the poem circles back to the rhetorical situation of the beggar and, in a deeply Barthesian sense, stages the origin of the poem not in its publication but in its reading and enunciation.[55]

Despite its appearance in *The Speaker*, a work "undertaken principally with the design of assisting . . . in acquiring a just and graceful Elocution," "The Beggar's Petition" makes no such use of textual effects and omits the Horatian epigraph as cues to its interpretation, oral performance, and origin (iii). The dashes, italics, and parentheses that appear throughout "The Beggar" are not in evidence. "The Beggar's Petition" standardizes its punctuation marks. The final line of the first and last stanzas becomes, for example, "Oh! give relief, and Heaven will bless your store" (4). For a volume whose express purpose in reprinting this and other texts is so that they may be spoken aloud, it seems counterintuitive to erase the marks from the source text that guide how it should be read, just as it seems counterintuitive to erase an epigraph that locates the poem's origin in its enunciation.

Enfield's "An Essay on Elocution," which begins the volume, however, addresses just these points in discussing the relationship between printed punctuation and pronunciation:

> The use of points is to assist the reader in discerning the grammatical construction, not to direct his pronunciation. In reading, it may often be proper to make a pause where the printer has made none. Nay, it is very allowable for the sake of pointing out the sense more strongly, preparing the audience for what is to follow, or enabling the speaker to alter the tone or height of the voice, sometimes to make a very considerable pause, where the grammatical construction requires none at all. (xx–xxi)

Enfield suggests that the oral performance of printed texts is itself an act of interpretation where one is encouraged to disregard the printed marks upon the page "for the sake of pointing out the sense more strongly."[56] The oral emphasis is separate from the grammatical construction indicated on the page as intended by either author, editor, or printer. Given this insistence on the role of interpretation in oral performance, then, the changes from "The Beggar" are necessary to the project of *The Speaker*. The textual effects of "The Beggar" offer an interpretation to reading the text that imposes emphasis on the reader, whereas "The Beggar's Petition" encourages one to engage with the text and make a choice in emphasis.[57]

Similarly, the omission of the epigraph in *The Speaker* relocates emphasis from the beggar in the poem as origin and locus of control to the speaker of the poem. Thus Cooper, in his "moving recitation of the 'Beggar's Petition'—acting the part of an old man wrapped in a faded cloak and leaning over his staff," does not merely recite the words of another but those words become his own; the implied actions and gestures of the beggar become his own (26). Cooper here, or others reciting the poem in multiple instances across the period, becomes very literally the medium for "The Beggar's Petition." Like all media, the speaker as medium acts upon the text in such ways as Enfield outlines in his reflection on punctuation.

Just as shifts in scholarly editing crystallized in the latter half of the period with an eye toward authenticity and a recognition of mediation, so too did the elocutionary movement cohere such that in the mid-eighteenth century, "elocution became quickly intertwined with developments in the theatre, art, criticism, politics and the church."[58] As Dana Harrington and Paul Goring have both shown, the elocutionary movement of the mid- to late eighteenth century emphasized embodiment and the marshaling of the body as medium.[59] The shift toward a sentimental mode of elocution, popularized by Thomas Sheridan, was essential in yoking verbal expression to bodily expression.[60] Enfield was both influenced by and occasionally (at least on library shelves) in competition with Sheridan.[61]

Necessary to both Sheridan and Enfield is an awareness and harnessing of the body as medium. This differs from what I've shown earlier in Malone and Nichols, whose task was to attend to the mediation of text only to render it transparent in search of the authentic text. Those elocutionists who followed in the wake of Sheridan emphasized and theorized mediation such that questions of authenticity and origin were not relevant. As such, those anonymous texts that were chosen for inclusion in elocutionary manuals rarely bore the name Anonymous.

Enfield's reflection, then, makes palpable the speaker as evident and obvious medium—there is no ignoring Cooper in his faded cloak. Whereas "The Beggar" seems to reduce itself to its textuality—which, in part, enabled its robust circulation—"The Beggar's Petition" is bound to its media context; indeed, the poem exists solely in that context. Through its appearance in *The Speaker*, Enfield models how "The Beggar's Petition" may be remediated and recontextualized. This occurred as it appeared in multiple collections, anthologies, and elocution manuals. It was further remediated and recontextualized as it was memorized, satirized, parodied, printed on handkerchiefs, and recited in schoolhouses. Along the way, the poem appeared with multiple attributions or no attributions at all and demonstrates the complex manner in which anonymity and mediation mutually reveal each other.

"The Beggar's Petition" circulated without authorial attribution throughout various anthologies and, as it was shaped by Enfield's elocutionary theory, bore with it interpretive flexibility for the reader and speaker. However, while "The Beggar's Petition" was popular in elocution manuals from its outset, it also circulated widely in a more didactic context through *A Father's Instructions to His Children* (circa 1776). Dr. Thomas Percival is the accepted author of *A Father's Instructions*. An English physician, Percival wrote primarily on medical matters; however, around 1775, he published the first part of what would become the wildly popular *A Father's Instructions*.[62] Published anonymously by J. Johnson, publisher of Enfield's *The Speaker, A Father's Instructions* includes "The Beggar's Petition" in its section "Compassion to the Poor."[63] While "The Beggar's Petition" receives no proper authorial attribution in *A Father's Instructions*, it does include a citation at its conclusion: "The Speaker, by Dr. Enfield" (44).

The text of "The Beggar's Petition" in *A Father's Instructions* is identical to that which was printed in *The Speaker*, and it is very likely, given the shared publisher, that *The Speaker* is the only source of the poem for *A Father's Instructions*. While the expressed purpose of "The Beggar's Petition" in *The Speaker* was to teach the elocution of "pathetic pieces," the purpose of "The Beggar's Petition" in *A Father's Instructions* is didactic. "The Author"[64] writes of the volume's "objects of instruction" in the preface:

> The first and leading one is to refine the feelings of the heart, and to inspire the mind with the love of moral excellence. And surely nothing can operate more forcibly, than striking pictures of the beauty of virtue, and the deformity of vice; which at once convince the judgment, and leave a lasting impression on the imagination. (13–14)

Whereas Enfield's "Essay on Elocution" in *The Speaker* focuses on externalization through oral performance, the preface to *A Father's Instructions* turns to the inward effect of the readings in the collection on the mind.[65] With its emphasis on tone and articulation, "Essay on Elocution" attends to refining the processes through which one makes the text external to the self through performance. *A*

Father's Instructions, however, following eighteenth-century theories of mind, attends to the internal processes through which one comes to moral judgment from external sources, such as the works in the collection.

The citation of "The Speaker, by Dr. Enfield" at the end of "The Beggar's Petition" is thus suggestive given the inward turn that "The Beggar's Petition" takes through *A Father's Instructions*. Percival's text borders on pedantic in its use of footnotes throughout the volume, and so the citation of the source of "The Beggar's Petition" is not unexpected. However, *A Father's Instructions* is the first context in which "The Beggar's Petition" receives any sort of citation of source or attribution to the poem. That any citation appears first in *A Father's Instructions* is significant to the circulation of "The Beggar's Petition," because the poem's appearance in the volume is a moment of divergence in the circulation of the poem that holds throughout the period. "The Beggar's Petition" circulates simultaneously as work to be read and performed aloud in elocution manuals like *The Speaker* and as poem to be read to oneself for moral edification, as in *A Father's Instructions*.

The poem's appearance in *A Father's Instructions* is not just a divergence in circulation; it is a remediation of the poem in which its mediation is rendered seemingly transparent. The palpable mediation of "The Beggar's Petition" as it circulates as an elocutionary text gives way to a fantasy of transparency in which the medium fades away and the words alone "leave a lasting impression on the imagination" (14). The curious attribution at the end of the poem, "The Speaker, by Dr. Enfield," however, works much like the acknowledgment of anonymity by gesturing beyond the text and possible author to its mediated nature. The attribution signals, ambiguously, the source and possible origin of the poem and, in doing so, locates it in an expressly mediated context that undoes any claim to origin. In oral performance, there is no such need for acknowledging origin or anonymity. One can identify and point to the source of the words of the speaker. The question of authorship or anonymity is effectively effaced by the speaker's embodied performance of the text. The medium is evident and sufficient enough to maintain anonymity as an unremarkable feature of the text, whereas when the poem diverges toward its didactic purposes via *A Father's Instructions*, there is a desire evident to acknowledge the anonymity of the poem or an attempt to name its author.

In its circulation, a rough pattern emerges of "The Beggar's Petition" and its attribution based on its intended reading and use. Volumes of poetry and instruction, such as *Lessons in Reading* (1780), *Profusiones Poeticae* (1788), *Elegant Extracts; or, Useful and Entertaining Pieces of Poetry* (1791), *Extracts, Elegant and Instructive* (1791), *The Beauties of Poetry, British and American* (1791), *The Poetical Epitome* (1792), *The Temple of Apollo* (1796), *The Selector; or, Miscellaneous Pieces from the Best English Writers* (1798), *The English Reader* (1799), *The Domestic Instructor* (1800), *The Beauties of English Poetry: Selected from the Most Esteemed Authors* (1804), *The Young Gentleman and Lady's Poetical Preceptor* (1807), *The Muses' Bower Embellished with the Beauties of English Poetry* (1809), *Pierpont's Introduction: Introduction to the National Reader; A Selection of Easy Lessons Designed to Fill the Same Place in the Common Schools of the United States* (1832), and *Cobb's Sequel to the Juvenile Readers* (1834), all attribute "The Beggar's Petition" explicitly to Anonymous, while volumes like *The Speaker, The Oratorical Instructor,* and other elocution manuals do not.[66]

"Anonymous" is thus not simply an expression of an already obvious anonymity nor a means of classifying a text. Rather, it is linked to the media context in which the poem appears. Where a speaker may occupy an authorial subject position, anonymous is not generally attributed. This is palpable mediation.[67] Where a silent reader is understood as the primary consumer of the poem, the anonymity of the poem is made explicit or some authorial attribution is given. Such attributions call attention not only to the anonymity of the poem but to its life as mediated literary artifact. This is in tension with the claims to immediacy of the poem wherein text is presented for the reader's moral edification. Moral edification presumes a directedness of text that necessarily implies transparency of the medium. A reader whose attention is drawn to the book as object or network of citation may miss the moral; the media may act on the poem and thereby affect its interpretation and internalization. Anonymous as an authorial name seems to establish a logic of substitution by pointing to some empirical individual to whom the text may be attributed, thereby anchoring the text and its meaning, but it often gives way not to individual humans but to instances of mediation.

One novel solution to the problem of didactic aims and the mediated (and remediated) poem was misattribution and reimagining the rhetorical situation of the poem. "The Beggar's Petition" did not circulate anonymously—either "by Anonymous" or tacitly without name—exclusively.[68] *The Orator* (Edinburgh, 1776) attributes "The Beggar's Petition" to Dr. Percival. "The Beggar's Petition" in *The British Poetical Miscellany* (circa 1799), published in Huddersfield and sold throughout Britain, again misattributes a version of the poem, with significant additions by F. J. Guion, to Percival.[69] The attribution of the poem to Percival well after Moss's 1783 claiming of "The Beggar" and various attributions of "The Beggar's Petition" to authors other than Percival in *Gentleman's Magazine* in the 1790s is worth noting; the context of the attribution within this volume is further compelling because the attribution appears alongside explicit attributions of works of unknown authorship to Anonymous.

The version that appears in *The British Poetical Miscellany* adds a narrative prefatory stanza at the beginning of the poem and two stanzas at the end, one in which the listener of the beggar's petition responds and the other of which narrates the beggar's response to the petitionee's charity. In doing so, the symmetry of the poem is altered such that the opening and closing stanzas are no longer the same. The stanza narrates the occasion of the beggar's petition, but it only narrates what is already evident in the words of the beggar. We learn of the events that have brought the beggar to his condition later in the poem. Likewise, we learn of the beggar's attempt to beg for alms at a house of "grandeur" shortly after the appeal for pity of the opening stanza. The narrative piece seems out of place in the context of the poem as it has been previously circulating to this moment. As the poem has circulated, it is a monologue spoken by the beggar. This form lends itself to the already noted oral performance of the poem. The additions by Guion mark the text as aimed at private reading. The addition of the narrative stanza is coupled with two additional stanzas at the end of the poem that transform the poem into a dialogue. The response of the listener is a dramatic change in form. The new stanzas have brought the additional voices of a narrator and listener to the solitary voice of the beggar in previous editions. Furthermore, this edition adds quotation marks and dashes heretofore absent from "The Beggar's Petition." As in "The Beggar," this edition of "The Beggar's Petition" uses textual effects to mark speech, but it does so not as cues to oral performance but as cues to the individual silent reader. As the editions of "The Beggar's Petition" in *The Speaker* and *A Father's Instructions* in the 1770s marked a divergence in the intended circulation and consumption of the poem, the edition in *The British Poetical Miscellany* attempts to resolve this divergence by using the orality inherent in the poem and altering its form to serve the private reader and ensure the proper moral is modeled.

In changing the form of the poem, Guion follows the imperative of Percival to make the poem suitable for "reflection and judgment." It is, of course, Percival to whom the poem is attributed. He has, as the changes suggest, authored the mode of understanding the poem that the changes in form reflect. The Guion-added thirteenth stanza of the poem in particular reimagines the question of moral judgment for the reader. In both "The Beggar" and "The Beggar's Petition," the reader or listener is left with the imperative: "Oh! give relief, and Heaven will bless your store!" to which she must form a judgment and respond. The expanded "The Beggar's Petition" removes the occasion for judgment and replaces it with the response from the fictional petitioned listener in the poem:

> "Enter, my aged friend!" reply'd the host,
> "Enter my humble mansion—child of woe!
> "No pompous grandeur does my table boast—
> "Such as I have, I freely will bestow—" (49–52)

The host responds with charity and compassion to the beggar. The reader is no longer presented with the question of how to respond. In adding the names Percival and Guion, the reader is further oriented toward the poem as anchored by its purported origin instead of its context of mediation. This rewriting of the poem coupled with its attributions attempts to subordinate the medium to the moral message.

The British Poetical Miscellany is committed to some form of authorial attribution for every poem in the volume. Those with named authors are attributed to those authors; those without named authors are attributed to Anonymous. This volume, then, presents an ideal case for considering the functions of named authorship and explicit anonymity and, by extension, that of tacit anonymity. Guion/Percival characterize mode of being for "The Beggar's Petition" in the world in a manner that Anonymous simply could not. Indeed, the logic of reimagining the poem is drawn from the logic of attribution at work in the poem and the volume more broadly. That is, anchoring the moral of the poem, as it appears with the added stanzas, builds upon the anchoring of the poem to its didactic father, Percival. Anonymous, on the other hand, points to the text's status as literary artifact. This expressly mediated status serves as a reminder of the competing agents, both human and nonhuman, involved in literary production and representation.

In its various attributions and transformations, "The Beggar's Petition" is a popular, yet understudied, example that allows for examining the function of Anonymous within literary texts. The attribution to Anonymous is connected to the mode of consumption and circulation imagined for the work. While tacit anonymity may seem to be connected to immediacy (the transparency of the medium), the opposite is true. Anonymity that bears no attribution to Anonymous is more typical of those forms of circulation where the mediation of the text is readily apprehended, whereas those forms that bear with them an ideology of medial transparency more often than not make their anonymity explicit. Attributing a text to Anonymous is different than attributing a text to a named author or not attributing a text at all. As we have seen throughout the chapter, marking anonymity calls attention to the absence of the author's name but, in doing so, also draws attention to the medium.

It is only after 1770 that Anonymous appears regularly as an authorial name on literary texts. It is tempting to think of the appearance of Anonymous as the logical extension of the professionalization of authorship and a movement toward the figure of the Romantic author.[70] I argue throughout this chapter, however, that Anonymous signals in fact the opposite: it is a movement away from the centrality of authors and persons and toward a network of mediation of which an author may be a part but of which she is not central.

As this chapter's study of the emergence of Anonymous is connected with the history of authorship, it is a history of authorship that is a history of its place within mediation rather than a history of origin, or liability, or property. The standard Foucauldian narrative in which the emergence of the author-function is bound to regimes of property and liability and the disappearance of anonymity is troubled by on-the-ground literary practices that suggest a far more diverse history, not of the emergence of single sovereign subjects, but of a growing awareness of mediation and subjects' complex relationships within mediation.

This chapter has identified the historical shift toward attributed anonymity in literary texts. "Anonymous," within literary contexts, is the form of the authorial name which functions not to "point a finger" toward someone or act "equivalent of a description" but to signal the objecthood of the literary artifact. The popularity of "The Beggar's Petition," if not its canonicity, makes it representational of the larger historical movement toward attributed anonymity and the work Anonymous does for a text. Within each literary example, Anonymous has served to remind one of the mediation, circulation, and possible reception of the text to which it is attached. This defamiliarization of anonymity, whereby tacit anonymity is made explicit, rather than pointing to an unease with the phenomenon and the desire for an author, indicates both an awareness of anonymity and an awareness of the medium.

2

"Acting Plays" and "Reading Plays"

Intermediation and Anonymity

As the previous chapter considered the explicitation of anonymity in the latter part of the eighteenth century, it also raised the question about the role of media in the legibility of anonymity. This chapter picks up on this question to consider the marked difference in patterns of authorial attribution in printed and staged drama. Attributed authorship was far from typical in the theater of the eighteenth century. In the 1726–27 season, for example, fully 60 percent of the new plays and theatrical entertainments presented on the London stage were (and remain) anonymous.[1] In general, this anonymity was wholly unremarkable; it was simply the nature of the medium. Some of the reasons for this may be found in James Ralph's *The Case of Authors by Profession or Trade Stated* (1758). Ralph, playwright and contributor to Henry Fielding's *The Champion*, rhetorically asks, "Have not we already transferr'd the Merit of the Composer to the Performer? Have not we gone farther still, and suppos'd the Merit of the personated Character to adhere to the real?"[2] If it is the case, as Ralph suggests, that eighteenth-century audiences had "already transferr'd the Merit of the Composer to the Performer," it is unlikely that authorial anonymity would have been notable to many in those audiences. This is because drama allows for the fantasy of immediacy over distanciation, that is, the unmediated presence of others over the mediated distance implied by the technology of writing. It does so in two ways: first, by placing the words of an author in the mouths of actors, it suggests an immediacy whereby both author and medium (the actor) dissolve—thus, for Ralph, this imagined audience not only "transfers merit" to the actor but supposes the actor to be no actor at all; he or she is, rather, "real"—and second, in the collective nature of the theatrical experience, both on- and offstage, the medium further fades by virtue of the social, interactive, and varied milieu of the theater of the eighteenth century. Thus, though heavily mediated, the theatrical experience may not have seemed as such. It follows, then, that authorship and anonymity—essential layers of mediation (at least for the literary historian)—was not necessarily notable to audiences.

In an obverse manner, literary and theater historians, too, often participate in this fantasy of immediacy when seeking to tell the history of authorship with and through the artifacts of cultural production. That is, though scholars distinguish between, for example, printed text and performance, they only rarely attend to *how* that difference might shape expectations about the presence or absence of an author and his name. Thus the critic is like Samuel Johnson, who claims in his preface to *Works of Shakespeare*, "A play read, affects the mind like a play acted."[3] Though critics are often presented only with the mediated evidence of authorial activity, it is treated as evidence for authorship itself.

If the majority of audiences in the theater did not take note of the absence of authorial attribution, dramatic catalogers of the Restoration and eighteenth century certainly did, by systematically cataloging printed anonymous plays *as anonymous* throughout the period. Beginning with Gerard Langbaine's *A New Catalogue of English Plays* in 1688, known more widely by its pirated title of *Momus Triumphans*, catalogers of plays and writers of the lives of dramatic poets regularly set aside anonymous plays as separate and distinct from plays whose authors were known or attributed. These writers clearly thought it notable that there was a body of plays for which no author could be named, and they deemed it necessary to create separate sections for anonymous plays in their catalogs.[4] Yet, save for Giles Jacob's *An Historical Account of the Lives and Writings of Our Most Considerable English Poets* (1720), there seems to be no attempt at such systematic cataloging of other anonymous literary forms.[5] While poetry and prose fiction do not become "by Anonymous" until the latter part of the eighteenth century, the anonymity of printed drama is made obvious much earlier in the period.

We have here a seeming paradox. On one hand, we have a largely anonymous theatrical tradition wherein anonymity is utterly unremarkable. On the other, we have a cataloging schema that serves specifically to draw attention to the anonymity of the play texts. To account for this difference in attribution between drama and other literary forms, Robert Hume has argued that there is a "double tradition" in performed and printed drama in the early eighteenth century, wherein performance and print diverge and the status accorded the author differs between the performance and the printed play text. He argues that "scripts were *titles* much more than they were 'works' by literary authors."[6] Theater, he argues, was just different; it emphasized actors over authors and performance over text.

What is at stake here for Hume, and others, such Paulina Kewes, is an interest in understanding the status of the dramatic author in the Restoration and eighteenth century and locating the "birth of the author" more generally. This status, they suggest, may be inferred by the prevalence of authorial attribution in either theatrical performance or printed play text. Kewes, however, differs from Hume on theatrical authorship to argue that "dramatists, no longer semi-anonymous scriptwriters or mere suppliers of live entertainment, as their early seventeenth-century predecessors had been, were increasingly thought of as individuals who carried their own identity and authority, and from whom the printed artefact originated."[7] Kewes, here, privileges the print text as evidence for the increase in status accorded authors in the late seventeenth and early eighteenth centuries. Scriptwriters were those who wrote for performance and were "semi-anonymous," but the new dramatic author was one who printed her work. It seems correct that where authorship is attributed, be it on the page or in the theater, one may thus infer the relative status of dramatic authorship. In other words, if proprietary authorship mattered, it follows that authors would be named, or at least guessed at. However, such arguments pose a question about the status of authorship and seem primarily to focus on either print or performance. In this singular focus, the highly mediated situation of both print and performance tends to be obscured and suggests therefore that individual agents, especially authors, were the central, though perhaps unacknowledged, organizing principles.

The eighteenth century was, as Allardyce Nicoll long ago noted, an age, "not of the author, but of the actor."[8] Hume, following Nicoll, apprehends a natural opposition between author and text and actor and performance, and he notes the tendency for literary scholars to view the play text through the lens of a relationship between reader and writer, to which he offers an invaluable corrective. However, the mode of categorical thought that privileges author and text over actor and performance is the same one that informs the very distinction between text and performance that Hume so crucially makes. In other words, we can only think of the primacy of the relationship between author and text once we have separated text from performance. I want to amend Nicoll, therefore, and suggest that the eighteenth century was an age, not of the author, nor of the actor, but of a complex and varied milieu encompassing persons, things, texts, agencies, and ideas. What emerges in the drama of the eighteenth century is the realization of meaning residing in action, and not just the action of the actors but instances like the collective authoring of pieces with the theatrical audience and the interplay between scenery, props, theatrical architecture—a series of actions that produce meanings that far exceed any embodied individual. The attempt in print to reorient the drama, postperformance, in an author or in the explicit presence of Anonymous is a disavowal of these various conditions of theatrical production.

The double tradition is taken to explain the differences in patterns of attribution between staged performance and printed text and to oppose the default anonymity of the theater to the tendency toward attributed authorship in printed plays. However, insofar as the double tradition explains the difference in attribution, it does so by creating that difference; it is thus another means of reorienting the drama toward the individual. The double tradition of staged and printed drama is not a natural or self-evident phenomenon that comes about simply because one has printed one's work. Rather, it is a way of thinking about drama that is first brought forth in print, then imported into the theatrical mode and naturalized. In this understanding of drama, print and performance are mutually reinforcing and defining. That authorial anonymity can be posed against named authorship and made to signify a lack of interest in authorship is a product of (1) understanding the empirical gap between printed words on the page and the performance of bodies on the stage and (2) privileging print where that absence of the name can be made most evident. This gap is first articulated in Langbaine's cataloging in the late seventeenth century, following the closing of the theaters during the Interregnum and the flourishing of the print market for plays, and becomes the dominant, though not exclusive, mode of cataloging plays throughout the eighteenth century.[9] The distance between stage and page and author and actor becomes a trope repeated throughout the theatrical writings of the early eighteenth century and taken as a truism in scholarship then and now. The argument is not whether theatergoing audiences and play readers of the early eighteenth century noticed the anonymity or authors of the pieces they saw on the stage or purchased in print but rather how they might have come to take note of authorial anonymity. Anonymity comes into being as a concern for theatrical texts, both printed and performed, only once a distinction between print and performance can be made. It is the attention to the difference in medium that enables the attention to anonymity, because this attention to the medium carries with it implicit claims about action and agency.

By positioning my study of anonymity across print and performance history in this way, I am guided by the notion of intermediation as it is deployed by Ted Striphas, who draws on the work of Charles R. Acland and recent work on eighteenth-century drama that has sought to reconceive the "double tradition" as a tradition of intermediation.[10] To narrate a history of anonymity, as this study does, we must attend to the historically situated expectations of authorship and anonymity within and among the media of the period. What working across media reveals is the manner in which different media introduce different agencies and differing and refracting intentions. Rather than positing analogies between the position of author and actor in relationship to written and performed text, as in Ralph, Nicoll, and Hume, such an intermedial view attempts to account for the nuanced complexities in the realms of both theater and print. In short, this method explores the ways in which we have folded multiple actions and agencies into individuals.

Lives of Poets and Catalogs of Plays

For Edward Phillips, the goal of writing history was the preservation of the names of great men. *Theatrum Poetarum* (1675), he claims, is an attempt to collect and preserve the names of only a select group—the poets—in one volume:

> Registers who have been studious to keep alive the memories of Famous Men, of whom it is at least some satisfaction to understand that there were once such Men or Writings in being. However since their works having by what ever casualty perisht, their Names, though thus recorded, yet as being dispeirc't in several Authors, and some of those not of the most conspicuous note, are scarce known to the generality, even of the Learned themselves, and since the later Ages the memories of many whose works have been once made public, and in general esteem, have nevertheless through tract of time, and the succession of new Generations, fallen to decay and dwindled almost to nothing; I judged it a Work in some sort not unconducing to a public benefit, and to many not ungratefull, to muster up together in a body, though under their several Classes, as many of those that have imploy'd their fancies or inventions in all the several Arts and Sciences, as I could either collect out of the several Authors that have mention'd them in part, or by any other ways could come to the knowledge of, but finding this too various and manifold a task to be manag'd at once, I pitcht upon one Faculty first, which, not more by chance than inclination, falls out to be that of the Poets, a Science certainly of all others the most noble and exalted.[11]

Theatrum Poetarum is explicit that it is not encyclopedic in its cataloging of authors; rather, Phillips has opted to focus on preserving those with the "Faculty" of poetry. *Theatrum Poetarum* is divided by both the era and gender of the poets. Male and female poets, in separate sections, are classed as either ancient or modern. Each section is organized alphabetically by the author's first name. Following the name of the author is a brief biographical note and, if available, the titles of works by said author. For example, for Dryden, we get a biographical sketch and list of major plays; while the entry for Fletcher emphasizes his association with Ben Johnson and Shakespeare and provides an encomium to his "courtly Elegance and gentile familiarity of style," it, however, makes no mention of his plays (108–9).

Phillips's *Theatrum Poetarum* differs from previous attempts to catalog authors and works, like *An Exact and Perfect Catalogue of Al the Plaies That Were Ever Printed; Together with All the Authors Names; and What Are Comedies, Histories, Interludes, Masks, Pastorals, Tragedies* (1656), because it organized the catalog by author's name, not by title of work.[12] In doing so, Phillips introduced the problem of what to do about anonymous poems and plays. Other catalogs had previously not differentiated anonymous plays from attributed plays. They were cataloged together and arranged by title. Recognizing this problem and, ever aware of the limitations of his register, Phillips addresses the absence of anonymous poems and plays in his preface:

> *Sorry I am I cannot pay a due respect to* Mr. Anonymus, *but he is the Author of so many Books, that to make but a Catalogue of them would require a Volume sufficient of itself; others there are who vouchsafe but the two first letters of their Names, and these, it is to be supposed, desire to be known onely to some Friends, that understand the Interpretation of those letters, or some cunning Men in the Art of Divination.*

Phillips argues that anonymous texts are so many in number that they would require a volume unto themselves. What he does not acknowledge, though it should be clear from the stated purpose of the volume, is that it is not the texts themselves that are of interest; rather, the poets behind those works are the true objects of attention and analysis. "Mr. Anonymus" affords no such object; the notion that texts could be "by Anonymous" seems something like a joke. The organization and execution of the catalog speak to the primacy of the named author. Indeed, the only way in which Phillips can account for anonymity is by referring to the phenomenon with the personated "Mr. Anonymus."

Following on the efforts of Kirkman and Phillips, Gerard Langbaine offered *A New Catalogue of English Plays* (1688) as a corrective to the less-than-perfect cataloging schemas of his predecessors. In his preface, Langbaine outlines the problems of previous efforts in three areas: they are out of print, they list plays that were not printed, and they are not methodical. Langbaine's innovations in *A New Catalogue* correct these errors by cataloging only printed plays and by demonstrating an unprecedented interest in the status of attribution of a play text through a new, methodical layout arranged by named, supposed, or anonymous authors. Though the catalog itself may not have been a best seller,[13] these two innovations in cataloging transcended *A New Catalogue* and the subsequent iterations of the *Lives and Characters of the Dramatick Poets* to become the dominant mode of understanding the dramatic past and present by asserting a primary difference between printed and unprinted plays.

Unprinted plays were of little interest to Langbaine because he *"designed* this Catalogue *for their use, who may have the same relish of the Drama with my self; and may possibly be desirous, either to make a Collection, or at least have the curiosity to know in general, what has been Publish't in our Language, as likewise to receive some remarks on the Writings of particular Men."*[14] The play as print object is Langbaine's primary interest; he writes first for those interested in what has been "Publish't" and second for those wishing "to receive some remarks on the Writing of particular Men." Langbaine inverts the work done by *Theatrum Poetarum* by privileging the play, specifically the printed play, over the author. In examining Langbaine's interest in originality and what she deems a proto-intellectual property, Kewes, too, notices Langbaine's emphasis on, and privileging of, the printed text:

> Langbaine welcomes the new possibilities attendant on the expansion of print and intends to take full advantage of them by exploring the affinities between plays and their sources. In this sense, his strictly textual approach might be said to privilege drama as literature rather than performance.[15]

Though she acknowledges he may have privileged it, Kewes still underestimates Langbaine's emphasis on the printed text. For a play to be included in *A New Catalogue*, it had to be printed. Langbaine is not interested in cataloging performance; he is interested in cataloging plays as material objects that may be collected, and he asserts the primacy of print, apart from performance, in accounting for drama. Such a sharp distinction between print and performance was available to Langbaine due to the increase in the private reading of plays during the Interregnum. With the theaters closed, a market for printed plays emerged.[16] Writing in the 1680s, Langbaine was able to articulate clearly the differences between the printed text and performance because they had been made so stark in the period before. By privileging printed texts, he is able to develop an approach that emphasizes bibliographic method and attends to anonymous plays as distinct from attributed plays.

Though *A New Catalogue* is organized by author surname and is the first, according to Kewes, to do so, its interest is in the completeness and the bibliographical, not in the biographical. Such regard for bibliographic precision over an interest in the author's biography is evident in Langbaine's discussion of the Kirkman catalog. In explaining the Kirkman catalog, Langbaine makes clear the problems introduced when there is no clear method at work:

> *The* first *Catalogue that was printed of any worth, was that Collected by* Kirkman, *a* London *Bookseller, whose chief dealing was in Plays; which was published 1671, at the end of* Nicomede, *a Tragi-comedy, Translated from the* French *of Monsieur* Corneille. *This Catalogue was printed* Alphabetically, *as to the Names of the* Plays, *but* promiscuously *as to those of the* Authors, (Shakspeare, Fletcher, Johnson, *and some others of the most voluminous Authors excepted) each Authors Name being placed over against each Play that he writ, and still repeated with every several Play, till a new Author came on. About* Nine *Years after, the* Publisher *of* this *Catalogue, Reprinted* Kirkman's *with emendations, but in the same Form. Notwithstanding the* Anonimous *Plays, one would think easily distinguishable by the want of an Author's Name before them; yet have both these charitable kind Gentlemen found Fathers for them, by ranking each under the Authors Name that preceded them in the former Catalogues.*

The problem inherent in the previous method of organization was not that it obscured the author and privileged the title of the play but that its layout, which included anonymous plays alongside attributed plays, encouraged errors of attribution. The emended Kirkman catalog introduced such errors so that formerly anonymous plays had "Fathers" found for them in the adjacent authors.

Langbaine's catalog demonstrates unprecedented interest in the status of attribution of a play text. This was a solution to the problems of attribution introduced into later Kirkman catalogs. *A New Catalogue* is organized into three major divisions: "Known or Supposed Authours," "Supposed Authours," and "Unknown Authours." "Known or Supposed Authours" refers to those plays whose authors' names are printed on the title page or those that may be solidly attributed to a named author. "Supposed Authours" comprises those plays whose authorship is attributed only with initials. "Unknown Authours" refers to anonymous plays. Each division within the catalog attests to the certainty with which a play may be attributed to a named author. The various levels of certainty are based, first, on the attribution of authorship on the text itself. Thus the greatest degree of certainty is placed upon print texts that declare their authorship on the page; supposed authors declare only their initials on the page; anonymous plays make no declaration on the page and cannot be reliably and retrospectively attributed. For Langbaine and those who followed, differentiating the printed play from the performed play both made visible and necessitated an attention to anonymity.

Throughout the eighteenth century, there were various attempts to catalog English drama, many of which drew upon Langbaine's method of listing printed plays and organizing plays by the author's name with anonymous plays set aside. Giles Jacob's *The Poetical Register: or, The Lives and Characters of the English Dramatick Poets. With an Account of Their Writings* (2 volumes, 1719–20) follows the model put forth in Langbaine's *Lives and Characters of the English Dramatick Poets* wherein Langbaine elaborates on *A New Catalogue* by providing a biographical and critical gloss on the life of each author. Jacob maintains the structure of *A New Catalogue,* organizing *Lives and Characters* by author's surname, listing possible sources, and including a listing of anonymous plays. Jacob, with an appreciative nod to Langbaine in his preface, updates this model by omitting the ancient poets and including those plays printed in the seventeenth and eighteenth centuries. Like Langbaine, Jacob's interest is in the printed plays, and he frequently notes those plays that were never acted in his listings. Jacob condenses Langbaine's organizational method by doing away with the categories of "known or supposed authors," "supposed authors," and "unknown authors." Instead, he divides his first volume into three sections. The first two are based loosely on a difference between older English dramatic poets and contemporary, what he calls "Modern," dramatic poets. The final section is for "Plays Written by Anonymous Authors." This section lists 211 plays organized alphabetically by title. Where available, Jacob provides the source of the play's plot material, its publication information, and, sometimes, its date of first performance. Most of the information provided in the listings, save for the source of plot material, would have been readily available on the title pages of the printed play texts or in catalog listings from booksellers.

Jacob's condensed Langbaine model is picked up again in *The British Theatre*, attributed to William Rufus Chetwood (Dublin, 1750; London, 1752). Like Jacob's earlier volume, *The British Theatre* acknowledges its debt to its predecessors in the preface but also notes the errors "both omissive and commissive" in the efforts of both Langbaine and Jacob. *The British Theatre* promises the accounts of more dramatic poets and plays and takes more interest in the stage by prefixing a history of the English stage to the volume. The organization of the catalog follows from this historical interest, and the authors and plays are organized chronologically. Thus the volume begins with authors from the sixteenth century in the "*Dramatic* Authors in the 1[6]*th Century*" section (1), and anonymous plays are grouped behind them in "Plays Wrote *by Anonymous Authors in the* 1[6]*th* Century" (21).

The British Theatre has three different sections for anonymous plays from the sixteenth, seventeenth, and eighteenth centuries. It lists 69 anonymous sixteenth-century plays, 122 anonymous plays from the Restoration to the end of the seventeenth century, and 77 anonymous eighteenth-century plays. Like Langbaine, and Kirkman before him, *The British Theatre* also includes designation of genre, if available, for each play listed. Table 2 offers a breakdown of anonymous and attributed eighteenth-century plays by genre listed in *The British Theatre*.

Table 2 suggests the publishing and cataloging strategies underlying *The British Theatre* and works like it. The major published

Table 2. Anonymous and attributed eighteenth-century drama by genre

Genre	Number of anonymous eighteenth-century pieces listed in *The British Theatre*	Number of eighteenth-century pieces attributed to authors in *The British Theatre*	Total	Percentage of anonymous pieces
Comedy	18	141	159	11.3%
Farce	27	71	98	27.6%
Tragedy	13	121	134	9.7%
Ballad Opera	4	21	25	16%
Opera	5	13	18	27.7%
Pastoral	1	3	4	25%
Other	9	25	34	26.5%

genres of drama all figure into the listing of anonymous plays, but those genres that tended to go unpublished—pantomime, burlesque, and entertainments—are all absent despite, as we will see, being predominantly anonymous. *The British Theatre* purports to be both a history of the English stage and a catalog of the lives and plays of the dramatic poets, but it is a selective history and catalog that draws on printed works to reconstruct its understanding of theater history and anonymous authorship.

Arriving decades later, *The Playhouse Pocket Companion* (1779) offers yet another variant on the Langbaine cataloging method. It promises on its title page "a Method entirely new, Whereby the AUTHOR of any DRAMATIC PERFORMANCE, and the TIME of its APPEARANCE, may be readily discovered on Inspection." Upon inspection, *The Playhouse Pocket Companion* does not offer an entirely new method; rather, it organizes itself by author's surname and lists that author's plays and dates. It differs from the chronological approach offered by *The British Theatre*, but it looks remarkably similar to Langbaine's *A New Catalogue* published nearly a century earlier. And, like the catalogs of Langbaine and his successors, *The Pocket Companion* includes a "Catalogue of Anonymous Pieces." The anonymous pieces are organized alphabetically by title, regardless of chronology, with genre, where available, noted. *A Playhouse Pocket Companion* is heavily indebted to *The British Theatre* for its lists to 1750. It appears that many of the listings of eighteenth-century anonymous pieces were borrowed entirely from *The British Theatre* and carried over any errors or variants in the earlier catalog.

The *Playhouse Pocket Companion*, however, adds its own content throughout the volume. Like its predecessors, it lists published drama almost exclusively, likely drawing from booksellers' catalogs, and specifies those plays that were printed but never acted. In total, *The Playhouse Pocket Companion* lists 47 anonymous sixteenth-century plays, 203 anonymous seventeenth-century plays, and 148 anonymous eighteenth-century plays. As with *The British Theatre*, I have divided in Table 3 the anonymous and attributed eighteenth-century pieces listed by genre.

The late-century *Playhouse Pocket Companion* nearly doubles the listings of anonymous eighteenth-century pieces from the seventy-seven listed in the mid-century *The British Theatre*. Like its predecessor, however, the relative number of anonymous plays divided by genre remains similar. Anonymous farces vastly outnumber anonymous tragedies and comedies. We can also see the changing tastes in preferred genre over time by comparing *The British Theatre* to *The Playhouse Pocket Companion*. Listings of anonymous operas more than triple from the earlier to the later catalog, coinciding with an increased demand encouraged by the Hanoverians' taste for, and patronage of, opera. Finally, as in *The British Theatre*, and those that came before it, the genres represented in the list of anonymous pieces are those genres that are printed. Despite the additions *The Playhouse Pocket Companion* makes, along with its claim to a new method, it still asserts that the way to know the theater is through its printed texts.

Coming right at the end of the period, John Egerton's anonymously published *Theatrical Remembrancer* (1788) marks a shift in cataloging practices that had been largely dominant for the last century.[17] Egerton organizes the catalog roughly by the date the plays appeared, decade by decade, with the author's name as header, but

Table 3. Anonymous and attributed eighteenth-century pieces listed by genre in *The Playhouse Pocket Companion*

Genre	Number of anonymous eighteenth-century pieces listed in *The Playhouse Pocket Companion*	Number of eighteenth-century pieces attributed to authors listed in *The Playhouse Pocket Companion*	Total	Percentage of anonymous pieces
Comedy	27	236	263	10.2%
Farce	41	107	148	27.7%
Tragedy	18	208	226	7.9%
Ballad Opera	5	16	21	23.8%
Opera	18	47	65	27.6%
Pastoral	2	10	12	16.6%
Entertainment	2	3	5	40%
Other	35	56	91	38.4%

he maintains the distinct separation of anonymous plays at the end of each decade. In a departure from the print-focused cataloging from Langbaine on, Egerton includes drama that was never printed and notes it as such with the abbreviation "n.p."

Egerton writes of the occasion of this new catalog in its advertisement:

> THE Arrangement for Sale of three very considerable Dramatick Collections, first suggested to the Publishers the Want of a Work of this Nature; and, at the same Time, supplied the Materials for its Composition. Several Publications of this kind at different Periods have been produced; but each being compiled, as it

seems; from the other, one excepted, are grossly erroneous and imperfect. At no time, it is supposed, hath an Attention to the Productions of the Theatre displayed itself so much as at the present. Of this the numerous Collectors of English Dramas now living, bear ample testimony. For the Use of these Gentleman this Performance is intended.[18]

The advertisement registers the unique tensions that gave rise to the particular shift in cataloging the *Theatrical Remembrancer* evinces. Its occasion is both the sale of three significant collections of playbooks—"Those of Mr. Henderson, Dr. Wright and Thomas Person, Esq."—and an increased "Attention to the Productions of the Theatre." On one hand, the collection sales point to the dramatic tradition as printed play text to be collected. On the other, the increased theatrical attention, following on the post-Garrick era and star system that had coalesced in the decades before, point to the dramatic tradition as the theatrical event.[19]

The inclusion of unprinted plays, rather than only those that were printed (as in Langbaine), registers, then, the hybrid nature of dramatic representation. This cataloging shift reflects the vogue for capturing play-as-performance, as in Bell's editions in the 1770s, which were oriented toward star actors in particular.[20] It is, however, also a practice oriented toward collectors who could then avoid the fool's errand of tracking down a play text that did not exist. Egerton's catalog is a suturing of traditions that had been pulled apart by Langbaine, but this suturing is in the service of, and in connection with, other print-based and collecting-oriented practices.

One of the immediate consequences of including plays that were not printed in the catalog is the heightened visibility of anonymous plays in the catalog. Whereas in the period from 1700 to 1750, *The British Theatre* lists 122 anonymous plays, in the same period, *The Theatrical Remembrancer* lists 221. In the period from 1700 to 1779, *The Playhouse Pocket Companion* lists a total of 148 anonymous plays, while *The Theatrical Remembrancer* lists a total of 454 anonymous plays from 1700 to 1780. Table 4 offers a breakdown of anonymous and attributed pieces listed in *The Theatrical Remembrancer*.

The departure from previous schemas of emphasizing and cataloging, almost exclusively, printed playbooks in *The Theatrical Remembrancer* brings into view the large number of anonymous pieces

Table 4. Anonymous and attributed eighteenth-century pieces listed by genre in *The Theatrical Remembrancer*

Genre	Number of anonymous eighteenth-century pieces listed in *The Theatrical Remembrancer*	Number of eighteenth-century pieces attributed to authors listed in *The Theatrical Remembrancer*	Total	Percentage of anonymous pieces
Comedy	88	329	417	21.1%
Farce	93	178	271	34.3%
Tragedy	30	357	387	7.7%
Ballad Opera	33	48	81	40.7%
Opera	31	124	155	20%
Pastoral	8	26	34	23.5%
Entertainment	18	42	60	30%
Pantomime	40	26	66	60.6%
Other	104	231	335	31%

that were performed but never printed. It further serves to highlight the relationship between medium, genre, and anonymity. In publication, plays were almost always attributed to an author, and those plays that were published were disproportionately those that fit into the familiar generic categories of tragedy and comedy and a four- to five-act structure. The anonymous, unprinted pieces, however, tend to be those that are not easily recognizable as typical plays: pantomimes, ballad operas, masques, farces, and entertainments. Importantly, in the eighteenth century, such pieces were performed onstage alongside such plays in a given evening and, indeed, make up a significant proportion of new dramatic pieces produced in the period, particularly after the Licensing Act of 1737 dramatically reduced the number of new plays performed in the patent theaters.[21]

What emerges from this genealogy of theatrical catalogs across the century is the simultaneous emergence of explicitly anonymous plays and their underrepresentation in the catalogs because of an emphasis on printed texts. Entire traditions of eighteenth-century theatrical practices are largely absent, and it is not until the Egerton catalog that there begins to be a more comprehensive view of what was presented in the theaters of the eighteenth century and thereby an attention drawn to the typicality of anonymous productions. The emergence of anonymity as a concern for play cataloging and its underrepresentation in those same catalogs may be explained by the necessary shift in medium from performance to print. In performance, as I show in the next section, anonymity and authorship were not typically central concerns due in part to the complexity of the theatrical milieu, and therefore those pieces that were never printed remain tacitly anonymous for much of the period. However, in the movement from theatrical performance to print publication, questions of origin and absence were raised, and they find their expression in cataloging practices and give rise to ways of thinking about texts as anonymous.

Claims about the importance of the these cataloging practices, which emphasized print as the primary means of making authorship and anonymity visible to both catalogers and the public, are incomplete without some evidence of how readers used these catalogs, if at all. Scholars have noted the widespread practice throughout the Restoration and eighteenth century of readers attributing authorship on title pages and correcting or supplying authors' names to catalog listings.[22] These catalogs both supplied attributions to curious readers and were themselves subject to attribution and correction. Much rarer, however, was the reader or bookseller who attributed anonymity to a text.

There is, however, the copy of *Love and Revenge; or, The Vintner Outwitted* held by the British Library (Figure 10). On its title page, below the appellation of its stage performance, "As Acted at the New Theatre in the Hay-Market," where an author's name would typically be printed, someone has written "Anonymous." Still further, following the publication information, in the same hand there appears the date "1729." *Love and Revenge* premiered November 12, 1729, and was performed a total of ten times in the 1729–30 season.[23] Its publication was advertised in the *Daily Post* on that same day.[24] Dating the ballad opera would not have been difficult. Despite the absence of the date on the title page, both *The British Theatre* and *Playhouse Pocket Companion* list the date as 1729. This is likely due to Chetwood's role in the production of *The British Theatre* and his knowledge as the prompter of the Drury Lane theater. Attributing authorship would, however, prove more difficult. Indeed, many current bibliographies and indexes, including *The English Short Title Catalog*, wrongly attribute the authorship of *Love and Revenge* to Christopher Bullock.[25] That this reader sought out and found both a date and an explicit attribution to Anonymous suggests that he consulted a catalog to learn of its authorship and publication date. *The British Theatre*, *Pocket Playhouse Companion*, and *The Theatrical Remembrancer* taught readers to think of this play as "by Anonymous," in the same way that current catalogs (wrongly) teach us to think of this play as by Bullock. This reader of *Love and Revenge* followed the practice of attributing authorship in his own hand common to the period and perhaps did so after consulting one of the catalogs described in this section.

Similar to this title page attribution to Anonymous, in John Philip Kemble's heavily annotated copy of Egerton's *Theatrical Remembrancer*, held at the Folger Shakespeare Library, there is an annotation to John Lyly's *Mother Bombie*. "Played sundry Times by the Children of Pauls. 4to. 1594. 4to. 1597." in manuscript hand: "this has been considered an Anon: play: it appeared without any author's name. See MS: addition at the end" (Figure 11).

This annotation demonstrates the use of these catalogs and the ways in which users of the catalogs were drawing on other catalogs as sources of knowledge and conceptual structures for cataloging and understanding anonymous drama. "This has been considered an Anon: play: it appeared without any author's name" signals an explicit attention to the former anonymous status of *Mother Bombie* in previous catalogs and on the title page of the play text. Kemble's annotations, and the many annotations in other hands in the volume, point to the ways in which these catalogs were both texts to

LOVE *and* REVENGE;

OR, THE

VINTNER *Outwitted:*

AN

O P E R A;

As Acted at the

NEW THEATRE

IN THE

HAY-MARKET.

Anonymous

L O N D O N:

Printed for *J. Clark* under the *Royal Exchange* in *Cornhill*; *T. Worral* at the *Judge's Head* near the *Temple-Exchange Coffee-House* in *Fleet-street*; *J. Jackson* near St. *James's* House; and Sold by *J. Roberts* in *Warwick-Lane.* *1729*

(Price One Shilling.)

Figure 10. Title page from *Love and Revenge.* Copyright The British Library Board (General Reference Collection 11775.c.67).

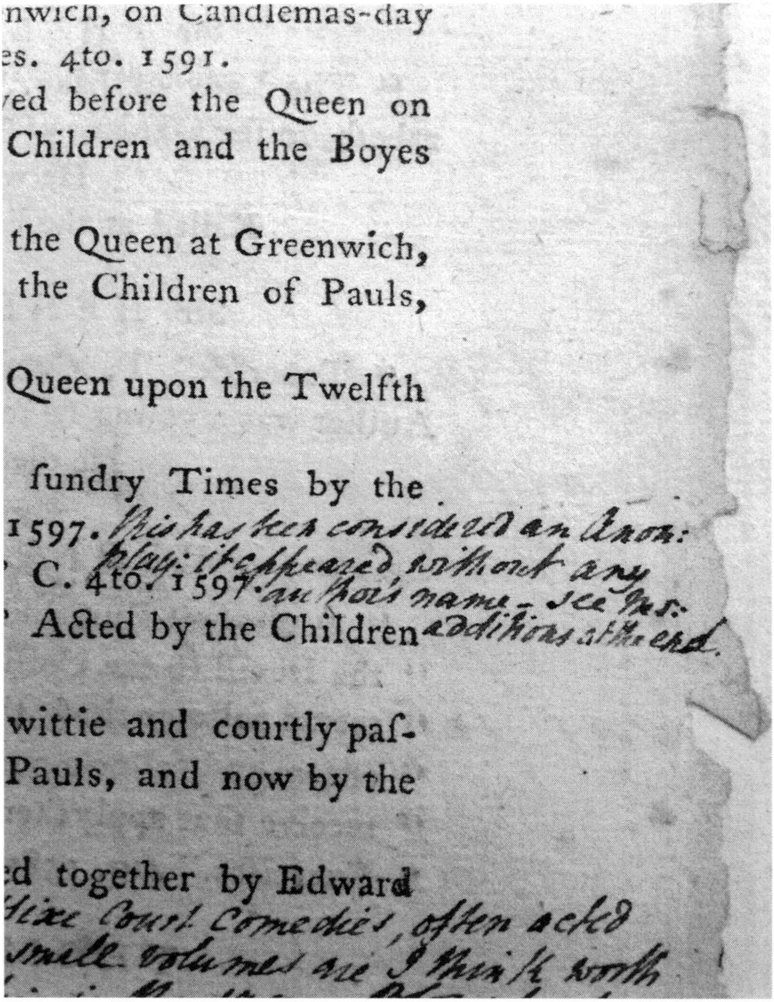
nwich, on Candlemas-day
es. 4to. 1591.
ed before the Queen on
Children and the Boyes

the Queen at Greenwich,
the Children of Pauls,

Queen upon the Twelfth

ſundry Times by the
1597. This has been considered an Anon:
C. 4to. 1597. play: it appeared without any author's name — see MS:
Acted by the Children additions at the end.

wittie and courtly paſ-
Pauls, and now by the

d together by Edward

Figure 11. Annotated page from *The Theatrical Remembrancer* (1788). Reprinted by permission of the Folger Shakespeare Library (Folger D.a.83).

be consulted and texts with which to work. Evidence of manuscript amendations pervade surviving seventeenth- and eighteenth-century dramatic catalogs. The catalogs invite a participatory scholarly interaction that further explains the attribution of anonymous pieces explicitly to "Anonymous" both within the confines of the catalogs and beyond, as on the title page to *Love and Revenge*.

While Langbaine's schema was the dominant mode of thinking about and cataloging drama throughout the period, it was not the only one. William Mears's *A True Catalogue of All the Plays That Were Ever Yet Printed in the English Tongue . . .* (1713) maintains the organization by play title first, then author if known. A later Mears catalog, *A Compleat Catalogue of All the Plays That Were Ever Yet Printed in the English Language,* 2nd ed. (1726), includes plays cataloged in two different organizational schemas: first the plays are alphabetized by author's name, then they are alphabetized by play title.

In one of the copies of this catalog is a manuscript continuation that picks up the schema of play title rather than author name (Figure 12). When given two cataloging schema in the same volume, this user chose title first. Significantly, this user of the catalog also re-creates the system of abbreviation for generic appellations. This suggests that title and genre, rather than author's name, were the central ways that the individual was thinking about the play text. Similarly, a manuscript nineteenth-century catalog of pre-1700 plays organizes itself on play title but does note those plays that

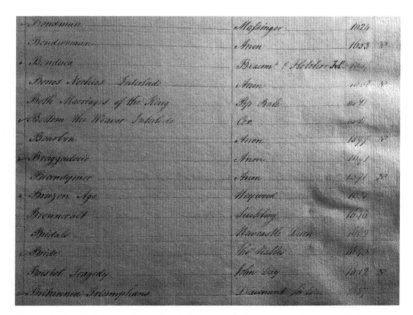

Figure 12. An alphabetical list of old plays antecedent to 1700 [manuscript], compiled circa 1820. Reprinted by permission of the Folger Shakespeare Library (Folger w.a.234).

are "Anon." What these pieces of evidence indicate is that there is not a massive sea change once the Langbaine schema takes hold. Rather, other practices and ways of thinking about play texts persist alongside it and suggest alternatives to the primacy of the singular, named author.

I have argued that the visibility and intelligibility of anonymous plays within the theatrical realm are dependent on the movement of, and understanding of, the difference between performance and printed text, which was first articulated in the work of Langbaine. We have seen that though catalogers may draw from performance history in their cataloging practices, their main point of reference throughout much of the eighteenth century remains the printed text. The emphasis on the printed drama made possible, for the first time, a separation of anonymity from named authorship. As these catalogs and registers taught their readers about named authors and attribution, they also taught them how to think about and name those play texts without authorial attribution. In short, they made remarkable in print what was utterly standard and tacit in performance. In what follows, I demonstrate just how standard anonymous authorship was in the theater of the eighteenth century and yet how, when anonymity or authorship is acknowledged, it is done by invoking the primary movement and distinction between print and performance.

"Acting Plays" and "Reading Plays": Intermediation and Anonymity

Scholars of Restoration drama are by now familiar with the oft-cited March 4, 1698[/99], letter to Elizabeth Steward in which John Dryden remarks,

> This Day was playd a reviv'd Comedy of Mr Congreve's calld the Double Dealer, which was never very takeing; in the play bill was printed,—Written by Mr Congreve . . . the printing an Authours name, in a Play bill, is a new manner of proceeding, at least in England.[26]

To Dryden, authorial attribution on playbills was an innovation in the late seventeenth century, but it was an innovation that did not catch on.[27] Playbills rarely attributed authorship throughout the eighteenth century. Only 6.1 percent of playbills from Drury Lane in the period between 1737 and 1774 offer the name of the author of the mainpiece; only 2.97 percent of the same playbills name an author of an afterpiece. At Covent Garden in the same period, 3.6 percent of playbills name the author of the mainpiece, and 1.9 percent of playbills name the author of the afterpiece.[28] While composers of performed musical pieces were often named, overwhelmingly the advertising practices of the eighteenth-century theater presented the dramatic pieces staged as tacitly anonymous.

Plays in the repertory, however, by authors of note may have received an authorial attribution, as in the August 15, 1702, advertisement for *Bartholomew Fair* in the *Daily Courant*:

> For the Benefit of Mrs. Lucas.
>
> At the THEATRE-ROYAL in Drury-Lane, on Tuesday next, being the 18th Instant, will be Presented that celebrated Comedy call'd, Bartholomew Fair; Written by the Famous Ben. Jonson. With several Extraordinary Entertainments, as will be express'd in the Bills. (2)

More often throughout the period, authorial attribution was absent, even in cases when the play was in print with the author attributed. An example is this September 18, 1702, advertisement for *Emperor of the Moon*:

> At the desire of the some Persons of Quality,
>
> this present Friday being the 18th of September, at the Theatre-Royal in Drury-Lane, will be presented a Comedy, call'd The Emperor of the Moon; wherein Mr. Penkethman acts the part of Harlequin without a Masque, for the Entertainment of an African Prince lately arrived here, being Nephew to the King of Bauday of that Country. With several Entertainments of Singing and Dancing, and the last new Epilogue never spoken but once by Mr. Penkethman. (2)

We learn from this advertisement that Mr. Penkethman will act the part of harlequin, notably without a mask, and that he will also deliver an epilogue rarely spoken. We also learn that this is a command performance for "the Entertainment of an African Prince lately arrived here." Yet the advertisement does not mention "Mrs. A Behn," author of the play printed in 1687.

It may be argued that familiarity with the printed text negated the need to attribute authorship to *Emperor of the Moon* in theatrical advertising, however, there are instances like the attribution of *Bartholomew Fair* to "the Famous Ben. Jonson," which was printed for Robert Allot in 1631 and included in the 1641 *Workes of Beniamin Ionson.* There seems to be no causal relationship between an absence or presence of authorial attribution in advertisements and attribution in printed play texts. Rather, attribution happened when an author's status, "the Famous Ben. Jonson," caused his or her name to be readily known. In other words, advertisements did not attribute authorship because an author was unknown or unprinted; theatrical advertisements attributed authorship because an author was already known through reputation. The typical practice was not to attribute authorship in playbills and advertisements.

Unlike playbills, printed play texts almost always attributed authorship. Curious theatergoers could indeed seek out the printed text to learn who an author was, and they would not have to wait long between first performance and first publication. In the early eighteenth century, the lapse in time between first performance and first publication of a play shrank to merely days and, in some cases, occurred simultaneously.[29] During the Restoration, the period in time between performance and publication decreased from six months in the 1660s to about a month by the 1690s.[30] This decrease in the lapse in time between first performance and first publication may suggest a lessening in the distinction between the performed play and the printed play, as they could be experienced nearly simultaneously as representations of each other. I would like to suggest, however, that the shortened time between first performance and first publication actually magnified the difference. One could almost immediately place the printed text alongside its performance, if one thought to do so, and understand them as fundamentally different forms. Such a difference would be obvious when the printed text did not represent all that was performed, nor could it capture the various performances that may have occurred in an evening. Printed play texts bore a relationship to performed pieces, but they were not, and could not be, understood as identical to the performances.

As the time between performance and publication decreased, the number of theatrical productions increased. The sheer volume of play and entertainment production contributed to theatrical writing that was less likely to be considered particularly worthy of literary value. Nicoll has characterized the period as rife with unliterary and anonymous writers who nonetheless seem to have pushed the form in new directions:

> In the early eighteenth century we are startled at the number of one-play writers. . . . There are twice as many individual dramatists in the one period as in the other, and more than four times the number of anonymous plays. Undoubtedly many of these unliterary authors aided at once in destroying the brilliance of the comedy of manners, and in introducing new motives and new themes destined to provide the basis for the modern stage. (8)

The increase in the number of anonymous plays that Nicoll notes is astonishing. Yet, it is unclear if he has excluded anonymously performed and printed plays that have been retrospectively attributed to an author, and thus the increase in the number of anonymous plays could be much larger. It is also unclear if his estimate of four times as many anonymous plays refers only to plays or to other theatrical entertainments presented on the stage. What we can say is this: anonymous plays and entertainments of various sorts were far less likely to appear in print. This is evident in the increased visibility of anonymous pieces in the *Theatrical Remembrancer* once Egerton includes pieces that were not printed. Furthermore, theatrical pieces aside from what one would typically consider a play were more likely to be anonymous in the period between 1700 and 1780. Such unprinted anonymous pieces might include a pantomime, a farce, a burlesque, or a droll. These pieces could be classed more broadly as entertainments, which have a written source yet seem to be unscripted, extemporal physical performances. What I offer in the following pages is a breakdown of the numbers and genres of anonymous plays and entertainments presented on the stage between 1700 and 1750 based on Nicoll's handlist of anonymous plays in *A History of English Drama*, vol. 2 (Table 5). Additionally, in the appendix, I offer a breakdown of new anonymous plays and entertainments performed in the period between 1700 and 1737 based on William Burling's *Checklist of New Plays and Entertainments on the London Stage, 1700–1737*.

Table 5 illustrates only very general trends in anonymity in the theater of the eighteenth century. I have maintained Nicoll's attribution of genre, which is largely drawn from the self-ascription of genre present on playbills, newspaper advertisements, and title pages. The works included in his handlist of unknown authors were truly without authorial attribution at the time of its compilation in the earlier part of the twentieth century. This means, however, that those pieces that were retroactively attributed do not appear in the listing of anonymous pieces despite their initial anonymous status in publication or performance; rather, they are listed in the section with named authors. Thus the number of anonymous pieces in a given period is likely much larger than depicted in the table. Even with these limitations (and limitations Nicoll is careful to acknowledge), the quantification of the number of anonymous pieces classified by genre in the period offers insight into the kinds of dramatic pieces that were more likely to be anonymous.[31] Furthermore, such quantification—when considered alongside similar tables from *The British Theatre* and *Playhouse Pocket Companion*—demonstrates the selective cataloging of works based on an eighteenth-century bias for printed texts of plays rather than actual performances. In the eighteenth-century catalogs of anonymous pieces, only *The Playhouse Pocket Companion* lists any entertainments (five), and none lists pantomimes, yet these genres are the most prevalent kinds of anonymous pieces throughout the period.

The three genres represented the most in the table of anonymous pieces between 1700 and 1750 are pantomime, entertainments, and burlesque. The vogue for pantomime hit its height in the 1720s and 1730s; this accounts for the larger representation of the genre in the table of anonymous pieces between 1700 and 1750. Pantomime and entertainment were genres that would not be the main presentation of an evening. Rather, a pantomime or an entertainment would be one part of a larger evening of performance that would feature a

Table 5. Breakdown of anonymous and attributed pieces by genre based on Nicoll's Handlist of Plays in volume II of *A History of English Drama*

Genre	1700–1750 Anonymous	1700–1750 Attributed	Total, 1700–1750	% Anonymous
Total	499	598	1097	45.5%
Tragedy	25	180	205	12.2%
Comedy (including tragic-comedy)	49	178	227	21.6%
Dramatic Opera	4	12	16	25%
Opera (includes comic opera)	19	23	42	45.2%
Farce	62	68	130	47.6%
Ballad Opera	58	70	128	45.3%
Masque	16	18	34	47%
Entertainment	65	7	72	90.2%
Pantomime	82	14	96	85.4%
Pastoral	9	9	18	50%
Political	16	0	16	100%
Drolls	58	0	58	100%
Other	36	19	45	80%

mainpiece, typically a play or opera, and then several afterpieces. For instance, a Saturday performance at Drury Lane on August 22, 1702, was advertised in the *Daily Courant* and offered a particularly robust program of play, entertainments, epilogues, and pantomime:

> At the Theatre Royal in *Drury-Lane*, this present *Saturday* the 22d of *August*, will be performed, A Comedy Call'd *the Jovial Crew; Or, The Merry Beggars*. and the famous Mr. *Clench* of *Barnet* will perform an Organ with 3 Voices, the double Curtell, the Flute, and the Bells with the Mouth; the Huntsman, the Hounds, and the Pack of Dogs. With vaulting on the Horse. A Dance between two French-Men and two French-Women, and other Dances. And Monsieur Serene and another Person lately arrived in *England*, will perform a Night Scene by a Harlequin and a Scaramouch, after the Italian manner. And M. *Pinkethman* will speak his last new Vacation Epilogue, being the last time of Acting till after *Bartholomew-Fair*. (2)

This evening at the theater featured one play, a comedy, alongside six other entertainments. Although there is some interest in naming the performers who will appear, there is no attribution of authorship of any of the pieces for the evening. What matters is who and what will be on the stage rather than who wrote the works presented on that stage. Given the sheer number of performances in an evening, it is unlikely that the audience noted the absence or presence of an author's name; rather, it was the embodied presence of the performers that demanded attention.

The genres that were primarily anonymous in the period between 1700 and 1750 were those that tended to emphasize the embodied nature of performance over its verbal component. Some pieces were entertainments, such as an unscripted musical performance like Mr. Clench's organ with three voices or a dance. Others, such as pantomimes, were scripted scenarios with spoken parts, directed action, and song that emphasized the physical movements of the actors over the spoken language of the scenario. John O'Brien, following Susan Stewart's notion of "crimes of writing," has suggested the following of pantomime: "to specify the particular order of threat that pantomime posed [to writing], we might rather think of it as a 'crime *against* writing,' an action that undercut the theater's desire to define itself as a space of language."[32] O'Brien attends to the physicality of pantomime and its emphasis on movement and spectacle as components of a practice that is less about language as a "transparent medium, but as a physical force" (62). In pantomime, and other pieces that similarly emphasized the bodies and movements of the performers, such as farce and some comedy, the locus of meaning was the performer, not an author.

While I generally agree with this assessment of pantomime, evidence from manuscripts and printed books of pantomime shows just how much language shaped such performances. Though they generally lack prolonged verbal performance by the actors, the actions, gestures, and staging were indeed heavily scripted. I therefore offer an amendment to O'Brien's account of pantomime that the physicality of the performance, while most visible within the theatrical milieu, and indeed in responses to pantomime, was the central but not exclusive feature of the event of eighteenth-century pantomime. Pantomime emphasized physical action over verbal action to the effect of obscuring the writing and forms of authorship that undergirded it; however, I suggest that this is a difference in degree, not in kind, from theatrical representation more broadly. What pantomime makes evident is the collectivity and multiple forms of action that make up the theatrical event, none of which is oriented around the named author or playwright.[33]

The popularity of pantomime and other entertainments did not go unnoticed during the period. In one of the most enduring and popular plays of the period, Henry Fielding ruthlessly satirized the preference for pantomime and other "Hurlo-thrumbo" entertainments in *The Author's Farce and the Pleasures of the Town* (1730).[34] *The Author's Farce* debuted in April 1730 and was published the next day by J. Roberts.[35] The 1730 London edition does not name Fielding as its author. Rather, in Scriblerian style, it is attributed on its title page to Scriblerus Secundus. *The Author's Farce* is a composite play that narrates the struggle of aspiring author Luckless to have his work published at a moment when wit and turn of phrase in writing for the stage are eclipsed by the spectacles of nonsense. Luckless is deep in debt to his landlady, but he loves her daughter. He is surrounded by hack writers whose writing is purchased by the bookseller Bookweight, while his writing is not. In a moment of inspiration, Luckless writes and has performed *The Pleasures of the Town*, a "Puppet-Show . . . to be perform'd by living Figures," which works as a play within a play in *The Author's Farce* (24). Early in *The Author's Farce*, Luckless's friend Witmore cautions Luckless on his incurable habit of "Scribling" (8). Witmore advises,

> S'death! in an Age of Learning and true Politeness, where a Man might succeed by his Merit, it wou'd be an Encouragement.— But now, when Party and Prejudice carry all before them, when Learning is decried, Wit not understood, when the Theatres are Puppet-Shows, and the Comedians Ballad-Singers: When Fools lead the Town, wou'd a Man think to thrive by his Wit?—If you must write, write Nonsense, write Opera's, write Entertainments, write *Hurlo-thrumbo's*—Set up an *Oratory* and preach Nonsense; and you may meet with encouragement enough. (8)

Witmore sets his remarks within the context of the ascendancy of the Hanoverian regime and Walpole Parliament, which brought with them party strife and, as the Augustans felt, debased culture.

The solution Witmore proposes is simply to give in to the taste of the moment and write nonsense. To write such pieces would be, as Luckless and Witmore both realize, to make a farce out of authorship. The writing of such pieces would indeed be writing, yet it would not be authored in the way that Luckless imagines his rejected play to be. Rather, this writing would contribute to a form of performance where language, meaning, and the author would be displaced by spectacle. As J. Paul Hunter has observed, "for the major Augustans, distrust of rope-dancing, juggling, and dumb show derived from theological concern about the displacement of the Word and the triumph of a world of art where no direct line existed between subject and object, between God and man."[36] This was at once a philosophico-religious concern, as Hunter suggests, that the very ways of understanding and representing the world were being turned upside down and also a practical concern, for Luckless (and Fielding), that one could not earn one's living as an author if there were no market for (good) writing.

Despite Witmore's caution, Luckless still attempts to sell his play to the bookseller Bookweight. Bookweight first asks if the play has been accepted for performance. Luckless says that it has not but inquires what he could be paid for its publication if it were to be performed. Bookweight defers by saying that he could not give a value without reading the play himself, because

> BOOKWEIGHT: . . . a Play which will do for them [the players], will not always do for us [the booksellers].—There are your Acting Plays, and your Reading Plays.

> WITMORE: I do not understand that Distinction.

> BOOKWEIGHT: Why, Sir, your Acting Play is entirely supported by the Merit of the Actor, without any Regard to the Author at all:—In this Case, it signifies very little whether there be any Sense in it or no. Now your Reading Play is of a different Stamp, and must have Wit and Meaning in it—These latter I call your Substantive, as being able to support themselves. The former are your Adjective, as what require the Buffoonry and Gestures of an Actor to be joined to them, to shew their Signification. (10)

Bookweight takes the linguistic utterance (instantiated here as the play) as the base of commonality between "acting plays" and "reading plays" which is registered in his recourse to the grammatical—"the latter I call your substantive, the former I call your adjective"—and he is attuned to the complexities in the shift in medium between performance and print and the manner by which in the mediation of the linguistic utterance the authority to "shew . . . signification" may shift from the writing subject to the speaking subject. Bookweight opposes the necessity of performance and performers in acting plays to the necessity of authors in reading plays. It thus seems to be a variation of the "double tradition" described by Hume: performed plays don't need authors; printed plays do need authors. Acting plays derive their meaning from performance, from the "Buffoonry and Gestures of an Actor," while the reading plays have wit and meaning derived from an author.

What is tacit in Bookweight's distinction between acting plays and reading plays is the crucial role played by publication. He is, after all, in the business of publishing plays. The necessary prerequisite for a distinction between acting and reading plays is the fundamental difference between a performed piece and a printed piece. As with Langbaine and his successors, Bookweight links authorship to the printed text that may be read and not to the performance, which is seen. Authors are not necessary for acting plays, which, as Albert Rivero has suggested, refer not only to those plays deemed not worthy of literary esteem but also to the broader category of popular theatrical entertainments like pantomime, farce, and opera.[37] The anonymity of these kinds of theatrical pieces bears out Bookweight's claim: acting plays did not need authors; if they were named at one time, their names were not preserved. Moreover, Bookweight suggests—and historical evidence demonstrates—that these pieces were by default anonymous and unlikely to be noted as such.

Failing to find a publisher for his writing, Luckless finally concedes and writes the kind of piece Witmore suggested. *The Pleasures of the Town* combines all the elements of opera, oratory, nonsense, the puppet show, and Hurlo-thrumbo into one nearly incoherent piece presented as a play within *The Author's Farce*. Though *The Pleasures of the Town* utilizes the genres it satirizes, it differs in one key way: rather than removing the author entirely from the performance, Luckless casts himself as Master of the Show. In this role, he acts both as author of the piece, acknowledging it as his own and explaining his motivation, and as a performer within the piece, introducing various acts.

Anthony Hassall has pointed to Luckless's role in *The Author's Farce* as one play among many in which Fielding makes use of what he calls the "authorial dimension," "the overt presence of the author or the supposed author" within a work.[38] Hassal, like C. J. Rawson and Hunter, views this presence as unusual within drama and suggests that it anticipates the much-noted authorial presence or intrusion within Fielding's novels.[39] However, Rivero suggests, I think quite correctly, that the authorial intrusion within *The Pleasures of the Town* is no intrusion at all; rather, it is a key part of the dramatic form of the play within a play (28). Luckless is, after all, an actor playing an author playing an actor. His presence "as author" is already mediated by the dramatic action of the framing of *The Author's Farce*.

Rivero has suggested that Fielding strikes a balance between the "acting play" and the "reading play" in the combination of *The Author's Farce* with *The Pleasures of the Town* through the distancing mechanisms of double satire and the authorial presence. This balance is key to the work of the play, so that it could not be taken as an endorsement of the theatrical and literary culture it satirizes (23). *The Author's Farce* and *The Pleasures of the Town*, however, maintain no such distinction. Bookweight's "acting play" and "reading play" distinction captures the complex of actions, objects, and meaning that is central to theatrical, and indeed all, representation. *The Author's Farce* in its own staging, which brings together multiple media forms and genres and collapses the frame play and the play within a play, does not actually allow for the kind of analytic cordoning off Bookweight suggests exists between the printed and the performed, word and action.

The play combines elements from those genres considered "acting plays," but in Luckless's emphasis of the authorship of those elements, it collapses the distinction between the anonymous and unliterary entertainments and the authored and literary framing comedy. *The Pleasures of the Town* emphatically argues, against the theatrical norm, that the meaning of the piece resides in the author, not in the action, but then consistently undermines this claim. Thus the often-confusing conclusion to *The Author's Farce*, which Frances Kavenik has called a nightmare dénouement, in which it is unclear whether the revelation of Luckless's royal lineage is part of the frame play or part of *The Pleasures of the Town*, blurs the boundaries between the frames to simultaneously suggest coherence and incoherence, authorial intention and theatrical intention, in the play amid the pieces that compose it.[40] With Luckless revealed as heir to the Bantamite throne, he will be an author and king, which serves as a counterpoint to the central action of *The Pleasures of the Town*, where the goddess Nonsense searches for a mate to share her throne. Authorship is thus bound, even in this seemingly triumphant account, to the ways in which meaning is made through theatrical representation.

While Fielding tried to assert the role of the author in performance, the Licensing Act of 1737, thought largely to be a response to Fielding's satire of the Walpole ministry in *The Historical Register for the Year 1736* and *Eurydice Hiss'd*, codified in law the operative and structuring distinction between performed and printed drama. The first two clauses of the Licensing Act pertain to the "more effectual punishing [of] such rogues, vagabonds, sturdy beggars and vagabonds," including those "players of interludes" without "legal settlement" (267).[41] The third clause for the preperformance licensing of plays is what effectively halted the production and performance of new plays:

> III. And be it further enacted by the authority aforesaid, that from and after the said twenty-fourth day of June, one thousand, seven hundred and thirty seven, no person shall for hire, gain or reward, act perform, represent, or cause to be acted, performed or represented any new interlude, tragedy, comedy, opera, play, farce, or other entertainment of the stage, or any part of parts therein; or any new act, scene or other part added to any old interlude, tragedy, comedy, opera, play, farce or other entertainment of the stage, or any new prologue or epilogue, unless a true copy thereof be sent to the Lord Chamberlain of the King's household for the time being, fourteen days at least before the acting, representing or performing thereof, together with an account of the playhouse or other place where the same shall be and the time when the same is intended to be first acted, represented or performed, signed by the master or manager, or one of the masters or managers of such playhouse or place, or company of actors therein. (267)

The third clause of the Licensing Act outlines the necessary steps required for a performance to be licensed. A company must send a "true copy" to the Lord Chamberlain for his approval with the proposed place of performance and the signature of the manager. Nowhere in the Licensing Act is the need for an author mentioned. There is no requirement for an authorial attribution on the script. Rather, because the act is focused on preventing unlawful performance, it focuses on those pieces of information key to the staging of a piece. The Licensing Act made a clear distinction between performance and print publication. Indeed, many plays that were not licensed for performance went on to be printed.

There is a scholarly tendency to cite authorial liability as an underlying motivation for anonymity, but with the Licensing Act, there was no authorial liability. The author was unimportant. Penalties and prohibitions were lodged against the manager or master of a company. There is therefore no connection between the acknowledgment of anonymity in the theatrical realm by the theatergoing public or catalogers of drama and the prohibitions of the Licensing Act. Such interest in anonymity, as I have shown in the previous section, predates the Licensing Act. The contribution of the Licensing Act to the public interest in the anonymity of drama, if there is one, was to further disassociate performance from print publication. Just as the closing of the theaters during the Interregnum popularized the reading of plays and made available a distinction between printed play text and performance that would be so crucial to Langbaine, the Licensing Act, in its sole interest in performance and silence on publication, enabled the publishing of theatrical pieces that could have no predecessor in performance and further separated the realms of the theater and printing.

While it is clear from advertising practices and legal proscriptions that named authorship and anonymity were not concerns within the eighteenth-century theater, it is less clear what the individuals who produced and attended the theater knew, or attended to, about the authorship or anonymity of the pieces they saw. Evidence of such knowledge is indeed hard to come by; however, theatrical records from Lincoln Inn's Fields and Drury Lane, eighteenth-century accounts of theatergoing, and images depicting the theatrical milieu give some suggestion of the range of interest and knowledge the various theatrical publics that composed the audience and company of the theaters possessed.

Take, for example, this anecdote from the Cross–Hopkins diary, the journals kept by the two consecutive prompters at Drury Lane Theater from 1747 to 1776, from February 1, 1773, about the first performance of the comic opera *The Wedding Ring*:

> The Wed. R. [The Wedding Ring] a Comic Opera of Two Acts wrote + Compos'd by Mr. Dibdin The Music very pretty—as the Author was kept a secret The Town fancy'd that [it] is one of Mr. Bickerstaff + and call'd out to know who was the Author. Mr. Garrick inform'd them that he had no power to declare

who the author was, but he cou'd assure them that it was not Mr. Bickerstaff this did not satisfy them at last Mr. Dibdin went on + declared himself to be the Author + made an Affidavit of it + then the Farce went on with Applause.[42]

In this case, Garrick knows who the author is. "The Town," or more precisely a small but vocal theatrical public, does not. This demonstrates a specific kind of interest in authorship, specifically that of playwright Isaac Bickerstaffe and whatever vitriol his biographical person may have drawn. It does not, however, indicate a general interest in authorship qua authorship; furthermore, in the misattribution of the comic opera, it indicates a general lack of information about authorship on the part of audiences.

As audiences were disinterested in or lacked information about the pieces they saw performed on London stages, so too did the managers and prompters of those theaters occasionally not know about the authorship of the pieces they staged. *An Account of Plays Acted at Lincoln's Inn Fields from 1714 to 1723* (more commonly known at "Rich's Register") offers particularly compelling evidence in this regard.[43] The ledger, like the Cross–Hopkins, lists the names of the authors of new plays. Moreover, it also includes what was performed at the competing Drury Lane theater on the same night and, when known, who the author was. There are many cases, however, in which the account book simply lists a new play at Drury Lane "Written by Mr." with the surname absent. For January 16, 1716/17, we see first evidence of this for a play at Drury Lane, "A new Comedy call'd *Three Hours after Marriage* Written by Mr," and on May 11, 1717, at Drury Lane, "A new Tragedy call'd *Lucius the Christian King of Britain* Written by Mr." Furthermore, Rich, or the keeper of the accounts, does not always know the authorship of plays performed at his own theater, Lincoln Inn's Fields, either. For example, on Tuesday, February 18, 1717/18, "A new Tragedy call'd Scipio Africanus Written by Mr." This play makes it to a third night, on February 21, "for the benefit of the Author." It is worth noting that despite the tradition of the third, sixth, and ninth nights, if a piece ran for that many nights, being a benefit for the author, the author was almost never named on either the playbill or the benefit tickets.

In these examples, the managers and prompters are thinking of these plays as authored or anonymous. However, the evidence for just how much their knowledge was limited demonstrates how even among interested and invested individuals—theatrical insiders— authorship may remain unknown and the play text engaged with, and experienced, without reference or regard to its authorship. This is due to the robust and varied conditions inherent in the theatrical milieu of the eighteenth-century theater. While the opposition of actor and author or stage and page begin to capture some of this dynamic, it also occludes the multiplicity of types of pieces presented on stage in a given night and the actions and reactions of actors, audiences, props, sets, and the architecture of the playhouse.

William Hogarth's painting and subsequent print of the third act of *The Beggar's Opera* (1731) is suggestive of just how the whole of the theatrical experience may not be reduced to merely actors and authors. Hogarth's painting depicts a scene from act III of *The Beggar's Opera* in which the hero and highwayman, Macheath, stands charged while Polly Peachum and Lucy Lockit plead for his life. Strikingly, it is not just the action of the stage that the image depicts. Onstage, in the boxes, alongside the drama, is a tableau of audience members, manager, and author with very little to suggest separation between actors and spectators.

A late eighteenth-century engraving of this image by Thomas Clerk makes this point even clearer. While the dimensionality of the painting presents in the foreground, slightly, Macheath, Polly, and Lucy, the 1790 engraving flattens the perspective to suggest a further flattening between audience and drama (Figure 13). This print goes further to identify the individuals depicted: first the performers, then the audience. In this depiction of performers and audience, it is evident how varied the attention of the audience is and the manner in which it echoes, if not interacts with, the varied attentions of the characters in the staged action. While to the right of Macheath, in the foreground, Polly's attention is fixed on Peachum, with whom she pleads, behind her, guards are in conversation with no indication, beyond their physical proximity, that they are attending to what is happening before them. So too, in the depiction of the audience on the lower right, the Duke of Bolton watches intently and, it seems, follows along with the book of the play.[44] Other audience members appear utterly disinterested in what is presented before them. Lady Jane

Cook, for example, on the lower left of the print, is turned away from the scene and lost in conversation. John Rich, manager of Lincoln Inn's Fields, in the background to the right, is similarly turned away in conversation with Mr. Cock, the auctioneer. Particularly striking is the manner in which John Gay, author of *The Beggar's Opera*, looks over the right shoulder of Rich toward the viewer but yet is almost entirely obscured. His displacement and near-occlusion in the image remind the viewer of the role, and lack thereof, of the author within the theatrical realm. Among all the persons depicted, he seems almost an afterthought, a presence, but one whose significance is minor in comparison with those who surround him.

Hogarth's representation of the varied and competing attention of the audience is echoed again in his *The Laughing Audience* (1733), which depicts a view of the audience in the pit and gallery, wherein we see the more modest pit attentive and enraptured by the performance and the upper-class boxes occupied with other concerns. An anonymous print late in the period from the perspective of the front boxes at Covent Garden (circa 1770) depicts the varied attention and the ways in which the totality of the theater may not be reduced to the action on the stage (Figure 14).

Figure 13. Engraving of Hogarth's *Beggar's Opera*, act III (1790). Copyright Victoria and Albert Museum, London.

Figure 14. *View from the Front Boxes of the Theatre-Royal Covent Garden,* Anonymous (circa 1770). Copyright Victoria and Albert Museum, London.

In this print, the representation on the stage is visible, unlike in *The Laughing Audience,* but it is not the subject of the image. Rather, the viewer sees what an audience member may see, if well-to-do enough to be seated in the front boxes. In the foreground to the left, two women and a man are in conversation, with another male spectator leaning in to join them. To the left of them, another male spectator is turned entirely away from the stage engaged in conversation and gesturing with his right hand at the stage. To the right of the image, other spectators seem to watch the stage with attention. It becomes clear, however, that they are also just as easily attending to the audience in the pit and other boxes. So, too, is it evident that spectators whose perspective the viewer is given are likewise as much objects of others' gaze as they are subjects of their own gaze upon both stage and audience. The prominence of the chandelier and candles throughout the image serves as a reminder that the houses of eighteenth-century theaters were not dark, as they are in our own moment. The neat division, therefore, between spectator and spectacle implied by the lit stage and darkened house does not hold, and, as in Hogarth's *Beggar's Opera*, the audience may well be as much of a spectacle as those onstage.

Eighteenth-century theater history is filled with moments wherein the audience either became part of the spectacle or themselves were the spectacle. Popular accounts and images of theatrical riots, like the Half-Price Riots in 1763 at Drury Lane and Covent Garden or the tumult over *The Blackamoor Wash'd White* at Drury Lane in 1776, indicate the ways in which the nature of theatrical representation and the space of the theater were so much more than what was advertised in a playbill or printed in a playbook.[45] Less violent and perhaps more ubiquitous than theatrical riots was the role of audiences as real-time critics of the dramatic representation. As in the case of the misattributed performance of *The Wedding Ring*, a small and invested group of spectators could, and sometimes did, stop the performance and dictate what was to happen onstage.

Instances, and even more so literary worries over, the "hissing pit" abound throughout the period. Certain small publics did indeed band together to damn and interrupt performances on their opening nights.[46] Hissing plays represents a move aimed at censuring an author (typically, it seems, over her presumed politics or other personal disagreements), but the hissing also appears to have an editorial function. Consider the run of the pantomime *The Rites of Hecate* from January 16, 1764, through February 6, 1764, at Drury Lane, as recalled in the Cross–Hopkins diary: "Saturday, January 28, 1764: *Venice Preserv'd, Rites of Hecate* [pant] and *Hymn* [interlude]: The Mad Scene in the Pantomime much hiss'd." In response to this hissing on Tuesday, January 31, 1764: "*Suspicious Husband, Hymen,* and *Rites of Hecate*. The Mad Scene left out." Finally, the following week, on Monday, February 6, 1764, the audience response comes to a head:

> In the last scene of the Pantomime for the Galleries some hissing; some Crying Off! Off! etc. Till Mr. King address'd the Audience as follows: Ladies and Gentleman. If this Token of your disapprobation Proceed from the Mad Scene being left out, give me leave

to Assure you; many applications have been made to the Managers to have it omitted—upon which they were quiet.

It is now customary to think about theatrical representation as a form of collective authorship wherein playwrights, actors, and managers all contribute in the making of a performance. These forms of audience participation and feedback suggest the degree to which the theater is a collective space of authorship not only on the side of production but on the side of reception as well. Audiences are actively participating in making, remaking, and revising the productions. Indeed, some of these audience responses point to knowledge and interest in authorship (though I would argue that in many cases, the interest stems from the particular biographical personages, not from the "Author"), and they also point to practices that move beyond individual authors and actors and that implicate the entirety of the theatrical milieu in the production of meaning.

Nonetheless, both eighteenth-century and contemporary critics return to the individual as figured in the author and the actor to account for the drama of the period. Nearly two decades after the Licensing Act of 1737 had reduced the production of new theatrical pieces and increased the reliance on pre-1737 repertory plays, dramatic authorship was in a sorry state. *The Case of Authors by Profession or Trade Stated,* published anonymously in 1758, and published again in 1762 with an attribution to James Ralph, bemoans the status of the profession of writing.[47] Authors, he claims, are not paid their due worth. This is especially egregious on the stage. Nearly thirty years earlier, *The Author's Farce* had attempted to take aim at the debased stage and championed the downtrodden Luckless. *The Case of Authors* continues this critique and focuses on what it sees as the dominant forms of writing—writing for booksellers, writing for the stage, and writing for political faction—advocating for authorial compensation based on artistic accomplishment.

Ralph echoes those complaints about writing for the stage voiced before the Licensing Act, but they took on new urgency when the Licensing Act reduced the number of patent theaters to two and, in effect, "reserved power in the hand of actor-managers like Garrick" to select and refuse new play scripts at their whim.[48] Of this control, *The Case of Authors* asserts,

> Whereas on the Stage, Exhibition stands in the Place of Compo-
> sition: The *Manager*, whether *Player* or *Harlequin*, must be the
> sole Pivot on which the whole Machine is both to move and rest:
> There is no *draw-back* on the *Profit* of the Night in *old* Plays: and
> any *Access* of Reputation to a dead Author carries no impertinent
> Claims and invidious Distinctions along with it. (25)

Ralph argues that the author is a mere journeyman supplying a
script that may or may not be bought. Central to the entire operation of the theater, instead, is the manager, who ensures that "Exhibition stands in the Place of Composition." Those genres that were
in ascendance—pantomime, opera, farce—at the time of *The Author's Farce* have been, by the time of *The Case of Authors*, established
as the dominant modes in theater and accompany "*old* Plays," which
need neither a license for performance nor payment to an author.

Older plays bear another significant advantage over newer offer-
ings: by the fact of a play's survival in the repertory, the good reputation of the author, if known, is assured. With reputation comes a
greater chance of financial security in a production. Thus we recall
the 1702 advertisement for *Bartholomew Fair*, "Written by the Famous Ben. Jonson." By taking the unusual step of announcing the
authorship of *Bartholomew Fair*, the advertisement traded on the
reputation of Jonson and his writing.

Ralph notes "access" of reputation, which suggests the reputation of dead dramatists may exceed the individual, now departed,
biographical person. Ben Jonson's name no longer refers to the individual but to the function of the name, whereas for new and living
authors—as in the case of Bickerstaffe, wrongly assumed to be author of *The Wedding Ring*—reputation is bound to the biographical
individual, his political and personal conflicts, and not necessarily
to his body of writing. Authorial reputation, of course, relies on
the name of the author to index the writing of the individual. Here
Ralph tacitly acknowledges the way in which authorial anonymity,
even of older plays whose authors are "known," permeates the en-
deavor of the theater.

The lack of proper acknowledgment of the author, Ralph claims,
is so bad that he notes, "I am ready to make my best Acknowledge-
ments to a *Harlequin*, who has Continence enough to look upon an

Author in the Green-room, of what Consideration soever, without laughing in his Face" (42). In this imagined backstage confrontation between author and harlequin, Ralph places the two competing figures—one representing the literary stage organized around authorship and language, the other the supposed unliterary stage organized around performance and embodiment—against each other, and it is clear that the harlequin comes out triumphant. In staging these two figures in conflict with each other, Ralph reduces the complexity of theatrical representations and locates them in singular, empirically observable, though imagined, figures.

The utility of such figuration to render thinkable the abstraction of the literary is evident when Ralph recasts this same confrontation in terms of the mind–body problem:

> In short; Tho' we talk of Soul and Body, we have but one Object; because the Soul is no Object at all—Hence Cooks, Taylors, Jewellers, Pimps, Flatterers, &c. &c. are always in request—Lawyers, Physicians, and Divines but when they are wanted—And Authors, or Dealers in Helps to improve and delight the Understanding, never. (46)

Here authorship is cast on the side of the soul, for its products are immaterial. The body, however, is aligned with material arts and with the production of goods: cooking, tailoring, prostitution, and so on. We may also add to that list of materially based professions acting or performing. As with the earlier imagined exchange between a harlequin and an author, what Ralph argues is privileged is the material, or the body, over the immaterial, or language.

The opposition Ralph attempts to draw between body and soul and the material and immaterial does not hold. Such dualism imagines the easy separability of matter from spirit and language from its mediated nature; indeed, Ralph even notes, "We have but one Object." That object is not the inert stuff of "Cooks, Taylors, Jewellers" but a hybrid comprising competing actions and agencies instantiated in material form. So, too, is the literature, dramatic and otherwise, of which Ralph writes. The goods of authorship are instantiated as material through print publication. It turns seemingly immaterial language into the object of the book. This movement imparts the fiction of transparency between author's mind and printed text object, even as Ralph and countless others recount the ways in which the words or actions of authors are refracted or mislaid in the medium of print. Such refraction is made even more palpable in the theatrical realm, where the obvious collective action of managers and actors, and the less obvious collective actions of audience, genre, props, and so on, combine to occlude authorship, much like Gay peeking over Rich's shoulder in the Hogarth print.

Despite the palpability of the layers of mediation in the theater, the medium of print is no less mediated, though it may seem so. The configurations and actors are different; the claim to transparency is greater, but the mediated nature remains. The name and figure of the author typically function to ensure illusions of transparency that seek to obscure such mediation. Anonymity, however, often works to short-circuit claims to the immateriality, purity, and transparency of literary language. The friction between the two media of representation of the drama—theater and print—makes even more obvious what anonymity may throw into relief.

Print publication, on one hand, obscures many of the complexities inherent in textual representation; on the other hand, it makes visible both the attribution of authorship and its absence. Print consolidates the complex layers of mediation into the named author or the explicitly anonymous text. The necessary precondition for that visibility is the distinction between a performed piece and a printed piece and thereby a sense of a media concept. When "the Merit of the Composer" has been transferred "to the Performer," the presence or absence of an author's name is unlikely to be noticed, or, at the very least, it seems that authors in the period perceived that no one noticed.[49]

This "double tradition" of attention to anonymity is not, however, a natural outcome of the division between publication and performance or author and actor. Medium matters to the history and intelligibility of authorial anonymity. Furthermore, awareness of the medium and the protocols surrounding authorship and anonymity matters. Once a dramatic piece, printed and cataloged, was understood as distinct and removed from the theatrical milieu, it may have raised concern and interest in the absence of the authorial name. Such absence, however, needed to be articulated and schematized in the form that writers such as Langbaine put forth. Such cataloging practices taught readers to notice and think about both the authorship and the anonymity of the published plays they encountered.

We cannot know for certain what theater audiences in the early eighteenth century knew about the authorship or anonymity of the pieces presented before them. From the publication of plays, registers, and catalogs, however, we can begin to gather what may have concerned collectors and readers in the period. Overwhelmingly, the plays, operas, pantomimes, and entertainments presented onstage were anonymous. At every level, from legal restriction to advertising practices, named authorship was of little interest to theatrical representation. Likewise, anonymity was of little consequence, for how could a default practice call attention to itself? To make these paired concerns visible, we must view them retrospectively through the printed text—an act that trades the harlequin and his bat for the author's name, or its absence, on a title page.

3

Attribution, Circulation, and "Defoe"

Authorial attribution is typically understood in terms of a binary logic: a text is either by a named author, or it is not; it is in a given author's oeuvre, or it is not. These commonsense views recognize the immense power attaching an authorial name to a text possesses; however, they tend to assume a uniform uptake and acceptance of the attribution. The material form and circulation of texts, however, necessarily complicate any totalizing narrative about the authorship or anonymity of a given text. In what follows, I first demonstrate this binary logic at work in the dispute over the attribution of *A Vindication of the Press* (1714) and the unquestioned acceptance of *An Essay on the Regulation of the Press* (1704) as Daniel Defoe's. I show the ways in which the pamphlets themselves stake a claim for the function of anonymity and how they resist the reduction of the work they do to that of a single, named author. I turn in the second part of the chapter to the late eighteenth century to consider the attribution of *Roxana* and *Moll Flanders*—both now accepted as Defoe's. In my account, authorial attribution is less a fact that may be verified or disproved and more of a network effect: not necessarily a binary process but one of contingency bound to processes of circulation, iteration, and the material form of the text.

"Defoe" the Pamphleteer: The Binary Logic of Attribution

In his introduction to *Defoe: The Critical Heritage*, Pat Rogers writes that Defoe was "chiefly regarded—understandably enough—as a polemicist and party writer" in his lifetime.[1] How strange it must seem to the contemporary, that is, the twenty-first-century, reader that Defoe, accepted author of some of the most canonical novels of the eighteenth century, was known primarily, if only, for the most ephemeral of his writings.

The great novelist Defoe, Rogers has suggested, is an invention of the nineteenth century, but as I argue, the process of Defoe's transformation into a novelist began in the late eighteenth century. This transformation was complicated and delayed by the original anonymity of Defoe's writing. The anonymous status of these texts in their original circulation has, however, been obscured by the nineteenth-century codification of the Defoe canon and biography that produce a teleological critical narrative in which the novels of Defoe represent the perfection of the craft of an "imaginative artist" (Rogers 1) honed by polemic and party writing.

I detail in the latter part of the chapter the means by which the name "Defoe" was circulated as a writer of novels in the late eighteenth century. Through the circulation and iteration of the name "Defoe" attached to novels, Defoe became like "Fielding, Smollett, Sterne, and all that class of perpetually self-reproductive volumes."[2] That is, the name of the author and the title of the novels were folded in together, author and texts abstracted as works, and a Defoe novelistic oeuvre was established. Thus the conditions under which those attributions were established fall away, and we are left with the abstract notions of Defoe as author and his works as novels unbound from their material instantiations. The consequence of this transformation is that though Defoe during his lifetime was regarded for his didactic and political writings, many of those same writings now receive scholarly attention only insofar as they are by Defoe "the novelist" and have some use value in narrating the biographical or literary development of the man named Defoe. Walter Scott's assessment of Defoe in the early part of the nineteenth century, for example, expressly sets aside his political writing to focus on his "Romance" writing.[3]

This reversal—from the political writings being the core of Defoe's writing to their occupation of a secondary or tertiary position—disavows the multivalent functions of these texts by consolidating them under the name "Defoe." Furthermore, through this consolidation, the boundaries of the canon are hardened, the inside–outside binarism of authorial attribution made more severe.

P. N. Furbank and W. R. Owens have warned of the "snowball effect" of attribution whereby once one text is let into a canon, it changes the perception of the author and allows for further attributions based on those changes.[4] I am in absolute agreement with Furbank and Owen's assessment of the dangers of willy-nilly authorial attribution (particularly those attributions based on internal evidence alone), and the ongoing discussions and whittling down of the Defoe canon are indeed much needed.[5] Lost, however, in the desire for verifying or disproving authorship is the in-betweenness many texts occupy over the course of their lives as they circulate in a culture wherein their agency and survival are associated less with their named author and more with their material form.

While Harold Love has theorized authorial attribution as the task of identifying and validating human agency, attribution also serves as a kind of shortcut for characterizing the nature of a work.[6] In this way, authorial attribution may foreclose study and analysis because the attributed work, if it is to be by the named author, must cohere—or be made to cohere—with a larger body of work. In the case of Defoe, whose ever-changing body of work refuses cohesion and whose novels, such as *Roxana* and *Moll Flanders*, are taken as an end point in a writing career, the singularity of a nonnovelistic text and its context or topicality may be sacrificed or ignored entirely because of the authorial name retrospectively attached to it. The critical tradition surrounding some of the pamphlets attributed (and deattributed) to Defoe is particularly exemplary in this regard. In this tradition, the pamphlets are made to matter as they may be made to fit into the biographical and literary development of the author—even if these pamphlets are later shown not to be by Defoe—and not as they may have mattered in their publication contexts. Even though attribution reinforces the inside and outside of an oeuvre, it does not ensure that those texts on the inside get read.

The Defoe canon demonstrates the ways in which the process of attaching names to texts privileges the coherent body of works over the singularity of the text and its context. Privileging the oeuvre over the individual text introduces a quandary: if Defoe's political pamphlets were not attributed to Defoe, they would likely be considered valuable only in the contextual writing of political history, if at all. Because they are attributed to Defoe, however, these pamphlets tend to be read by many critics solely (if at all) for their relevance to his biography and literary development. In other words, we may read attributed texts *because* they have been attributed—for what they have to tell us about their creator—rather than for the work they do, or did, in the world.

While *A Vindication of the Press* has been subject to much worrying by Defoe scholars over its attribution, *An Essay on the Regulation of the Press* has been unproblematically attributed to Defoe. Attribution of these pamphlets to Defoe or arguments over attribution replicate a reading practice similar to the structures of press regulation to which these pamphlets respond that seek to attach names to the text; in effect, they represent a shortcut whereby reading is unnecessary. The critical habit of reading them entirely as part of a biographical and literary narrative about Defoe is precisely the reading strategy that the pamphlets themselves caution against and the reading strategy that is complicated by anonymity. This critical reading practice predicated on the importance of the name is informed, in large part, by the late eighteenth- and early nineteenth-century creation of Defoe as novelist. I wish to move away from this narrative and instead explore the work anonymity does for these pamphlets in the early eighteenth century and detail a method that expands accounts of attribution beyond its binary form.

Within these pamphlets, we have the identification of two possible functions of the author's name, one that refers to an individual person with partisan politics and another that refers to the body of works—both of which eclipse the text itself—and the aim of the pamphlets themselves: a disavowal of those functions in favor of engaging with the content of the text. Within this context, anonymous authorship works alongside textual production and asks for a reading of the content of the text. That it should be common for political pamphlets is not surprising, as this form demands attention to the current political context to stake a claim for valuation.

Though we think of attribution to a known author as leading to an otherwise unknown or unremarkable text being read and studied, *An Essay on the Regulation of the Press* is fascinating because its history of attribution rests on its not being read. *An Essay* has remained in the Defoe canon unchallenged since Defoe's first biographer, George Chalmers, included it in his list of works by "De Foe."

J. R. Moore's introduction to the facsimile edition constructs a useful and common, it seems, narrative of the text's attribution:

> One striking result of the rarity of the tract has been that it has been almost unknown to biographers of Defoe. It has been assigned to him since 1790, when Chalmers included it, at the end of his expanded *Life of Daniel De Foe*, in "A List of Writings, which are considered as undoubtedly De Foe's." Chalmers' assignment must have been based on some acquaintance with the overwhelming internal evidence of Defoe's authorship, but there is no other indication that he had seen the pamphlet. Professor Trent owned a copy, but it was purchased eight years after his chapter on Defoe was published in the *Cambridge History of English Literature* and four years after the publication of his *Daniel Defoe: How to Know Him*. Trent's bibliography for his chapter on Defoe lists the title, but his published writings indicate no personal acquaintance with the tract. In 1830 Wilson wrote: "Not having been able to procure the pamphlet, the present writer is unable to state his argument; . . ." Lee merely guessed at the contents from the title (which was known from the booksellers' advertisement). Chadwick, Minto, and most later biographers have made no mention of it. Wright offered only a wild surmise: "Daniel is at them in a moment, and with his *Essay on the Regulation of the Press* mangles their argument like a bull-dog"—a statement more helpful in understanding the habits of bulldogs than in following Defoe's line of reasoning.[7]

Moore's introduction is striking in the way it works through all of the key Defoe biographers and bibliographers who have never looked at the pamphlet. Chalmers, it seems, attributed *An Essay* to Defoe based on internal evidence, and subsequent biographers and bibliographers accepted that attribution without looking for further evidence. The absurdity of relying on internal evidence for authorial attribution has been well argued by Furbank and Owens.[8] In the case of *An Essay*, its content and style have been guessed at based on its title and attribution to Defoe. However, such guesses at content and style, it appears, are the only bases for its attribution to Defoe.

Scholarship on the emergence of British copyright, most notably that of Jody Greene, has invigorated the study of this pamphlet.[9] In *An Essay*, Greene reads the clearest articulation of the rights and responsibilities of authorship that would be codified in the Act of Anne.[10] Greene offers a compelling reading of the text but avoids the problem that this essay, which calls for the owning of texts by their authors, circulated anonymously and that much of its attribution to Defoe rests on a long history of its not being read. Indeed, for Greene, much of the force of her argument, that the origins of copyright lie in authorial liability, relies on the relationship between the biographical incident of Defoe being pilloried for the anonymous *The Shortest Way with Dissenters* (1702) and the anonymous *An Essay*, which argues that if an author is to be held liable for his work, he should also be able to profit from it through ownership.

As a counterpoint to the unread-until-recently *An Essay on the Regulation of the Press, A Vindication of the Press* has been read, reread, and ultimately rejected from the Defoe canon because of its anonymous publication and its late addition to the Defoe bibliography.[11] Setting aside the problem of whether the text was actually written by Defoe, scholarly discussion of the place of the pamphlet within the Defoe canon, and hence its value as an object of study, reveals much about the critical reading strategies employed when an author is "known." Otho Clinton Williams's introduction for the 1951 facsimile edition notes, "*A Vindication of the Press* is one of Defoe's most characteristic pamphlets and for this reason as well as for its rarity deserves reprinting."[12] Here Williams slots the pamphlet within the canon on the basis of its "characteristic" marks of the individual author. Still further, Williams notes,

A Vindication of the Press is chiefly important for the corroboration of our knowledge of Daniel Defoe. It presents nothing that is new, but it gives further evidence of his pride in authorship, of his rationalization of his actions as a professional journalist, and of his belief in the importance of a free press. Many of his characteristic ideas are repeated with his usual consistency in point of view. Although the critical comments in the essay are thoroughly conventional, they offer evidence of contemporary literary judgments and reveal Defoe as a well-informed man of moderation and commonsense. (v)

Williams notes the importance of the text because it "corroborates" what Defoe scholars already know about the individual named Defoe but admits the conventionality of the commentary contained therein. Two strains appear in this argument: one points to Defoe as a "proud" individual author, whereas the other points to the commonplace nature of the arguments and thus to a larger cultural sentiment that remains unexamined and may undermine the attribution.[13]

In arguing against the attribution of *A Vindication* to Defoe, Furbank and Owens take the unextraordinary critique as proof of its authorship by someone other than Defoe:

> What is characteristic of this pamphlet is that is does not seem to have any particular target in view, and for the most part the ideas it contains—on the benefits of a free press, on the harmfulness of much contemporary criticism and on the qualities of good writing—are commonplace platitudes. (356)

In identifying both its characteristic and its conventional elements, the reading of the content of *A Vindication* ceases at the moment when attribution or deattribution can be established. The binarism of attribution is apparent in its insistence that the text is either characteristic of an individual author or conventional within a period. Indeed, a text may possess both qualities, but drawing them out requires explicating the meaning, content, or context of these pamphlets. Attribution, here, stops short of such explication.

While Donald Foster has noted the impasse anonymous or contested authorship poses to the critical process, with *An Essay* and *A Vindication*, we repeatedly see the cessation of critical reading following authorial attribution.[14] In these cases, attribution enables not further critical engagement but rather critical disengagement. What is of critical interest is not what the pamphlets argue but who did or did not write the argument. Both *An Essay* and *A Vindication*, however, articulate the very problem that naming the author of a text very often precludes the reading of a text. The named author, these pamphlets claim, stands directly in the way of reading and engaging with the content of texts.

An Essay on the Regulation of the Press was written in response to a bill on licensing the press, introduced into the House of Commons on December 15, 1703, that sought to restrain discussion of political decisions in the press.[15] An Essay rejects licensing because of its arbitrariness and, perhaps more importantly, its ability to be easily corrupted by "Frauds, Briberies, and all the ill practices possible" (8). Most emphatically, the text worries the current state of politics and fears the control of the press by one party who would appoint a licenser:

> Then suppose this or that Licenser, a Party-Man, that is, One put in, and upheld by a Party; suppose him of any Party, which you please, and a Man of the opposite Kidney, brings him a Book, he views the Character of the Man, O, says he, *I know the Author, he is a damn'd* Whig, *or a rank* Jacobite, *I'll License none of his Writings*; here is Bribery on one Hand, partiality to Parties on the other; but get a Man of his own Kidney to own the very same Book, and as he refus'd it without opening it before, he is as easie to pass it now, not for the Good or Ill in the Book, but on both Hands for the Character of the Author. (10–11)

Here we are presented with a very different function of the author's name than the model of Foucauldian penal appropriation by which the author's name is attached to the text so that the author can be held liable for its contents. Under partisan politics, the author is meant to answer not for his text but rather for his or her "Character" (11). The text in this view is irrelevant; rather, it is the political allegiances, "*damn'd Whig or . . . rank Jacobite*," of the author that determine authorial liability. The complaint of the text here is that writings will not be evaluated on content but on the name of the author and his personal allegiances. The name of the author, then, is not a function within discourse; it is instead the name of an actual person situated within a political discourse.

The text's worry about partisan control of the press is further articulated in its insistence of the neutrality of the press:

But 'tis pitty the Press should come into a Party-strife: This is like two Parties going to War, and one depriving the other of all their Powder and Shot. Ammunition stands always Neuter, or rather, *Jack a both Sides*, every body has it, and then they get the Victory who have most Courage to use it, and Conduct to manage it. (16–17)

The "Neuter" nature of the press that is pressed into partisan service further works to highlight the importance of *An Essay* as a text that was circulated anonymously. Like the press itself, *An Essay*, for it to be effective, must be approached as politically neutral. The name of the author, as the text demonstrates earlier, taints the text with the "Character" of the author.

Given this reading, it is hard to reconcile the turn in the last four pages toward the pamphlet's call for "a Law be made to make the last Seller the Author, unless the Name of Author, Printer, or Bookseller, be affix'd to the Book, then no Book can be published, but there will be some body found to answer for it. Whoever puts a false Name, to forfeit . . . &c." (22). Here the function of anonymous publication seems to be erased in a regulatory impulse. However, if anonymous publication is not read in terms of liability but readability and political efficacy, the argument coheres. Within this scenario, the "chain of liability," as Greene calls it, cannot be activated until a text has been read and offense caused. In arguing against prepress censorship, the pamphlet allows for a proliferation of texts that may be read and, if prosecution is to happen, must be read. In this manner, *An Essay* responds to the threat of prepress censorship by posing both anonymity (in its publication) and named authorship (in its argument) as modes that ensure that texts can be read.

A Vindication of the Press is even more emphatic in its attention to the effects of the author's name on readership. The text first bemoans the effect of named authorship impeding reading due to authorial reputation:

In respect to Writings in general, there is an unaccountable Caprice in abundance of Persons, to Condemn or Commend a Performance meerly by a Name. The Names of some Writers will effectually recommend, without making an Examination into the Merit of the Work; and the Names of other Persons, equally qualified for Writing, and perhaps of greater Learning than the Former, shall be sufficient to Damn it; and all this is owing either to some lucky Accident of writing apposite to the Humour of the Town, (wherein an agreeable Season and a proper Subject are chiefly to be regarded) or to Prejudice, but most commonly the Former. (20–21)

Here the name of the author is noted as a sufficient impediment to critical engagement with the content of a text. If the author's name is not already of repute or not of "the Humour of the Town," the text is condemned without ever being read. The name here refers not to an individual person but rather to a group of texts bearing her name that informs her place in cultural valuation.

In *A Vindication*, however, we have the emergence of another function of the author's name that echoes *An Essay*'s earlier discussion of the problem of partisanship and the press:

The Question first ask'd [by the "lower Order of Criticks"] is, whether an Author is a Whig or a Tory; if he be a Whig, or that Party which is in Power, his Praise is resounded, he's presently cried up for an excellent Writer; if not, he's mark'd as a Scoundrel, a perpetual Gloom hangs over his Head; if he was Master of the sublime Thoughts of *Addison*, the easy flowing Numbers of *Pope*, the fine Humour of *Garth*, the beautiful Language of *Rowe*, the Perfection of *Prior*, the Dialogue of *Congreve*, and the Pastoral of *Phillips*, he must nevertheless submit to a mean Character, if not expect the Reputation of an Illiterate. (18–19)

Again, the unnamed author's name refers to an actual person with political allegiances, and again, such allegiances prevent reading of the text as an aesthetic object. Here we also see the authorial name as a means of organizing texts. Each named author, Addison, Pope, Rowe, and so on, is not named to refer to the individual; rather, each name stands in for the texts in which the formal elements the pamphlet wishes to praise are found. Even as the text uses the authors' names as a kind of shorthand, it presents its own desire to move beyond the name and to the aesthetic object that is the text with its "fine Thoughts . . . flowing Numbers . . . [and] the beautiful Language." The text is clearly interested in names, but as with *An Essay*, the anonymous publication of *A Vindication* thematizes its own interest in the problem of the authorial name.

The critical engagement with these pamphlets amply demonstrates the power of retrospective attribution and the durability of an authorial name to profoundly shape, limit, and restrain the readings of a text. The original anonymity of both *An Essay* and *A Vindication* is taken merely, if at all, as an afterthought or obstacle to the critic who wishes to place, or displace, the texts within the larger Defoe oeuvre. This is not the case, of course, with all texts published anonymously whose authors are then discovered. However, certain genres and forms are more vulnerable to this cessation because they cannot be understood within the framework of the rise of the dominant literary forms, as in the case of the novel, unless they are attributed to literary apprenticeship.

As these examples show, one such vulnerable form is the political pamphlet. Responding, in some cases immediately, to contemporary political events and generally ephemeral, it is no surprise that these texts have limited contemporary readership and literary value. They do, however, present the need for and utility of a critical strategy that is not arranged around a single author but rather can contend with the cultural–historical language world in which they operated and the notion of authorship they put forth. The anonymity of these pamphlets, and indeed of any anonymous text, cannot be taken as an afterthought or an obstacle. Rather, their anonymity is central to the work they do as texts. The refusal to recognize the anonymity of these pamphlets is a refusal to read these texts as discrete historically situated documents and rather to subsume them within the oeuvre of the novelist Defoe in which their specificity, and thus their possible meanings, are lost.

In demonstrating the workings of attribution, deattribution, and their effect on canon construction, I am putting pressure on the explanatory power allowed to a body of works. The oeuvre, like the works from which it is composed, is a historically contingent, and highly malleable, construct. Central to the construct is the attribution of authorship. The name of the author is required to group and give meaning to a body of works. Subsequently, that body of

works must internally cohere such that works deemed uncharacter-
istic are (1) changed to meet the perceived ideology of the author or
(2) deattributed and removed from the canon. I argue the necessity
of teasing out the various "lives" of the texts themselves from the
life and craft of the author and, in doing so, attending to anonymity
and the processes of attribution in our understanding of the cultural work these texts do.

"Defoe" the Novelist

The familiar stories about Defoe and his relation to the novel have
placed his works as central to the rise of the novel in the eighteenth
century, and yet "the novelist" Daniel Defoe is an invention of the
nineteenth century.[16] These two stories seem at odds with each
other. Each is, however, about attribution: the former is a story of
the attribution of genre, the latter of the attribution of authorship.
From the beginning, describing the rise of the novel meant placing
the novels of Daniel Defoe in a lineage alongside those of Samuel
Richardson and Henry Fielding. However, before Defoe could be
part of the rise of the novel, his works needed to be recognized as
novels, and he needed to be the author of those novels. Although
Robinson Crusoe was quickly attributed to Defoe upon its publication, his other popular fictions circulated anonymously well after
their initial publication.[17]

   We are accustomed to thinking of authorial attribution as an act
of bibliographic scholarship that is grounded in evidence either internal or external to the text.[18] Rooted in a long history of scholarship of pseudoepigrapha,[19] authorial attribution as a practice has
involved putting anonymous or pseudonymous texts in relation to
each other and a named, biographical author. Attribution, however, also has a contingent, often social, dimension. Even in the
absence—or on the basis of the scantiest bit—of textual evidence, we
speak of readers "knowing" the identity of an anonymous author.
Knowledge of authorship may circulate among readers—as gossip,
for example—independent of the text in question and leave no textual trace. External evidence may allow some access to an instance
of the social dimension of authorial attribution, but it does so by relying on a particular attribution recorded in a text. In the example

of our gossiping readers, a diary entry, letter, or transcript of the conversation could serve as such a piece of external evidence that captures an instance of authorial attribution but does not capture its popular acceptance. By moving away from emphasizing a single instance of authorial attribution as evidence for authorship and to the broader contexts in which these attributions may have occurred, we can begin to understand the ways in which authorial attribution is not a binary process but one bound to the effects of networks.

Attribution requires repetition. A single instance of naming the author or genre of a text may not constitute a lasting attribution. However, as it circulates repeatedly bearing this attribution, a stable association may develop between an author and a text or a genre and a text. As a text moves through space and time with the name of an author or genre repeatedly attached to it, the text is more readily known to be by the named author or in the named genre. Circulating a text requires, however, a network through which it moves among its readers. Here McKenzie's imperative to attend "to the roles of institutions, and their own complex structures," becomes useful as a means of looking beyond an individual human's actions and motives to the networks in and through which texts and knowledge about those texts circulate (15). I examine the institution of the Francis and John Noble's circulating libraries to argue that popular knowledge of Defoe's authorship of *Roxana* and *Moll Flanders* derived from the entirety of the institutional context in which the attributions occurred. While we are accustomed to thinking that authors make books, I am arguing, in effect, that books, through their circulation, make authors.

Since the unsettling of the Defoe canon by Furbank and Owens, the attribution of the pamphlet and periodical writing associated with Defoe has remained vexed; the novels of Defoe, because of their long-standing anonymity, too, share this problem of attribution.[20] While much scholarly attention has been paid to properly attributing or deattributing the texts associated with Defoe, less attention has been paid to the process of attribution itself and the context in which these attributions were made. Defoe became known as the author of *Roxana* and *Moll Flanders* through the circulating libraries and bookshops of Francis and John Noble. The Nobles were two of the largest and most successful circulating library proprietors, booksellers, and publishers in eighteenth-century London. In the history of Defoe attribution studies, Furbank and Owens have paid particular attention to this institution: "If it be asked indeed how [Defoe] came to be popularly thought of as a novelist—the answer is, through the activities in the 1770s and 1780s of a rascally publisher named Francis Noble."[21] The Nobles ran a "three-tier operation" as publishers, booksellers, and circulating library proprietors and became "leading producers of novels from the mid-1750s to the mid-1770s."[22] Their enterprise fostered the popular knowledge of Defoe's authorship by repeatedly circulating the physical texts of *Roxana* and *Moll Flanders* in their commercial libraries, by advertising and cataloging them as Defoe's novels, and by promoting forms of sociability around the libraries themselves.[23]

The name "De Foe" became attached to "his novels" as they circulated in the libraries and bookshops and were represented in the catalogs and advertisements of the Nobles in the 1770s and 1780s. The Nobles' libraries enabled the lasting attribution of the previously anonymous *Roxana* and *Moll Flanders* by repeatedly circulating them with the name Defoe attached. No single instance of attribution, nor several, established the name "De Foe" as a writer of these novels. They needed to be circulated within an established network that would serve as a source of both books and ideas about those books; the institution of Nobles' libraries provided such a network. Crucially, the Nobles' libraries played both a virtual role in circulating ideas among otherwise unconnected patrons and an actual role in circulating books from physical locations. Authorial attribution, as it depends on a relationship between the virtual knowledge of authorship and the actual textual evidence of that authorship, could thus be fostered in the circulating library and could establish Defoe as the author of *Roxana* and *Moll Flanders*. Like the novels themselves, the circulating libraries of the Nobles straddled these two realms as both physical locations for the renting of books and a figure for loci of knowledge or, depending on the reviewer, scandal.[24]

Noble first attached Defoe's name to the title pages of *The History of Mademoiselle de Beleau; or, The New Roxana, the Fortunate Mistress: Afterwards Countess of Wintselsheim. Published By Mr. Daniel De Foe* (1775) and *The History of Laetitia Atkins, Vulgarly Called Moll Flanders. Published by Mr. Daniel De Foe* (1776), both sold by "F. NOBLE, in *Holborn* and T. LOWNDES in *Fleet-Street*."[25] The Nobles had earlier published *Moll Flanders* in 1741 and *Roxana* in 1742. In their catalogs and on their title pages, Defoe's name was not present.[26] Though both manifest dramatic changes from the 1724 *Roxana* and 1722 *Moll Flanders* and the earlier Noble editions, they purport to be "from Papers found since his Decease, it appears greatly altered by himself [Defoe]," and they are prefaced by introductions explaining the alterations, each signed "Daniel Defoe."

The alterations introduced into both *Roxana* and *Moll Flanders* since their first publication are not minor. Indeed, *Roxana* had already been transformed repeatedly after its 1724 publication.[27] John Mullan's introduction to the Oxford World Classics Edition of *Roxana* carefully maps out the revisions throughout the eighteenth century and notes that the anonymous publication of the novel is key to its constant revision.[28] Robert Griffin has further argued that the publication history of *Roxana* allows the scholar to see a text in motion where each edition defies conventional thinking about narrative closure and the generalized text.[29] In the Noble editions, the 1775 *Roxana* ends in a sentimental resolution in which Roxana returns to England and marries Mr. Worthy, while her servant Amy weds his valet. The 1776 *Moll Flanders*, too, undergoes a dramatic revision—the heroine is not a pickpocket or a thief, as in the 1722 edition; rather, she is mistaken for one. These revisions to each narrative may have been intended to suit the tastes of the Nobles' customers and make them ideologically coherent with the more widely known Defoe works, such as *Robinson Crusoe* and *The Family Instructor*.[30]

The title pages alone did not announce Defoe's relationship to *Roxana* and *Moll Flanders*. Advertisements evince an increasing clarity about Defoe's authorship of the novels following their publication. A December 13, 1776, advertisement in the *Public Advertiser* announces the publication of "THE HISTORY of LÆTITIA ATKINS, vulgarly called MOLL FLANDERS. Published by Mr. Daniel Defoe . . . Printed for the Editor, and sold by F. Noble, in Holbourn; and T. Lowndes, in Fleet Street. Where may be had, by the same Author, Roxana; or, The Fortunate Mistress." Here Defoe is identified as publisher, editor, and, perhaps, author.[31] Defoe's relationship to the text, some forty-five years after his death, is unclear—perhaps deliberately so. The Nobles make the relationship between Defoe and the novels more explicit in an advertisement two years later, in a March 7–10, 1778, issue of *St. James's Chronicle*. The advertisement for *Memoirs of Countess of D'Anois* available from both Francis and John Noble also lists "Modern Seduction, 2 Vols. 6s. bound," "Fortunate Mistress, by Daniel De Foe, 3s. bound," and "Moll Flanders, by Daniel De Foe, 3s. bound." The ambiguity of the relationship between Defoe, *Roxana,* and *Moll Flanders* in the prior advertisement is clarified by the mode of attributing authorship in the 1778 advertisement. Both *The Fortunate Mistress* and *Moll Flanders* are "by Daniel De Foe."

A final advertisement illustrates how the representation of authorial attribution may be standardized through repetition and suggest a coherent body of work. The November 25, 1785, *Morning Herald and Daily Advertiser* announces the publication of *The Lady's Tale; or, The History of Drusilla Northington* by Francis Noble and lists other books that one might purchase. Among the list are "Amoranda; or, The Reformed Coquet, 2 vols. 6s," "Adventures of a Cavalier, 3 vols, 9s," "Roxana; or, The Fortunate Mistress, 3s," "Moll Flanders; or, Laetitia Atkins, 3s," and "History of the Great Plague, 6s," with the note, "N.B. The four latter written by Daniel Defoe." In this advertisement, Defoe's authorship is attached to texts in the aggregate. Noble has, for perhaps the first time, identified a body of works that may, as a whole, be attributed to Defoe rather than needing individual attributions for each text listed. The mode of attribution in this advertisement suggests a coherence in the Defoe oeuvre that was previously absent. The representation of title, *Roxana* and *Moll Flanders*, and author, Defoe, has been standardized by articulating a clear relationship between named author and works. This advertisement is thus a moment of crystallization in an ongoing process of variously representing the relationship between the name "De Foe" and the texts to which that name was attributed.

In the catalogs of the Nobles and other libraries and bookshops of the period, there is a similar pattern of dispersed and gradual authorial attribution of Defoe's, and others,' texts. The anonymity of the earlier Noble editions of *Moll Flanders* (1741) and *Roxana* (1742) would likely not have been notable within the circulating library. Generally speaking, most novels and romances in the eighteenth-century circulating library were anonymous, and they were particularly so in the Nobles' libraries.[32] The Nobles' catalogs make clear the limited importance and utility of the author's name to their presentation of these texts. Rather, the physical form of the texts is primarily used to organize them. For example, John Noble's *A New Catalogue of the Large and Valuable Collection of Books (Both English and French)* (circa 1761) lists its primarily anonymous texts categorized by size and subject. The material form of the book is asserted as the primary taxon; this is a pattern that continues throughout the period. For the most part, even when their authors are known, texts appear, like "Adventures of Joseph Andrews in 2 vol," with no authorial attribution.[33] When authors' names do appear, they may be placed before the title in the possessive, as in "Cervantes's Don Quixote," or after the title, as in "Amelia, by Mr. Fielding." In this catalog and others, the author's name is more likely to appear in the possessive when the text is accorded an elevated status. Thus "Cervantes's Don Quixote" (41) may be differentiated from "History of Don Quixote, by Motteux" and "History of Don Quixote, by Jervais" by the possessive use of the name "Cervantes" to mark an originary source and a regarded author (46). *Don Quixote* can be owned and elevated by Cervantes in a way that the "History of Don Quixote" can never be owned by its translators.

The circa 1761 catalog lists both the 1741 Noble edition of *The Life of Moll Flanders* (48) and the 1742 Noble edition of *Roxana, or the Fortunate Mistress* (51), but it does not attribute them to Defoe. Indeed, even after the 1775 and 1776 editions of *Roxana* and *Moll Flanders* were published with Defoe's name attached to their title pages, contemporary circulating library catalogs did not always list *Roxana* or *Moll Flanders* as a work by Defoe. Thomas Lowndes, who published the 1775 *Roxana* along with Francis Noble, published a catalog for his bookshop in 1778 in which "Roxana, or the Fortunate Mistress, *new*," dated 1775 and "Moll Flanders, *new*," dated 1776, are listed among "*Miscellanies. TWELVES*," where neither bears an attribution.[34]

A survey of catalogs from booksellers and estate sales similarly reveals a varying pattern of authorial attribution for the novels consistent with the gradual process of acceptance that I have outlined.[35] For example, *Lackington's Catalogue for 1784* lists both the

1724 *Roxana* as "Roxana, the Fortunate Mistress, *neat,* 2s 3d Ditto 1s 6d 1724" (49) and the 1775 *Roxana* as "History of Madam de Boleau [*sic*], or Roxana, by DeFoe, *new,* 1s 6d" (61). The editions are listed separately with an attribution to Defoe only for the later edition. The Lackington catalog, however, is a bit unique in this regard; a 1791 catalog by Thomas and John Egerton, for example, lists "*Roxana,* or the Fortunate Mistress, by Defoe, eleg. 3s 6d 1742" (244). In this catalog, the earlier edition that was not attributed to Defoe picks up the attribution in its catalog listing. It seems here that the catalogers are drawing from a body of social knowledge rather than any attribution on the printed book—a body of social knowledge like that associated with the circulating libraries and bookshops of Francis and John Noble.

More than ten years after the publication of the Noble editions of *Roxana* and *Moll Flanders,* Francis Noble offered up a list of "NOVELS *Printed for* F. Noble" that appears to be the first extant evidence of the standardized attribution of Defoe's "novels" as an oeuvre in a catalog bound with the third volume of *Daniel De Foe's Voyage Round the World. By a Course Never Sailed Before*[36] (1787) (Figure 15). Also found in the first volume of *Daniel De Foe's Voyage* is "The Life of the Author, by William Shiels, ESQ.," which Furbank and Owens have identified as a plagiarism from the *Life* by Robert Shiels of 1753 but with updates to include the recent Noble publications by "De Foe."[37] These publications include all the fictional works available for rent or sale from Noble and now bear authorial attributions to "De Foe."

The catalog standardization of Defoe's "novels" by Noble was delayed by more than a decade following the attribution of *Roxana* and *Moll Flanders.* The 1787 list "NOVELS *Printed for* F. Noble" represents a reimagining of Defoe as an author of novels rather than a political pamphleteer and author of *Robinson Crusoe.* It is a moment, much like the 1785 *Morning Herald* advertisement, where a body of work coheres with Defoe's name attached. As we have seen, however, such a process is gradual and requires multiple repetitions across the literary marketplace before it coheres into a form recognizable as the Defoe canon. The circulating library, with its publishing, advertising, and lending practices, enabled this necessary steady repetition of author and text. In doing so, the library helped

NOVELS *Printed for* F. NOBLE.

Bubbled Knights, 2 vol. ——— 6s
Belle Grove, or the Fatal Seduction, 2 vol. 6s
Benjamin St. Martin, a Fortunate Foundling,
  2 vol. ——— —— 6s
Crusoe Richard Davis, his Life and Adven-
  tures, 2 vol. ——— 6s
Captive, or the History of Mr. Clifford,
  2 vol. —— —— 6s
Contrast, or History of Miss Weldon, 2 vol. 6s
Conflict, or History of Sophia Fanbrook,
  3 vol. —— —— 9s
Country Cousins, or Maria and Charlotte,
  2 vol. —— —— —— 6s
Clementina, or History of an Italian Lady, 3s
Capricious Father, 2 vol. ——— 6s
Derrick's Letters from Bath and Tunbridge,
  2 vol. —— —— —— 6s
Double Disappointment. A Farce, *stitched*, 1s
Du Verney on the Organ of the Ear, *with*
  cuts, —— —— —— 3s 6d
Distrest Virtue, or History of Harriot Nelson,
  3 vol. —— —— 9s
Devil upon Crutches in England —— 3s
Dean of Coleraine, a moral History, 3 vol. 9s
Disinterested Marriage, 2 vol. —— 6s
De Foe's Adventures of a Cavalier, 3 vol.
  calf, lettered, ——— —— 10s 6d
De Foe's Adventures of Roxana, *calf, let-*
  tered, —— —— 3s 6d
De Foe's Adventures of Moll Flanders, *calf,*
  lettered, —— —— 3s 6d
De Foe's Adventures of Captain Singleton,
  calf, lettered, —— —— 4s

De Foe's

standardize the attributions by repeatedly making available many instances in which an author's name appears attached to a text, both the physical book and the advertisements and catalogs representing the book.

It is worth pausing briefly to consider the role of eighteenth-century Defoe biography and bibliography in the shaping of the Defoe oeuvre. George Chalmers, Defoe's first biographer and bibliographer, assembled his "LIST of WRITINGS, which are considered undoubtedly DE FOE's" in the 1790 edition of *The Life of Daniel De Foe*, which is based on a variety of sources including, as Furbank and Owens note, cautious attention to catalogs of booksellers and large libraries (52). Chalmers's "LIST" is neither a starting point nor an end point in the construction of the Defoe canon; rather, it is one critical point among many that crystallize Defoe's works and offer attributions of previously anonymous writings. Chalmers offers little evidence for most of his attributions in *The Life*, and it is quite possible that his textual sources of attribution for *Roxana* and *Moll Flanders* were the Noble editions or catalogs. However, given the dispersed and social nature of authorial attribution, it is also possible his source was not the Nobles.

I have shown how the Nobles represented the relationship between Defoe, *Roxana*, and *Moll Flanders* with increased clarity beginning in 1776 and culminating in the standardization of Defoe's works in the catalog pages of 1787. The Nobles reoriented the relationship between the author and genre of *Roxana* and *Moll Flanders*. Through the attribution of authorship to Defoe, *Roxana* and *Moll Flanders* were no longer simply novels listed among other circulating library novels. With the addition of the name of the author, these texts became works.[38] They could thus be understood as novels among other Noble novels but also placed within the emerging Defoe oeuvre as articulated in the 1787 catalog listing. This process is aided by the abstraction of the physical text: the individual edition or volume of *Roxana* or *Moll Flanders* matters less than the idea of "De Foe's Adventures of Roxana" or "De Foe's Adventures of Moll Flanders."

Each instance of Defoe's name attached to *Moll Flanders* and *Roxana*—on title pages, in advertisements, and in library catalogs—contributed to the notion of "De Foe's Adventures of Roxana" or "De Foe's Adventures of Moll Flanders" apart from any physical edition.

Through repetition, author and title became virtual entities because each instance of repetition was also an instance of representation detached from the physical book and content of *Roxana* or *Moll Flanders*. Author and title as virtual entities could circulate more widely than the actual Noble editions bearing Defoe's name and thus become attached to other editions of *Roxana* and *Moll Flanders*, propagating the knowledge of Defoe's authorship. The processes of repetition and virtualization are not, I suggest, incidental to the advertising practices of the Nobles' circulating libraries as they participated in the larger print marketplace. Rather, these processes are central to the premise of the circulating library.

As a central node for distributing texts, the circulating library is virtual and repetitive, more so than the bookshop. The sale of a book entails the acquisition of private property, whereas the renting of a book involves many people in the common enterprise of sequential possession. The material practice of renting books carries with it the idea that books are interchangeable and exchangeable and thus function in the abstract both as commodities and as texts.[39] Though the trade is of the material form of the book, the discrete book does not matter as much as its ability to be exchanged or stand in for another book, or, in the case of *Roxana* and *Moll Flanders*, other, variant, editions. The idea that Defoe could have works that supersede the individual edition (and have little relationship to the original edition) is fostered in the institution of the circulating library, which insists that the material, discrete edition does not matter as much as exchangeability. The system of circulation contributes to the actual, physical book becoming a virtual entity shared among readers. The ideological assumptions of and about the Nobles' circulating libraries are drawn from the circulating libraries' function as a node of textual circulation. This network of circulation renders both text and work abstract notions.

The Nobles' libraries were among many in the London literary marketplace whose practice of lending books helped form a reading public centered on the libraries. Keith Manley has suggested that, "although buying books is a commercial activity, lending, at a price, adds new levels of social and economic dynamics, especially since many of the largest circulating libraries became social centres in their own right."[40] Manley alerts us to the key structural difference between the selling and the lending of books: by its very nature, the circulating library book must pass repeatedly through the hands of many readers, all of whom have in common the institution of the library. Similarly, Raven has written about the forms of sociability fostered by proprietary and commercial libraries that allowed for participation in an imagined literary community.[41] Barbara Benedict has further reflected on the virtual, or imagined, connection between readers in the circulating library.[42] She distinguishes between the books in subscription libraries, which were available only to the limited set of readers who also were owners and who had some relationship with each other, and the connection between commercial circulating library readers, which entailed the shared status of being customers of a common enterprise and sharing the collective experience as readers. As Raven has further suggested, "by reading, the reader assumed links with numberless others also reading the text, extending the notion of a participatory culture."[43] Charlotte Stewart-Murphy has similarly pointed to the social project of literary commonality embedded within the structure of the circulating library.[44] The nature of the connection between customers of the circulating library was one of a virtual literary public engendered by a shared collection of texts and ideas circulated by the institution of the library.[45]

The circulating library further contributes to the understanding of works not only as physical books but as abstractions because, it was hoped, authorial attribution would lead to greater renting and purchasing of books. Furbank and Owens have suggested that by attaching Defoe's name to the novels, Francis Noble hoped to increase the circulation of his novels in his circulating library and bookshop.[46] Jan Fergus's study of the records of Midlands booksellers has borne out the similar conclusion that provincial readers, at least, preferred to borrow and buy books with known authors.[47] One of the effects of increasing the number of times a given volume is borrowed is that the wear and tear on the volume is also increased. The most-read books were thus the least likely to survive in their material form.[48] Their texts, however, were most likely to survive, detached from their material form, as works. In effect, attaching the name "De Foe" to these novels ensured the degradation or displacement of the material text but ensured the longevity of the work.[49]

Charles Lamb meditates on this relationship between the book as material object subject to degradation and its relationship to the work in his *Detached Thoughts on Books and Reading* (1822). He draws on the condition of circulating library books to exemplify his point:

> How beautiful to the genuine lover of reading are the sullied leaves and worn-out appearance, nay, the very odour . . . if we would not forget kind feelings in fastidiousness, of an old "circulating library" Tom Jones, or Vicar of Wakefield! How they speak of the thousand thumbs that have turned over their pages with delight!—of the lone sempstress whom they may have cheered (milliner, or hard-working mantua-maker) after her long day's needle-toil, running far into midnight, when she has snatched an hour, ill spared from sleep, to steep her cares, as in some Lethean cup, in spelling out their enchanting contents! Who would have them a whit less soiled? What better condition could we desire to see them in?
>
> In some respects, the better a book is, the less it demands from binding. Fielding, Smollett, Sterne, and all that class of perpetually self-reproductive volumes—Great Nature's Stereotypes—we see them individually perish with less regret, because we know the copies of them to be "eterne."[50]

Lamb relishes the material proof of reading: the smell of pages well thumbed and the degradation of binding. The degradation of the book testifies to its circulation and thus, for Lamb, its literary esteem. Interestingly, Lamb transitions from speaking of titles of books to the authors of books. The passage begins by recalling the smell and appearance "of an old 'circulating library' Tom Jones, or Vicar of Wakefield" but moves to authors' names, "Fielding, Smollett, Sterne, and all that class of perpetually self-reproductive volumes," to make a case for the less durable binding of works that have become "eterne."

For Lamb, the name of the author renders a text eternal; that is, the name makes a book a work. Works with the names of "Fielding, Smollett, Sterne" do not need preservation through durable binding or limited circulation; they have passed from the concerns of the text as discrete material object. These books, as Lamb calls them, have moved from material text to work. The material text may, and indeed must, fall away to be become the work. The work is "perpetually self-reproductive." Its life is in the literary imaginary, not simply on the bookshelf of the circulating library or the bookseller's stall. The work is a construction of title and author that may or may not recur to the material form of the text. One edition is interchangeable with the next as long as its author and title remain fairly stable and recognizable. The material form of the text is thus disavowed even as it is absolutely depended on for its physical circulation.

The degradation of the material text and the emergence of the work requires a network that circulates both the material text and ideas about texts. The circulating library is the central node through which those texts and ideas move. It is a source of kinds and genres of writing—"the circulating library novel"—not simply physical books.[51] The circulation of physical books through the library facilitates the circulation of ideas that make texts largely interchangeable. Thus one could rent *The Fortunes and Misfortunes of the Famous Moll Flanders* (F. Noble 1741) or *The History of Laetitia Atkins, Vulgarly Called Moll Flanders* (F. Noble 1776) and think of them both as *Moll Flanders* "by Defoe."

As institutions, the circulating libraries of the Nobles worked powerfully as figures for circulation even more so than as physical places for the renting of books. As such, their role in circulating ideas—such as the name of a previously anonymous author—was highlighted in critics' responses to circulating libraries and their novels. A 1772 print exchange between the Nobles and a critical anonymous reviewer illustrates the manner in which the ideological basis of the institution of the circulating library, its insistence that circulation is not solely the movement of physical objects through time and space, is ultimately taken up and turned against the circulating library proprietors. In the November 1772 issue of *London Magazine,* two new novels published by the Noble brothers were reviewed: *"The Way to Lose Him; or, The History of Miss Wyndham. By the Author of The Way to Please Him* and *The Way to Please Him; or, The History of Lady Sedley. By the Author of the Way to Lose Him."* The reviews were not positive. Of *The Way to Lose Him,* the anonymous reviewer claims that it was "written solely for the use of the circulating library, and very popular to debauch all young women who are still undebauched." *The Way to Please Him* fared no better: "See the last article. The same character will do for both."[52]

Francis and John Noble were not pleased. The brothers issued two appeals in the following months attacking *London Magazine* and the anonymous reviewer and vindicating their novels from charges that they were fit only "to debauch young women." In the first, they published an appeal to the public and reprinted the letter they had sent to "Mr. Baldwin, the publisher of the Magazine in which the injury had been done."[53] Along with charges of scurrility against the anonymous reviewer, the Nobles also reprinted positive reviews of *The Way to Lose Him* and *The Way to Please Him* that spoke to their stated mission "to publish only such Novels as have for their objects, what their writers ought ever to have in view, amusement, instruction, decency, and morality" (6).

Rather than receiving the expected apology, the Nobles, who had cornered the market on anonymous, largely ephemeral novels of romance, found in the January 1773 issue of *London Magazine* an even more scurrilous attack by the anonymous reviewer on themselves, their novels, and their libraries. In *An Appeal*, the Nobles reprint this attack and offer ongoing commentary refuting its claims in their footnotes. The reviewer claims that the letter from the Nobles was "replete with those barbarous expressions *(b)* familiar to men, whose business it is to puzzle heads, and to corrupt hearts *(c)*." In note c, the Nobles respond that they do not understand if the reviewer means to refer to their "business" as that of "Booksellers and Publishers; or that of keeping a Circulating Library; or whether all together." The note continues on to repeat the claim that "our Libraries abound with authors of the first character, in almost every useful art and science; and are, therefore, calculated to diffuse knowledge, and improve the mind, instead of corrupting the heart" (10–11).

The familiar attack on the corrupting nature of the novels of the circulating library continues throughout the anonymous reviewer's response to the Nobles' letter, in which the reviewer excuses the Nobles for the "aspersions" they "have applied to him, because he [the reviewer] believes they are not accustomed to talk otherwise" (13). The reviewer then claims,

> Scandal is the property of mean and illiberal minds, and the Circulating Library is its palace. *(g)* But he cannot suppress his [the reviewer's] inclination to inform them [the Nobles], that an Act of Parliament is soon to be passed, by which Circulating Libraries are to be suppressed, and by which the owners of them are to be declared, like the players, "rogues and vagabonds," the debauchers of morals, and the pest of society. *(h)* (13–14)

The reviewer offers two competing critiques of the circulating library: it is a place of scandal, and it is not a place at all. While the circulating library may be a figural home to scandal, ignorance, and folly, its status as an actual location in the world seems much less clear to this reviewer in his reference to "an Act of Parliament . . . by which Circulating Libraries are to be suppressed, and by which the owners of them are to be declared, like the players, 'rogues and vagabonds'" (14). The reviewer invokes earlier critiques of the stage and likens the Nobles to itinerant performers; they are corrupters of morals who roam throughout the land without a home. Furthermore, like players, the Nobles are the medium for the words and ideas of another. The reviewer's double critique points to the abstraction of the Nobles' circulating libraries where the physical location of the libraries is obscured and their role as medium is made central.

The Nobles seize upon the claim that they are without a place in their response and ask:

> Prithee, friend, how is this same Act to make it appear that we are wanderers, have no visible way of living, or settled habitation? See what it is not to consult your Dictionary! Or, perhaps, you thought that, because we keep a Circulating Library, *we* must necessarily *circulate too,* and, like our books, perpetually wander about from place to place. (14–15, emphasis original)

The Nobles identify in the reviewer's rhetoric the conflation of the circulating library as place and the circulating library as idea. He has, they claim, likened the brothers to their books that "perpetually wander about from place to place" (15). The idea of circulation that is central to the work of the circulating libraries and, even more, the circulation of ideas that is achieved by the circulation of books is made to represent the circulating library while disavowing its material conditions, much in the way Lamb disavows binding. The Nobles, then, wish to offer a corrective by moving away from the notion of the library as a medium that perpetually circulates folly, ignorance, and scandal, insisting instead on the literal place of the libraries "near *Middle Row, Holborn,* and *Saint Martin's Court,* near *Leicester Square*" and the circulation of books with physical dimensions, like the duodecimo *The Way to Please Him*.[54]

Though the Nobles protest adamantly against the notion that their libraries could be reduced, like the players, to mere circulation, the rhetoric the reviewer employs shares the assumptions they themselves employed in the representations of their libraries. In the frontispieces of their catalogs, they idealize their libraries as figures with little correspondence to physical reality, particularly because it is likely that access to the stacks was limited.[55] These frontispieces blur the boundaries between the actual and the virtual. As I will show, these images portray the library as a source of enlightenment; the images privilege the library not for their physicality but as mediating institutions that put ideas into circulation. Despite the Nobles' attempt to defend their enterprise by appealing to its physical location, the library gained in significance (whether as an agent of debauchery or enlightenment) in line with the recognition of its virtuality. In this way, the Nobles' circulating libraries reinforced a powerful set of ideas and conventions about literature that supersede the material texts and the libraries themselves.

The Nobles embraced the notion of the circulating library as a figure for the circulation of ideas and incorporated it in their representations of their libraries. *The Yearly and Quarterly Subscriber; or, A New Catalogue of a Large Collection of Useful and Entertaining Books, All of Which Are Lent to Be Read by F. and J. Noble* (circa 1746) features an engraving by Jacob Bonneau that presents itself as a representation of the interior of their circulating library in St. Martin's Court (Figure 16). Raven writes of this frontispiece, along with others from the period, that they "highlight large book stacks on open shelves. These rare surviving prints of early circulating libraries also reveal the attention given to access and fashion and depict a very respectable clientele."[56] Though Raven contends that "for commercial reasons these library trade cards and catalogue engravings of the interiors undoubtedly offered romanticized pictures to subscribers, many of whom lived in country parts," he argues that these images are not entirely fanciful and thus offer a fairly accurate representation of the interiors of these libraries and their means of controlling access and thus readership (186). Manley, who first brought the Bonneau engraving to scholarly attention, is less convinced, however, that this image is a representation of the interior of the library at all, "since circulating libraries were closed access, and customers had to order their choice of books from the catalogue" (75).[57] This question of how accurately these images represent the interior of the library and the possibility of patron access captures many of the place–no place dynamics of critiques of the libraries within the period. What this suggests is historical continuity in approaches to thinking about the actuality and virtuality of the circulating library such that the two are inseparable.

Raven's reading of the frontispiece has asked us to attend to the foreground of the print; I am interested, however, in the background of the image and its relationship to the catalog in which it appears. While the image may index the interior space of the circulating library, I contend that this frontispiece is a visual representation of the catalog itself. Near the visual center of the print, but shrouded in shadow, is the text "THE CIRCULATING LIBRARY." This text appears to be carved into the wall above the built-in bookcase. Similarly, each bookshelf has its subject contents carved into it. The top shelf is labeled, "HISTORY. VOYAGES." the shelf under it, "NOVELS. ROMANCES." then, "MATHEMATICKS." "PHISICK. SURGERY.," and finally, partially obscured by the figures in the foreground, "POETRY PLAYS." The remaining two shelves are similarly labeled but almost fully obscured. Furthermore, the books are not organized by subject alone but by size as well. On the very top shelves are what appear to be folio editions, below them quartos, below the quartos, octavos. The 1746 circulating library catalog of the Noble brothers, like most circulating libraries' and booksellers' catalogs throughout the eighteenth century, followed an organization of books based on size and subject. A typical catalog began with folio editions and went through octavo editions.[58] In the circa 1746 Bonneau engraving, the books on the shelves in the background follow this mode of organization almost exactly.

Figure 16. Frontispiece from F. and J. Noble's *The Yearly and Quarterly Subscriber* (circa 1746). Rare Books and Special Collections, McGill University Library, Z998 N63 1746.

The minute details of the organization of the bookcase in the background seem secondary to the composition of the image until we compare it to the text of circulating library catalogs. For, once juxtaposed, the organizational logic of the bookcase that appears in the image underneath "THE CIRCULATING LIBRARY" is nearly identical to that of the catalog itself. The left hand of the foreground figure appears to rest on what Raven has suggested is the catalog of the circulating library itself (or a similar finding guide), while with his right hand he points to the space before him, perhaps to the shelf labeled "SURGERY" from which another figure is taking a book. On the basis of these details, I suggest that this frontispiece is an indexical image of self-reference.[59] When we look more closely at it, we see that like his right index finger, the foreground figure's left index finger also is pointing—in the first case, to the catalog of the circulating library, in the second case, to the interior of the circulating library itself, an image of which is reproduced on the catalog's frontispiece. The effect is to establish, within the framework of an image, a correspondence between the actual space of the library and the virtual space of its catalog. What this suggests is that to read the virtual representation of the library—that is, its catalog—is to enter the actuality of the library. But the opposite is also true, because the actual library space contains the bookshelves we see on the frontispiece of the catalog, whose books are, like the catalog itself, virtual representations of an actuality that lies beyond them. Outside the frame of the frontispiece, of course, what I've called the "actual library space," is the virtual image of the material space of the actual library in which a spectator might be standing, confronted simultaneously by that material space and by a material catalog displayed on a table much like that pictured in the frontispiece.

A second Bonneau frontispiece from John Noble's circa 1761 circulating library catalog further illustrates the insistence on the virtual nature of the circulating library (Figure 17). In this engraving, no attempt at mimesis is made in the representation of the library. Instead, a patron approaches a pedestal of circulating library books with one of the classical figures pointing at the books whose subject matter is represented by the stylized figures and their accoutrements: on the top, a lyre (hence poetry), on the bottom, a shaft and shield (hence history and antiquity). The second classical figure points at either (or both) the books and the patron in a gesture that suggests invitation to the profundity of the books. The suggestion may account for the expression of awe evinced by the splayed fingers of the patron who stands before them. At the base of the pedestal is a piece of parchment that reads "J. Noble's Circulating Library." Then, in a near-inversion of the 1746 frontispiece, the books are stacked by size, folios at the bottom, with what appear to be quartos at the top. The absence of the structure of the bookshelves and this arrangement is evocative of sculpture and furthered by the presence of classical figures. The books simultaneously retain their "bookishness" while also serving as abstractions for what it is books do and how the circulation of books works. This frontispiece, even more so than the 1746 frontispiece, depicts the book-as-abstraction which is at the heart of both the work of the circulating library and the processes of authorial attribution that I have described. This engraving, then, takes the nonmimetic representation of the library to its logical extreme. Rather than representing a library with an exact correspondence between catalog and stacks, the image represents the library as an ideal summed up by the Horatian epigram on the engraving to "delight while teaching."

These frontispieces emphasize the nature of the libraries as a virtual space and medium for the circulation of ideas, as implicated in their role in the actual distribution of physical books. Though more pronounced in the second (1761) frontispiece, each image presents the library as a virtual space with an indication of the actuality of both the catalogs that they preface and the libraries that they (the frontispieces and catalogs) represent. This occurs through the finger of the figure pointing toward the bookcase in the foreground in the 1746 frontispiece and the fingers of the stylized classical figures pointing toward the stack of books in the 1761 frontispiece. It is as if the 1761 frontispiece further abstracts the 1746 representation of the enterprise of the Nobles' libraries. At each level of abstraction in these images lies an instance of repetition where the viewer is simultaneously asked to think of the representation of the library, the actual library, the actual catalog, and the uses of both the catalog (as finding aid for books) and the library (as medium for books). This complex figuration of the virtual and actual nature of the libraries is not only a product of the Noble brothers' self-representations in their catalogs. Much of the discourse about their circulating libraries in the period, as we have seen, testifies to popular understanding

S. Wale inv.^t　　　　J. Bonneau sc^t

Lectorem delectando pariterque monendo.

Hor.

Figure 17. Frontispiece from J. Noble's *A New Catalogue* (1761). Reprinted by permission of the Folger Shakespeare Library, Z997.N7 1761 Cage.

of the libraries not only as places where books were rented but also as a way of understanding the abstraction of circulation. The circulating library came to stand for the virtual circulation involved in not only the renting (or buying) of books but also the reading of them. In the conflation of the circulating library with the circulation of its books, what seems to be a misapprehension of institution and its goods is in fact a recognition of the processes of mediation. The circulating library in popular thought became a flashpoint for understanding and thinking about how the abstract and material interacted and intertwined in productive processes.

The notion that an institution could enable the perpetual circulation of ideas is what made the attributions of *Roxana* and *Moll Flanders* so significant. These attributions were not of a singular instance or bound to single editions. Rather, the attributions occurred within an institution whose very premise was based on the repeated circulation of both books and ideas to a reading public. Defoe the writer of novels may have been, as Rogers has claimed, "an invention of the nineteenth century," but the conditions under which the transformation was made possible—the attribution of authorship— crystallized in the world of the late eighteenth-century book trade (4). Because attribution is a process that depends on its repetition and circulation, its effects are neither immediate nor widespread. Attribution is, rather, a slow transformation that, as instances accrue, gains traction. This process of transformation is such that even by the early nineteenth century, Defoe's literary production was deemed obscure enough by Lamb that in a letter to early Defoe biographer Walter Wilson, he could claim, "He is quite new ground, and scarce known beyond Crusoe."[60]

The book-length studies of attribution and the Defoe canon by Furbank and Owens have placed in the foreground the problems in attribution posed by any work said to be by Defoe. Though most pronounced in Defoe studies, the issues of anonymity and attribution pervade the publication history of eighteenth-century novels. Anonymity and attribution, their function and effect, then, must be taken into consideration in the study of the eighteenth-century novel. What this section has demonstrated is the very historical contingencies that made possible the lasting attributions of *Roxana* and *Moll Flanders* that have so shaped the post-eighteenth-century reception of the author and his works. In his *Detached Thoughts on*

Books and Reading, Lamb does not account for how a text or author becomes "eterne," but he suggests some intrinsic merit to a text that shines through. It is, however, not the intrinsic factors of a given text that guarantee its durability and perpetual self-reproductivity. Rather, it is the extrinsic factors, the conditions in which a text may or may not circulate and with which, if any, name attached that determine whether a text disappears as passing ephemera or is preserved, detached from its material form, in the literary imagination.

In this chapter, we have seen the centrality of authorial attribution to the formation of canons and its effect on the individual works contained therein. The ease of attributing *An Essay* and the difficulty of attributing *A Vindication* demonstrate an end point to the steady and historically contingent process of attributing *Roxana* and *Moll Flanders.* The novels had to have been attributed to Defoe before the pamphlets because they gave meaning and value to these otherwise ephemeral political writings. As the individual editions of *Roxana* and *Moll Flanders* fall away once attributed to Defoe, the specificity and content of the pamphlets fall away. Furthermore, we have seen how the anonymity of *Roxana* and *Moll Flanders* went unmarked for more than fifty years, while *An Essay* and *A Vindication* immediately called attention to their anonymity by thematizing its utility in their arguments. Such a difference speaks to the importance of attending to generic differences in the study of anonymity. Though purportedly written by the same author, Defoe, these four texts are each anonymous for very different reasons, and their anonymity is attended to, or not, by readers because of differences in generic expectations, audience, and context.

Daniel Defoe was undeniably a biographical personage. "Defoe" the novelist, pamphleteer, journalist, and so on, is, on the other hand, an effect bound to networks of circulation that enable the attachment (and sometimes detachment) of the name to the text. Key to both attribution and deattribution is iteration. Even in the case of *A Vindication of the Press,* which for now appears to be out of the Defoe canon, deattributing this pamphlet requires its continued circulation with the acknowledgment of its contested authorship. Thus the inside–outside binary logic of attribution cannot capture fully the ways in which attribution is an ongoing and continual process, not a one-time practice, static ever after.

4

Motive, Intention, Anonymity

Thus far I have refused to answer the most common question posed about anonymous texts: "what was the motive for the author's anonymity?" From what has come before, the reason why ought to be clear—my primary interest is in actions, not subjects; in observable exterior reality, not supposed interior life. Literary scholars have long attempted to disarticulate the interior life of the author from the text she wrote, beginning at least with Wimsatt and Beardsley's "Intentional Fallacy," continuing with poststructural postmortems of the author, and into our moment with a return to formalism and a renewed interest in materiality. And yet, anonymity is the situation par excellence in which scholars typically, against any other held critical ideology, seek to inquire about the interior life of an author.

The case studies I draw together in this chapter—Frances Burney's 1778 *Evelina* and Walter Scott's 1814 *Waverley*—are an odd fit; in most ways, an epistolary novel of manners and the ur-historical novel have very little to do with each other beyond their designation as novels. Both novels are, however, famous for their anonymity; moreover, the accounts of their authors' anonymity rely on, often conflicting or uncertain, accounts of Burney's and Scott's motives to explain it. Seemingly well documented in the period and often studied, it appears we know the reasons why Burney and Scott were anonymous.

Discussions about motives for anonymity rest on the assumption that the absence of the author's name is a conscious act by an individual—typically the author. To speak of motives is to offer reasons for acting. The necessary difficulty for critics is in defining anonymity as a choice or an action and then attributing that choice or action to an author. Strictly speaking, not attaching a name to a text is the absence of an action. This is particularly true within the broader publishing context of the eighteenth century, in which new novels were anonymous by default. Though we typically take anonymity to be something out of the ordinary and deliberate, from the mid- to late eighteenth century and into the nineteenth century, it was utterly common.

Both *Evelina* and *Waverley* are distinct in drawing attention to their anonymity in a market full of anonymous novels and thus suggest an intentional character to their anonymity; this does not mean, however, that we must recur to the motives of Burney or Scott to explain why the novels were anonymous. Rather, we can consider the intention, and therefore meaning, *in* the anonymity of the novels. In this chapter, I argue that we must move from prioritizing the author and his claimed or inferred motive for anonymity (as an interior mental state) to considering, within a broad literary historical context, intention in anonymity (as manifest in external action). Thus anonymity is presented as much as a generic and collective phenomenon as it is an individual choice, and intention is expanded beyond the sole province of human action.

Despite the relatively long history of questioning the importance of authorial intention and motive, discussions of the anonymity of literary texts inevitably return to the explanatory force of authorial motive. These accounts seek to explain the seeming aberration of authorial anonymity through recourse to the sometimes stated, sometimes inferred motives of an author. John Mullan's *Anonymity: A Secret History of English Literature* (2008) offers an example of this critical habit of mind by organizing many of its chapters under a rubric of implied motives for authorial anonymity. Chapter titles such as "Modesty," "Mischief," and "Danger" suggest that the absence of the author's name may be explained by some understanding of the author's motive. Often discussions of, and attention to, underlying motives for anonymity carry with them two central assumptions: (1) that authorial motive is accessible, knowable, and believable and (2) that anonymous publication is atypical. In these assumptions, the former explains the latter: they take anonymity as an outlier and insist that some underlying authorial motive may be adduced to explain said outlier.

The desire to explain anonymity through recourse to authorial motive and thereby group anonymous works finds its clearest articulation in Samuel Halkett and John Laing's *Dictionary of
Anonymous and Pseudonymous English Literature*, which remains the
standard dictionary of its kind.[1] "Notes on Anonymity and Pseudonymity," which prefaces the 1926 edition, announces,

> Anonymous and pseudonymous books and pamphlets may be
> grouped, in the first place, according to the motive which led
> to the suppression of the author's name. Generally the motive
> is some form of timidity, such as (*a*) diffidence, (*b*) fear of conse-
> quences, and (*c*) shame.[2]

And a bit later: "The great majority of anonymous and pseudonymous books will be found to fall under these groups. But one can
imagine a variety of other possible motives, some of which may
operate in addition to one of these main groups."[3] Motive here has
replaced author as the central principle of organization in this explanation. Without the name of author, the (also unnamed) authors
of the "Notes" choose the most proximate cause for the absence of
the name—"motive"—to "group . . . in the first place" texts.

In this schema, they trade the quandary of the absent name for
the quandary of categorical organization that they seek to resolve
by turning to motive. An anonymous text may raise the question,
if one thinks to ask it (and the *Dictionary* does), who wrote this? For
the authors of these "Notes," and, indeed, for many scholars, this
question transforms from one of knowledge about an author's name
to two related ontological questions: (1) how did this text come to be
if we cannot name the author? and (2) how do we categorize this
text without its author's name? The answer posed by the "Notes"
to these questions is first to assume an author (a fair assumption)
and then to ascribe a mental state to that author—motive—to explain the absence of her name and thereby categorize the text. With
the absence of an empirical fact—the name—we are asked to "imagine" mental states, decidedly not observable, to glean "a variety of
other possible motives" to explain that absence.[4]

Motive, the authors suggest, may be evinced from the content
of a given text: "Shame may be supposed to be the motive which

often leads writers of pornographic books to withhold their names, and the same motive must be at least partly responsible for the frequent anonymity of spiteful personal attacks and lampoons."[5] In this move, they fold together the content of the text with the causal explanation for the anonymity of the text. These are in fact two different matters. To ask about the content is to ask about what is in the text. To ask of motives for anonymity is to ask about a state of mind (motive) antecedent to an action that did not happen (the attachment of the name). They have confused the meaning of an action (or perhaps a lack of action) with textual meaning. These issues do indeed intersect in the space of the text, but in doing so, they do not recur solely to the author as the arbiter of meaning for both.

Discussions of authorial motive for anonymity acknowledge the writing context but deny its significance by locating motive in the individual. This project of ascribing motive to explain anonymity is already committed to ascribing agency to the context, in addition to the individual agent; it just does not acknowledge it. In the instance of the pornographic writer's "shame" in the *Dictionary,* such shame does not originate because of the text or in the writer. It is activated by the larger cultural milieu with which the writer and the text are associated. Though "shame" in the *Dictionary* is imagined as emanating from the individual's response to his writing, one cannot be ashamed without the larger culture acting with the individual to engender such a sense of shame.

To emphasize the individual and motivated character of anonymous publication is to assume the typicality of named authorship and the anomalous nature of anonymity. As I have already shown, anonymity was not atypical. Accounts of the widespread nature of anonymous publication across all kinds of texts in these periods complicate our sense of authoriality and anonymity by asking us to imagine a publishing context in which signed authorship was not the norm. In turning from anonymity as an anomalous individual choice to a typical practice throughout literary history, then, I suggest that our discussions of motive as an explanatory force may not be as useful as we had once thought. Anonymity may not be an individual choice driven by knowable motives just as publishing a late eighteenth-century novel in a three-volume duodecimo format is not exclusively the choice of any one individual involved in the production of the book. That is, anonymity may be productively understood not exclusively as a phenomenon tied to the actions of an individual author but as a complex collection of forces—some institutional and generic—that may have little to do with the actions, motives, or intentions of any human individuals.

Evelina's Intention, Burney's Motive

Evelina presents a compelling case to explore questions of motive and intention because the anonymous novel written by Burney exists alongside varying accounts of her wariness about the novel and novel writing. It would seem that one is not left to imagine Burney's motives for anonymous publication because her letters, journals, and novels document them. This is tempting, and often compelling, evidence on which to base an explanation of *Evelina*'s anonymity. However, this evidence offers conflicting accounts of Burney's motives and intentions and has enabled a critical tendency to conflate Burney with *Evelina* and Evelina. This tendency to collapse author, text, and character signals an attempt to shore up the unstable but absolutely necessary category of named authorship in the face of anonymity. As the *Dictionary of Anonymous and Pseudonymous English Literature* produces categorical stability by imputing authorial motives for anonymity, the conflation of Burney, *Evelina*, and Evelina imagines a unity of motive and intention and locates this unity in the author to explain the supposed aberration of anonymity. My aim in drawing on *Evelina* is to demonstrate how even when it seems we are not left to imagine authorial motives for anonymous publication because we have documentary evidence, we are still engaging in a practice of inferring authorial motive that does not account for competing actions, intentions, and contexts.

To be clear, I am not arguing that anonymous texts do not possess or are not subject to authorial motive or intention. What is necessary is to separate out motives for anonymous publication from intention in the text. The former is antecedent to the text; the latter is manifest in the text. *Evelina*, then, presents the ideal example of such a text where discussions of authorial motive lead only to seemingly contradictory accounts of what Burney thought about what she was doing, while discussions of intention point to actions and productions that seem to function counter to an authorial motive for anonymity. The intense interest in making anonymity explicit within *Evelina* indicates its intentional character, not in the fact of the anonymity of the novel (the absence of a name on the title page) but in the work done within the novel to highlight its anonymity. Burney's motives for the absence of her name on the title page mean very little in my account; however, the manner in which attention is drawn to that absence is deeply significant for the work the novel does in positioning itself within the cohering canon of the eighteenth-century novel.

Catherine Gallagher has questioned the narrative critics have articulated about anonymity being a kind of concealment that reflects Burney's stated concern with reputation. Gallagher notes that throughout *Evelina*, the anonymity of the text both points to no name and indicates the importance of names and naming.[6] Anonymity in this instance is thus not purely the absence of the name but a way of actively signaling that absence. This argument productively moves away from the topos of authorial modesty manifest in the earlier criticism and imagines greater agential engagement with the novel's reception on Burney's part.[7]

My reading attends both to the broad context in which *Evelina* was published and to work done within the novel to distinguish itself from that context. Of the sixteen new novels published in 1778, fourteen (including *Evelina*) were published anonymously.[8] Certainly fourteen anonymous novels out of the sixteen published (or over 87 percent) is a remarkable number if we tend to think of the novel as attached to a named author; however, we must also contextualize it within the broader trends in the rise of the novel.[9] The overwhelming anonymity of novels published in 1778, and more broadly across the period, rendered *Evelina*'s anonymity far less remarkable than literary critics have often thought. Anonymity was a typical and tacit feature of the novel. Because novels were published anonymously more often than not in the period, and because anonymity is usually the absence of positive evidence of a name, it was neither a notable nor an obvious feature unless explicitly mentioned. This is especially true of those novels published by circulating library publishers, as *Evelina* was by Thomas Lowndes. *Evelina*'s anonymity was not exceptional.[10]

However, *Evelina* positions itself not among those other fourteen

anonymous novels but among the more prestigious novelistic tradition signaled by the names "Rousseau, Johnson, Marivaux, Fielding, Richardson, and Smollett" in the novel's preface.[11] The novel
does so, crucially, by demanding that the reader acknowledge the
absence of its author's name. It turns the absence of the authorial
name into positive knowledge. *Evelina* does not allow or imagine
the typicality of the novel in its generic and medial coherence to
stand in place of, or draw attention from, the anonymity or authorship of the text. Instead, the text presents a persona who is reducible
neither to Frances Burney nor to the novel itself. The function of
this persona is, in part, to make the novel's anonymity explicit. The
expression of anonymity as a positive knowledge of the absence of
the author's name marks the novel as being in a state of transition
from its origins as entertainment to its rarified status as literary.
In doing so, it begins to explain why we read *Evelina* and not other
circulating library novels that resemble it.

This attention to the novel's anonymity begins with the dedicatory poem in the first volume "To ——— ———." The poem is
dedicated, if we know that Frances Burney is the author of *Evelina*,
to Burney's father Charles Burney. The text presents it as a keyed
dedication that foregrounds the absence of the name of its dedica-
tee. By foregrounding this absence, the poem further implies that
the unnamed Charles Burney, by the absence of his name, is the
anonymous "author of [the author of *Evelina*'s] being!" (1). Here we
have not only the anonymous author of the poem and the novel in
which it appears but the very possibility of the poem and novel's
existence predicated on another anonymous author—her father.

The doubling of anonymity evident in the opening stanza of the
poem continues in its fourth stanza when the poem admits its author's "incapacity" to trace the "num'rous virtues" of its subject:

> But since my niggard stars that gift refuse,
> Concealment is the only boon I claim;
> Obscure be still the unsuccessful Muse,
> Who cannot raise, but would not sink, your fame. (1)

Operating in this stanza is both the narrator of the poem's understanding of her "concealment" of both herself and her subject and
her ability to further "obscure" herself. The anonymity of both

subject and author is absolutely necessary to the project of this poem, because if one were named, the other could easily also be named. The effect of this doubling of anonymity, however, is to focus attention precisely on the doubly missing names. By reflecting on the multiple absences of names in both the title and content, the poem's use of anonymity, the stated purpose of which in the poem is to "obscure" or "conceal," ceases to do so and instead poses anonymity like the blanks in the title, "To ——— ————," as something to have its absent names filled in.

The dedicatory letter "To the Authors of the Monthly and Critical Reviews" that follows the poem likewise does similar work to call attention to the anonymity of its author. In asking for the patronage of the critics, she writes, "Without name, without recommendation, and unknown alike to success and disgrace, to whom can I so properly apply for patronage, as to those who publicly profess themselves Inspectors of all literary performances?" (3). The line "without name" plays with the double notion of obscurity offered in the dedicatory poem whereby its author is without name insofar as she is an unknown to the world of literature (a somewhat dubious claim for Burney) and the literal fact of the dedication and the novel being offered anonymously. As Margaret Anne Doody has suggested, there is a bit of ironic mockery in this dedication, as Burney was, in fact, known to many of the critics at the *Monthly* and *Critical Reviews*.[12] This moment in its ironic doubling demonstrates the emergence of an anonymous persona in the text who is not the same as the biographical person known to the critics as Frances Burney and whose ambitions for the novel *Evelina* may be very different from those stated in Burney's letters and journals.

The editorial persona manifest in *Evelina* is not reducible to Burney and may in fact exceed her intention; however, that is not to suggest that her own knowledge of the publishing world of the late eighteenth century is absent in the work that persona has done. Both Gallagher and Doody have noted that Burney was embedded in, and knowledgeable about, the literary culture of the period. Doody shows just how much Burney was privy to the various processes and competing interests involved in publishing and promoting one's work. In going to extraordinary lengths to ensure she could not be identified with *Evelina*, Doody observes, Burney may have forgone the interpersonal aspects of these processes, but they manifest in the construction of the anonymous editorial persona who seeks in the prefatory materials to differentiate *Evelina* from the other fourteen anonymous novels published in 1778 by demanding that the absence of the author's name be noticed.

The dedicatory letter seeks to appeal to the critics for their protection of the novel it prefaces. In doing so, it positions the novel among other literary texts through the interpolation of lines from William Shakespeare's *The Merchant of Venice* and Alexander Pope's *Epistle to Dr. Arbuthnot*. This appeal does not locate the novel and its author in the realm of interpersonal exchange with the actual critics of the reviews in the same way that quoting Shakespeare and Pope does not imply a personal relationship between those authors and Burney. Rather, it positions the novel and its anonymous persona in a relationship with the contemporary literary world, represented by the anonymous critics to whom it appeals, as well as the English literary tradition, here represented by Pope and Shakespeare, neither of whom is named. The signature at the end of the epistle, "*** ****," further signals, then, not a place for the name of an actual biographical person, because none could conceivably fit there, but the place of the unnamed authorial persona, the "editor" as she names herself in the preface, who exists in her relationship to *Evelina* and *Evelina*'s relationship to the broader literary landscape of the late 1770s (5, 9).[13]

This epistle is thus marked by its impersonality because it understands, deeply, the broader literary context into which *Evelina* appears and wishes to stake a claim to its import and quality despite its origins and resemblance to other anonymous novels bearing the name of their heroines in their titles. The preface continues this work of differentiation by placing the novel within a paternal literary lineage. It begins by remarking on the "inferior rank" of the "humble Novelist" within the "republic of letters" (7). The figure of the "republic of letters" reiterates the premise of the epistle to the critics that the entrance of the novel into the world is not, like Evelina's entrance into society, the actuality of its biographical writer stepping forth into the world. Rather, the novel's entrance is into the virtuality of the "republic," which is shaped and informed by all the material practices of publishing by human actors but is not identical to it. Instead, the novel and the novelist—as persona, not biographical individual—enter into a series of relations with the reviews, other novelists, and other novels. Like the work of the dedication, the preface seeks to manipulate those relations in an attempt to shape the novel's reception. Having noted the low status of the novel, the preface resituates *Evelina* not among the (perceived) low circulating library novels but among the emergent and respectable prose fiction tradition:

> Yet, while in the annals of those few of our predecessors, to whom this species of writing [the novel] is indebted for being saved from contempt, and rescued from depravity, we can trace such names as Rousseau, Johnson, Marivaux, Fielding, Richardson, and Smollett, no man need blush at starting from the same post, though many, nay, most men, may sigh at finding themselves distanced. (7)

This tradition is marked by "names," not by the titles of works. The catalog of authors named stands in direct contrast to the situation of *Evelina*'s own anonymous publication and novels like it. "Rousseau, Johnson, Marivaux, Fielding, Richardson, and Smollett" are all authors of novels, though the generic appellation is loosely applied in some cases, whose names are known and have been preserved, unlike the bulk of new novels in the later eighteenth century. Thus to invoke the name of the author within this context is to invoke the entirety of the oeuvre of imaginative prose fiction.

There is, then, a clear difficulty for an anonymous novelist to stake a claim within a tradition represented by named authors. The preface, like the rest of the prefatory materials, takes on this problem by making explicit the anonymity of the novel:

> The following letters are presented to the public—for such, by novel writers, novel readers will be called,—with a very singular mixture of timidity and confidence, resulting from the peculiar situation of the editor; who, though trembling for their success from a consciousness of their imperfections, yet fears not being involved in their disgrace, while happily wrapped up in a mantle of impenetrable obscurity. (7)

By once again pointing to the anonymous status of the novel as "impenetrable obscurity" in this passage, the preface envisions the audience for the novel as "the public." This notion of the public, is, however, immediately qualified as a public of novel readers rather than the entirety of the public sphere or even the vastness of "the republic of letters." Here the preface indicates a clear sense of *Evelina*'s place within the larger literary landscape in which it will appear by locating it both within a reading public, who would typically not expect an attributed novel, and within the novelistic genre in which the author is posed as the editor of letters rather than the author of them.

This passage is further striking in its understanding of *Evelina*'s entrance into the world as marked by "a very singular mixture of timidity and confidence, resulting from the peculiar situation of the editor." This "very singular mixture of timidity and confidence" speaks to the creation of the anonymous persona, "the editor," that creates a gap between the biographical person Burney with her "timidity" and the anonymous narrator with her "confidence" about the novel. "The peculiar situation of the editor" may suggest the underlying context from which Burney published the novel. That is, she is publishing as one who is deeply connected to the literary marketplace, and yet, if we wish to speak of her motive, in her "timidity," she elects to "wrap . . . up in a mantle of impenetrable obscurity" and publish anonymously. However, this line also signals the peculiarity "of the editor" who is thus "situat[ed]" both in the text and between the text and its biographical author.

By drawing attention to *Evelina*'s anonymity, by making it remarkable, "the editor" is able to position the novel in a lineage with the named authors invoked in the previous paragraph. *Evelina* understands itself not as a commodity whose authorial labor is made absent through its anonymity, nor as a "history" whose anonymity would bolster its truth claim.[14] Rather, in understanding itself as an explicitly anonymous fictional prose narrative and creating an authorial persona apart from its biographical author, *Evelina* appears like other anonymous circulating library novels but acts, or more precisely reads, like a novel within the emergent prose narrative tradition of Richardson, Fielding, and so forth.

It is worth noting that prefatory letters to critics and other prefaces are not unique to *Evelina*. The anonymous *The History of Eliza*

Warwick (1778), for example, includes a modest address of three pages to the critics by its claimed female author. This address, much like that in *Evelina*, seeks to stave off the harsh criticism that often met new novels. While the author of the prefatory letter in *The History of Eliza Warwick* makes mention of her gender, she makes no mention of the novel's anonymity; it is wholly tacit. What is different in *Evelina* is the manner in which the absence of the authorial name is foregrounded and the manner in which persona is called attention to. The central preoccupations of the prefatory materials to *Evelina* are its anonymity and the development and expression of an editorial persona who functions within the "republic of letters" but who is not, and cannot be, reducible to either Frances Burney or Evelina.

Though published in the impersonal realm of the literary marketplace, *Evelina* is represented throughout much of the criticism as an extension or version of Burney herself, not as an impersonal fiction of which she is the author. The anonymity of the novel is therefore explained by recourse to the author's motive—typically modesty. However, such an approach neglects much of the context in which *Evelina* was published—the circulating library of Thomas Lowndes—in favor of the biography and characteristic modesty of its author.[15] My insistence on a broadening of horizons follows from the call to look "beyond *Evelina*" to its literary contexts.[16] Certainly we must look to the novel's literary contemporaries and antecedents, just as we must look to its historical moment, its place among the market, its author, her gender, and so forth. To do so is to make visible the connections already present in *Evelina*. It is to situate the text among the multiplicity of such interlocking contexts. Thus we can speak of the so-called editorial persona of *Evelina* operating within the text itself (apart from Burney), within the literary tradition that is invoked, within the reading public invoked, in short, within the entirety of its cultural circulation.

The tendency surrounding *Evelina* to understand the novel and its author in their singularity has taken it as a case of a female novelist publishing her first novel (about a young woman) anonymously in a world hostile to both women and women authors. Read in this way, the anonymity of *Evelina* seems like an immensely personal choice, and the evidence from Burney's letters and journals supports these claims about Burney's modesty. In her journal for June 23, 1778, for example, Burney writes upon getting her father's approval of the novel,

> I had written my little Book simply for my amusement; I printed it, by the means first of my Brother, Charles, next of my Cousin, Edward Burney, merely for a frolic, to see how a production of my own would figure in that Author like form.[17]

Here Burney represents *Evelina* as a private exercise in novel writing "for a frolic." This entry alludes also to the lengths to which Burney went to disguise her authorship; she employed her brother, then her cousin, to deliver it to the publisher Thomas Lowndes. Famously, Burney even changed her hand when writing the manuscript so that publishers, who knew her to be the amanuensis for Charles Burney, would not recognize her hand and attribute authorship of the novel to her. When her father, who did not know Burney had written it, learned of her authorship and approved of it, Burney was delighted and relieved.

In this entry, Burney writes of her "little Book," her "production," and how it would "figure in that Author like form." Betty Schellenberg has suggested that in this moment, Burney links the printed text with authorship in these lines as a "narrowly print-based view of the author."[18] I would add, however, that while "that Author like form" may allude to a print-based concept of the author, it also suggests that the "form" (the shape of the novel) may itself be "Author like." Rather than simply offering an idea of the individual author within what may be called print culture, "Author like form" may also attenuate our notion of how the form of the novel itself may be semi-autonomous and self-authorizing as it is connected to its broader generic, media, and market contexts. The novel is "Author like" insofar as it constitutes the text's mode of being in the world.

Foucault has linked such a function with the authorial name, but genre, form, and medium (among other attributes of a text), as I suggested earlier, may work in a similar way. Identifying or categorizing a novel as a novel as it is connected to the context of the literary marketplace of the late eighteenth century shifts the emphasis that the contemporary (twenty-first century) critic presumes to be on the author as individual actor to the broader network of texts, humans, and contexts of which the novel is a part. The novel need not refer back to its writer to define its nature. By the late eighteenth century, the novel coheres in both genre and medium such that a three-volume duodecimo bearing the name of a young woman in its title "authors" the text. Burney's own entry registers this tension between the individual labor of creation and the semi-autonomy of the book within the world through her language of "my little Book" and "a production of my own" alongside the notion of "that Author like form." The possession signaled by "my" is thus undone by the suggestion that "form" is itself "Author like."

As Burney's journal entry articulates the tensions between individual production and possession and the nature of the form of the novel, it also evinces, at least on its surface, a claim for limited ambition and modesty. This surface claim for limited ambition and modestly is further evident in a December 1, 1778, letter to Catherine Coussmaker in which Burney writes, "Little, indeed, did I imagine, when I parted with Evelina, what Honours were in reserve for her! I thought that her only admirers wd be among school girls, & destined her to no nobler habitation than a Circulating Library."[19] Burney did not, however, destine *Evelina* "to no nobler habitation than a Circulating Library." She sent off the manuscript of the half-completed novel first, not to Lowndes, its eventual publisher, but to James Dodsley, who was an up-market publisher and not a circulating library proprietor, "but Mr. Dodsley declined looking at anything anonymous; and the young group . . . next fixed upon Mr. Lowndes, a bookseller in the city."[20] Schellenberg has noted Burney's "disingenuous . . . denying [of] ambition" in her letters and journals, and this letter certainly seems to be one of those moments.[21]

Of Burney's attempted dealing with Dodsley, George Justice writes,

> The more prestigious publisher [James] Dodsley had refused to consider the manuscript of the novel for publication because the author refused to reveal her identity: anonymity, especially in relation to the transaction of business prior to publication, was the preserve of the mighty, even the titled.[22]

Justice here thinks through the presumption, on Burney's part, of anonymity as it is connected with the status of the author; however, what I would like to consider is anonymity as it relates to the status of the publisher. For Dodsley to publish, or consider publishing, an anonymous novel, particularly one which, as Justice notes, resembled circulating library fare, would be to lower the status of his own brand of publications.[23] By the late eighteenth century, anonymity was not the province of the modest and titled, nor was it ever exclusively. Anonymity, rather, is reinforced as a tacit feature of the novel in its role as an entertainment. Dodsley's rejection of *Evelina* need not be entirely about the perceived pretensions of Burney's anonymity but instead his own interest in preserving the status of his name and catalog.

Furthermore, much has been written about Lowndes as a publisher of ephemeral works. Gallagher notes, for example, that "to publish a novel, especially one for the circulating libraries, in the late 1770s was to embrace all that was most impermanent and insubstantial about the literary marketplace; it was not to court immortality but to solicit a big audience of little people for a short time."[24] In 1778, the year of *Evelina*'s publication, however, Lowndes published, or co-published, twenty-six books, including Samuel Johnson's *A Dictionary of the English Language,* Daniel Defoe's *The Life and Surprising Adventures of Robinson Crusoe,* and John Milton's *Paradise Lost.* Despite the unsettled ground of the vernacular canon in the late eighteenth century, one would be hard-pressed to claim that any of these texts were particularly ephemeral. Thus, even though Lowndes operated a circulating library and was associated with circulating library novels, many of his publications were still sufficiently literary enough to complicate the narrative of modest aspirations that Burney draws for us in her journals and letters.

Evelina retains its ambitions, as evidenced by Burney's decision to offer the manuscript to Dodsley first, even though the novel eventually found a "habitation" in Lowndes's "Circulating Library." I argue that this is a consequence of the novel's repeatedly calling attention to its anonymity and its thematization of the search for origin as a central feature of its plot. *Evelina*'s anonymity is not about deferral of authorship, or bashfulness, or modesty, or disownment. However, Burney's anonymity may well have been. *Evelina*'s explicit anonymity is a statement of valuation through the pose of seeming dispossession in a publishing context in which anonymity was something unremarkable, something to be ignored or forgotten. By demanding that attention be paid to *Evelina*'s anonymity, the effect of the prefatory materials is to court immortality against the assumed typical ephemeral nature of the circulating libraries' other anonymous novels.

This is not to argue that the biographical person, Frances Burney, did not have very personal reasons for wishing not to attach her name to the novel. Nor is it to deny the difficult position of writing women in the late eighteenth century that may have encouraged anonymous authorship.[25] The persona that is present in the prefatory materials of the novel is, however, not necessarily the same as the biographical person. Nor are whatever motives she may have had for the anonymity of the novel manifest in that persona. If we wish to impute intention to Burney, we may say that she crafts this anonymous persona precisely because it may guard against the mode of criticism that conflates persona with person, which the prefatory materials anticipate and which much twentieth- and twenty-first-century criticism continues to do.

This distinction between Burney as biographical person and the narrative persona manifest in the prefatory materials indicates a crucial separation, to borrow from Quentin Skinner, between authorial motive *for* anonymity and the intention *in* anonymity. Burney's motive for anonymity, as I have shown, is difficult to tease out reliably, and I would argue that motives for anonymity are always inscrutable and rarely useful if we wish to understand the history and function of anonymity within literary culture. Intention in anonymity, however, may be accessible as it is made manifest in the text. But here is where I depart from Skinner: for, while he connects intentions to authors as biographical personages, I argue that intentions in texts may, and often do, exceed or efface those of their biographical authors. Intention, as it is manifest in the prefatory materials to *Evelina* in the letters, poems, and dedications, is not bound to or possessed by Burney; it is rather associated with "the editor" of *Evelina* (if, indeed, we need to pin intention to an acting subject), who may be thought of as a figure who works in parallel to Burney but who is not self-identical to Burney. The persona of "the editor" of *Evelina* operates across the text and within the broader network of textual production and circulation. Neither individual context can be understood to fully realize or make available the motive of the author.[26]

Looking to *Evelina*'s context of publication, we see that anonymity was hardly a rarity within the circulating library. Indeed, it was typical of novels published by and for the circulating libraries. That *Evelina* was anonymous in its 1778 publication was not remarkable; it was to be expected. The critical approaches that fold the biography of Burney in with the publication history of *Evelina* understand authorship to be typical of novel publication and *Evelina*'s anonymity to be exceptional. This simply does not reflect the history of the novel in the late eighteenth century in general or the history of the novel within the circulating library in particular.

What is remarkable about *Evelina*'s anonymity is the lengths to which the novel draws attention to its anonymity. The prefatory materials repeatedly, and almost obsessively, make visible the absence of its author's name. Moreover, as much of the criticism has suggested, naming is a central concern of the narrative itself. Such attention to anonymity, against the norms of the circulating library novel, seems to be in tension with Burney's stated claims to limited ambition and modesty and indicate the difficulty of ascribing motive to Burney to understand *Evelina*'s anonymity. Thus, to offer an account of the anonymity of *Evelina*, or indeed any anonymous novel, we must turn from what happens within an author's head to what happens in the world.

A Long Eighteenth-Century Coda: *Waverley* and Motive in the World

Perhaps no other novel of the long eighteenth century is as noted for its anonymity as *Waverley* and the Waverley novels that followed. I have shown already how supremely common the anonymity of novels was during this period. The anonymity of *Waverley* follows generic convention, where, as Garside notes, "the general tendency during the period as a whole was towards anonymity."[27] Such convention is further suggested by that fact that, as Paula Feldman has shown, Scott had published his poetry under his name and then published *Waverley* anonymously.[28] Yet, as Mullan suggests in Scott's "obstinancy," there are intentions expressed in the anonymity of the novels that exceed the typicality of convention.[29] Indeed, the introduction to *Chronicles of the Canongate* notes, shortly after Scott had been publicly identified as the "Author of Waverley," that "it was my original intention never to have avowed these works during my lifetime."[30] Much like *Evelina* some thirty years earlier, *Waverley* makes explicit its anonymity in the text, paratexts, and epitexts in distinction to the typically tacit novels of the period.

As is common, particularly for famous cases of anonymous texts, much has been made of Scott's possible motives for the anonymous publication of the Waverley novels. Seamus Cooney details eleven possible motives, Thomas R. Dale adds yet another in his response to Cooney, and Mullan implies Scott's motive in his chapter titled "Mischief."[31] Yet, while the lists of possible motives present a sense of certainty and are based on statements that appear in many of the Waverley novels and Scott's correspondence, even Cooney notes that they are merely inferred with no certainty of their truth, "largely because [Scott] admits that he does not fully understand his own motives."[32] That is, while some motive or motives exist as antecedent to the action or inaction involved in not attaching his name to *Waverley* and the Waverley novels, neither the critic nor Scott himself is able fully to articulate what those motives were.

The history of the anonymous status of the *Waverley* novels was indeed complicated, and as Claire Lamont has noted, it was a "partial anonymity" owing to Scott's prior publications bearing his name and the sense that some indeed knew Scott to be the author of the novels.[33] It is clear, then, that there are intentions *in* the anonymity of the novels even as Scott's accounts of his motives *for* the anonymity of the novels remain inconsistent at best. *Waverley* further offers its own theorization of motive, one that recognizes the difficulty of reliably accounting for the motives of individuals. Early on in the novel, for example, in distinguishing the politics of Sir Everard and his younger brother Richard, we are told,

> Painters talk of the difficulty of expressing the existence of compound passions in the same features at the same moment: It would be no less difficult for the moralist to analyze the mixed motives which unite to form the impulse of our actions.[34]

In this passage, the central problem of motive is made very clear: accounting for the—often mixed—reasons for action in others is like representing the mixed emotions in painting: it is difficult. In both instances, the task is for one to interpret and represent the internal, unobservable mental states of another as legible, external phenomena. Given this account of motive, then, it seems unsurprising that much of the first *Waverley* novel is concerned with the difficulty, if not the impossibility, of sussing out the motives of its characters. Indeed, the novel imagines that there may well be actions that occur without antecedent motive:

> But there are men in the world who will not believe that danger and fatigue are often incurred without any very adequate cause, and therefore who are sometimes led to assign motives of action entirely foreign to the truth. (178)

The belief that the motives of others are accessible and knowable leads not to truth but to error. Yet *Waverley* also offers another account of motive, one drawn from the conceit of the historical novel, in which motive is not solely the province of individual humans:

> I beg pardon, once and for all, of those readers who take up novels merely for amusement, for plaguing them so long with old-fashioned politics, and Whig and Tory, and Hanoverians and Jacobites. The truth is, I cannot promise them that this story shall be intelligible, not to say probable, without it. My plan requires that I should explain the motives on which its action proceeded; and these motives necessarily arose from the feelings, prejudices, and parties, of the times. (26)

Motive here is not exclusively as phenomenon of an individual mind; it is located first as "feelings," which, while they may recur to the individual, exceed them, as they are represented as a historical sensibility "of the times." "Prejudices" similarly indicates a collective, shared sense that exceeds the individual. Party-as-motive further abstracts away from the individual to collectives joined toward a purpose. Motive, then, is knowable through historical distance, and the task of the novel is to account for the reasons for actions in history, not in human individuals alone. Such an account of motive and causation in the historical novel is similarly found in Georg Lukács's discussion of historical necessity in Scott's historical novels and James Chandler's discussion of characterization in *Waverley*.[35] In each, the literary character is given animation and form by forces that far exceed the individual and her psychology.

Considered in the light of *Waverley*'s theory of motive, the seeming inconsistency of Scott's accounts of his own motives for anonymity makes more sense—those that refer to internal mental states are wholly unreliable; yet motive may be understood as historical forces in the world from which action proceeds and may therefore be explained. Thus, whereas the first half of this chapter disregarded the individual's motives *for* anonymity in preference for intention *in* anonymity, Scott's reimagining of motive as historical force renders it as an impersonal and externalized notion that may indeed be known. This allows me to account for both the historical motives for the Waverley novels' anonymity—as distinct from whatever motives Scott may have had—and the intentions in the anonymity of the novels.

In what follows, I revisit the varying accounts Scott and his personae offer of their motives for publishing anonymously. The aim, in part, is to offer a new answer to the question, posed long ago by Cooney, "what, we ask ourselves, might it have been that made Scott feel his fiction writing was bound up with his anonymity?"— without recurring to Scott's individual psychology.[36]

In its first edition, *Waverley* offers very little in the way of explanation for its anonymity—it needn't; the novel of the late eighteenth and early nineteenth centuries was an anonymous form. Instead, the postscript, which identifies itself as inverting "the usual arrangement," does the retroactive work of shoring up the narrative persona at the end of the novel—not in its preface—with no mention of the novel's anonymity (365).

Although there is no account of the novel's anonymity in its initial publication, scholars have drawn on Scott's letters from 1814 to tease out his possible motives. In a letter to John Morritt, he writes, "I shall not own Waverley—my chief reason is that it would prevent me of the pleasure of writing again."[37] Established already as a renowned poet and as a clerk of sessions, Scott wonders if it would be "decorous" to be known as a novelist. Here one could educe a personal motive for the anonymity of *Waverley,* one that could be identified as "reliev[ing] him of the danger of being thought professionally indecorous."[38]

Of course, only a month after this letter, in August 1814, *The British Critic* offered a positive review of *Waverley* that noted:

> A very short time has elapsed, since this publication made its appearance in Edinburgh, and though it came into the world in the modest garb of anonymous obscurity, the northern literati are unanimous, as we understand, in ascribing part of it at least to the pen of W. Scott. As that gentleman has too much good sense to play the coquet with the world, we understand that he perseveres in a formal denial of the charge; though from all we can learn, the *not guilty* which he pleads to the indictment, proceeds almost as faintly from his mouth, as from the tongue of a notorious offender at the bar of the Old Bailey.[39]

The anonymity of *Waverley* was, as this review and other evidence suggests, an open secret and an attribution only "faintly" denied. So while Scott may have had personal and professional reasons for anonymity, his actions suggest only a limited investment in maintaining that anonymity.

In the same letter to Morritt, Scott offers another account of the anonymity of *Waverley,* one that dislocates anonymity from a matter of personal choice motivated by professional reasons to one of literary tradition:

> I think an author may use his own discretion in giving or withholding his name. Harry Mackenzie never put his name in a title page till the last edition of his works and Swift only ownd one out of his thousand and one publications.

Whereas the editorial persona of *Evelina* sought to locate the novel in a named tradition of novelists including "Rousseau, Johnson, Marivaux, Fielding, Richardson, and Smollett" despite its anonymity, Scott locates his novel in an anonymous tradition, but one he signals by recourse to MacKenzie's and Swift's names.

That names should be used to signal a tradition of anonymous writing suggests a paradox wherein the name persists despite the claimed absence of the name. This is precisely the course that the anonymity of *Waverley* and its successors takes, where Scott's authorship is effectively an open secret and yet the novels remain anonymous. Scott, then, is named, but the novels and the personae who inhabit, and function outside of, them are anonymous.

The preface to the third edition of *Waverley* in October 1814 continues the work of crafting these anonymous public personae, who first appear in the postscript, noting its out-of-order nature. It is the preface to the third edition that calls attention to the novel's anonymity, and it does so by implying both multiple personae and multiple motives:

> He has heard, with a mixture of satisfaction and humility, his work ascribed to more than one respectable name. Considerations, which seem weighty in his particular situation, prevent his releasing those gentlemen from suspicion by placing his own name in the title-page; so that, for the present at least, it must remain uncertain, whether WAVERLEY be the work of a poet or a critic, a lawyer or a clergyman, or whether the writer, to use Mrs Malaprop's phrase, be, "like Cerberus—three gentleman at once."[40]

This passage proposes a multiplicity of occupations for the supposed author and then, through an invocation of the memorable Mrs. Malaprop from Richard Sheridan's *The Rivals*, suggests that such multiplicity may be resolved in one being. This most obviously refers to Scott's own situation as both poet and clerk of sessions. The lines of Malaprop, however, in her mistaken notion of Cerberus—in fact, a dog with three heads—offers an image of multiplicity and singularity, formally embodied in the same being, and situated within the literary and media culture. "Like Cerberus—three gentleman at once" became by the late eighteenth century a commonplace for thinking about the ways that multiple personae (or occupations) may operate in a single being. Its invocation here also signals the manner in which theater and theatrical history figured into the ongoing anonymity of the Waverley novels. The preface puts forth an account of its "Author" that invites the creation of multiple personae who inhabit the literary and theatrical realms and bear some connection to "the Author" but are not reducible to Scott.

The multiple accounts of possible motives in the preface stemming from "different situations in life" extend from this claim of multiplicity and singularity:

> The Author, as he is unconscious of any thing in the work itself (except perhaps its frivolity) which prevents its finding an acknowledged father, leaves it to the candour of the public to choose among the many circumstances peculiar to different situations in life, such as may induce him to suppress his name on the present occasion. He may be a writer new to publication, and unwilling to avow a character to which he is unaccustomed; or he may be a hackneyed author, who is ashamed of too frequent appearance, and employs this mystery, as the heroine of the old comedy used her mask, to attract the attention of those to whom her face had become too familiar. He may be a man of a grave profession, to whom the reputation of being a novel-writer might be prejudicial; or he may be a man of fashion, to whom writing of any kind might appear pedantic. He may be too young to assume the character of an author, or so old as to make it advisable to lay it aside. (62)

The persona within the preface immediately disavows anything in the content of the novel that might incline its author to publish anonymously. This seems an unnecessary move given the typicality with which new novels were published anonymously, regardless of content. It does serve, however, a specific purpose to suggest that one may begin to develop an account of motives for anonymity not from within the novel, nor even from within the mind of its author, but from without—from the position of the author in the world.

Rather than the consolidation of authorial consciousness through an immediate suggestion of motive, this passage offers multiple possible subjects in different positions, each with his own unique reasons for acting (or not acting to attach his name). This then complicates the vision offered by Mrs. Malaprop's "Cerberus"; not only minds but bodies and occupations are multiple. Such multiplication of possible "situations in life" and motives that follow from them may suggest that the preface takes seriously the possibility of knowing motives. In referring the reader to the possible positions of the author in the world—rather than the text—as a starting point for inferring motive, the reader is asked to work from the knowable position of an individual in the world backward toward "his" mental states in what seems a reasonable exercise. However, the reader is presented with not one possible subject position but six, each which may suggest very different reasons for acting. In refusing singularity, the preface refuses an individual's motives. Given these choices, one can neither reliably identify a single individual to whom one may attribute motive nor posit motive to imagine a singular authorial consciousness.

Shortly after being identified as the "Author of Waverley" by Lord Meadowbank at the Theatrical Fund dinner in Edinburgh in February 1827, Scott published *Chronicles of the Canongate* with an introduction retelling the story of his avowal of the novels and meditating on the possible motives for their anonymity. Although it is suggested in the introduction that it is in the "confessional" mode, what emerges is an account of the loss of Scott's "incognito" as another form of historical fiction.[41]

The retelling of the scene at the Theatrical Fund dinner in the introduction turns the historical event into a historical fiction and aligns with what follows: a crediting of the sources from whom and from which the characters in the novels are drawn. The "Author of Waverley" notes, "I have always studied to generalize the portraits, so that they should still seem, on the whole, the productions of fancy, though possessing some resemblance to real individuals" (xii). While the express concern here is that some of the characters may have too closely resembled acquaintances of Scott and therefore led to his discovery, I want also to argue that this is an account of the various authorial personae who operate throughout the Waverley novels. That is, those personae "possess . . . some resemblance" to Scott but are nonetheless fictional persons acting in manners that may in fact exceed Scott's own intentions.

Thus the theorizing about the relationship between historical persons and their fictional counterparts becomes the terms through which this persona accounts for "his" anonymity. The initial account of motive is marked by its resistance to positing an interiority for the writing persona:

And now the reader may expect me, while in the confessional, to explain the motives why I have so long persisted in disclaiming the works of which I am now writing. To this it would be difficult to give any other reply, save that of Corporal Nym—It was the humour or caprice of the time. (xxii)

"It was the humor or caprice of the time" disavows any prior mental state. The absence of the possessive—*my* humor or caprice—and the use of the pronoun *it* suggests a supreme impersonality in this account of motive and its externality. "The motives," decidedly not *my* motives, are not a mental state possessed by this persona, nor do they even reference interiority. They are, rather, contingent forces in the world, "of the time," much like the accounts of motive offered in *Waverley* some thirteen years earlier.

Much of what follows this declaration recounts a familiar story of authorial modesty and concern for critical reception—perhaps odd given Scott's previous poetic endeavors—and thus might suggest deeply personal reasons for anonymity, but this section closes by troubling the very account of motive just offered: "I have now frankly told my motives for concealment, so far as I am conscious of having any" (xxv).

Even here, writing an introduction signed "Walter Scott," the persona seems not to know his own reasons for acting. As G. E. M. Anscombe notes, "the question whether the light in which one so puts one's action is a true light is a notoriously difficult one."[42] This seems precisely the case; the motives available and reliable are those that are impersonal and external—the "humour or caprice of the time"—not Scott's interior thoughts.

Furthermore, the very existence of the introduction to *Chronicles of the Canongate* becomes an allegory for contingent historical forces beyond the control of the individual human actor:

As for the work which follows, it was meditated, and in part printed, long before the avowal of the novels took place, and originally commenced with a declaration that it was neither to have introduction nor preface of any kind. This long proem, prefixed to a work intended not to have any, may, however, serve to show how human purposes, in the most trifling as well as the most important affairs, are liable to be controlled by the course

of events. Thus, we begin to cross a strong river with our eyes
and our resolution fixed on the point of the opposite shore, on
which we purpose to land; but, gradually giving way to the tor-
rent, are glad, by the aid perhaps of branch or bush, to extricate
ourselves at some distant and perhaps dangerous landing-place,
much farther down the stream than that on which we had fixed
our intentions. (xxvii–xxviii)

Thus, while a person may intend one thing, other actions or forces
may redirect those actions regardless of her motives or intentions.
As the introduction begins by rendering a historical event, the Theatrical Fund dinner, as historical fiction, it concludes by rendering
itself, much like *Waverley*, both as a consequence of historical events
and charged with explaining the causes, beyond one individual's
motives, of those events.

The introduction to *Chronicles* begins the work of "owning"
the Waverley novels while offering a complicated account of the
personae and motives that lie behind the novels; this is picked up
again in the 1829 general preface to the "Magnum Opus" edition of
the Waverley novels. The preface begins with a biographical account
giving the author's penchant for storytelling and his love of books
and then moves to recount the composition and initial publication
of *Waverley* in 1814, where "the title-page was without the name of
the author, [and] the work was left to win its way in the world without any of the usual recommendations."[43] It then moves to rehearse
the controversy about the anonymity of the novel and those that
followed it and acknowledges the varying amount of knowledge the
public and intimate acquaintances had of Scott's authorship.

As the 1827 introduction seeks to account for Scott's motives and
does so unsatisfyingly, the 1829 edition continues the work of frus-
trating the desires of those who wish to find some psychological
cause:

But although the cause of concealing the author's name in the
first instance, when the reception of *Waverley* was doubtful, was
natural enough, it is more difficult, it may be thought, to account
for the same desire for secrecy during the subsequent editions, to
the amount of betwixt eleven and twelve thousand copies, which

followed each other close, and proved the success of the work. I am sorry I can give little satisfaction to queries on this subject. I have already stated elsewhere that I can render little better reason for choosing to remain anonymous than by saying with Shylock, that such was my humour. (94)

The preface suggests that one may reasonably infer a motive for anonymity when *Waverley* was new and its success not guaranteed—indeed, this practice was in line with the general tendency toward the anonymity of new novels. Once the novel became a best seller, however, the continued anonymity is more of a mystery and one that Scott cannot account for beyond claiming, "Such was my humour."

Here there is a clear echo back to the 1827 introduction in which the account of motive is similarly offered as a Shakespearean "humour or caprice of the time" (xxii). Where the 1829 general preface departs is in its claiming of the "humour" as the writer's own. Thus the preface is marked by a closer association with Scott the biographical personage—further elaborated in the sketch of his early reading and writing experiences—than with prior prefatory and postscript materials. This is evident from the opening lines of the preface, in which Scott reflects, "The Author, under whose name they are now for the first time collected, feels that he has the delicate task of speaking more of himself and his personal concerns than may perhaps be either graceful or prudent" (86). Recognizing that the third person tends to distance persona from person, "he proceeds in the second paragraph to make use of the first" (86).

Such toggling between first and third person pronouns registers the history of the multiple personae across the Waverley novels in which the "I" and "he" of the narrative voice in the paratexts does not always refer to Walter Scott. The "I" of the general preface seems to do so, however, and offers unprecedented access to the man behind the novels. And yet, even when it seems we have Scott "unmasked" at last, his account of his motives for anonymity seems as fleeting and unreliable as all those offered by prior personae—a mere "humour."

I want to close by suggesting that the unsatisfying account of motive Scott offers, even when it appears he writes in his own voice in the general preface, follows from the particular way in which masking and unmasking are theorized in the first instance of Scott identifying himself in print as the "Author of *Waverley*" in the introduction to *Chronicles of the Canongate*. The relationship between masking and unmasking is figured in the character of Harlequin or, as the introduction gestures back to *Commedia dell'arte*, "Arlechino" (i).

The introduction begins by recounting the story of an Italian actor in France convinced to play Harlequin without that "unmeaning and bizarre disguise," his mask: "He played Harlequin barefaced, but was considered on all hands as having made a total failure" (ii–iii). The introduction recounts that without the mask, the actor "lost the audacity which a sense of incognito bestowed" (iii). The introduction, then, suggests that "perhaps the Author of Waverley is now about to incur a risk of the same kind" in laying "aside his incognito" (iii).

As I have already argued, this introduction produces more of an account of fictional personae bearing a relationship to history than it does an account of biographical persons and their personal motives. This anecdote of the Harlequin does a similar kind of work in its absence of particularity. Frank Jordan, for example, admits to not knowing the source of this anecdote but points out that "more than one player in France was compelled or seduced into playing without a mask" and suggests an allusion to Giovanni Bissoni or the English Harlequin, William Penkethman.[44]

While the leaving off of the mask may suggest revelation and truth or a vulnerability of the actor, it actually works as a reminder of the multiplicity and collectivity in any performance. Harlequin as a character further invokes a particular performance tradition stretching from the Italian *commedia* to the continually popular English pantomime, which was, as I showed in chapter 2, a largely anonymous form and which makes evident the collectivity and multiple forms of action that make up the theatrical event. Furthermore, even without the mask, the actor *is still acting*; persona is multiplied, not reduced—a clear echo of "three gentleman at once" in the 1814 *Waverley* preface—and located within a palpably mediated event. The mask enables one sort of play; its absence enables another; neither is wholly reducible to the actor.

Pantomime and its characters, particularly Harlequin, bear with them the sedimented intentions that have come before—the *technē* of the form—which is most evident in the mask worn by Harlequins.[45] In the Harlequin figure, we position the human actor in relation to an entire accreted history of its performance; Penkethman or Bissoni, if they are indeed being alluded to in the introduction, are in a long lineage among many acting in any given scenario. Harlequin in the introduction, then, bears a relationship to the allegory of the man in the river with which it concludes. Just as the actor playing harlequin is acted on by the impersonal forces of gestures, antics, costumes, and masks that have come before such that his actions are shaped, reshaped, and redirected by those forces, the man crossing the river sets out with one intention and finds himself acted upon and redirected by the competing actions and intentions of the river.

The further unmasking, or true unmasking, of Scott in the 1829 general preface bears these traces of the prior unmasking in 1827 and prior, informal unmaskings. In each instance, the reader is reminded that one's actions are never quite one's own, nor do the intentions expressed in those actions always meet their goal. Motives, then, antecedent to those actions may be difficult, if not impossible, to account for, even when expressed by those who ought to best be able to account for them. "Humour" as it is passing, fleeting, and capricious might be as close as one can get to the interior depth and motives of Scott or any author. The contribution of the Waverley novels might well be that they provide a means of thinking about the detachment of motive from an individual—as historical force, not the possession of a psychology. In this way, Scott redeems motive from its unknowability while still foiling critics who seek to account for his own motives.

When we ask why a text is anonymous, we invariably ask why an author chose to publish anonymously. We ask for an explanation of the individual's motive for action as if such motives were knowable and such actions occurred outside of their broader context, that is, the world. Motives are generally not knowable. If they are announced to interpret an action, they may not be reliable. Actions, however, occur in the world and may be described by intentions. Looking exclusively to Burney or Scott to explain and interpret the anonymity of *Evelina* or the Waverley novels serves only to confound explanation. Nor does motive tell us about the history of authorship or anonymity. To answer these questions, we must turn away not only from the author as the origin for the text but also from an emphasis on individual human action as a whole in the production of the novel. This chapter, and the book as a whole, calls for a rethinking of how we orient authorial subjects within a literary landscape comprising material and ideal objects. To do so, we must attend to the network comprising novels, authors, publishers, media, and so forth to understand the collective action inherent in the formation of any of these literary artifacts.

Epilogue

Anonymity and Media Shift

In a November 29, 2010, opinion piece for the *New York Times* titled "Where Anonymity Breeds Contempt," Julie Zhuo, then a product design manager at Facebook, writing about the supposed culture of anonymity fostered in online environments and the benefit offered by social media platforms like Facebook, where "people's faces, real names and brief biographies . . . are placed next to their public comments to establish a baseline of responsibility," made the curious argument that "until the age of the Internet, anonymity was a rare thing. When someone spoke in public, his audience would naturally be able to see who was talking."[1] By now, I hope it is obvious that such a claim is patently false. If anything, anonymity is far rarer than it ever has been before. While it may be the case that public-facing online activity allows a feeling of anonymity—less in the sense of an absent name and more in the sense of impersonality—in the wake of revelations about NSA spying and growing awareness of the ubiquity of dataveillance by both governments and corporations, actual anonymity, in both senses of the term, is a near-impossibility.[2]

Zhuo's argument is, however, a familiar one. It links the ideology of media shift—the belief that "one form of human communication inexorably succeeds or displaces another"—to an attention to anonymity.[3] The opinion piece demonstrates the ideology of media shift in its comparison of oral speech in the market to online communication. It very obviously omits multiple forms of media in the shift it traces: print, analog, and other forms of digital media are all absent. Yet in the yoking of media shift with an argument about the ubiquity (or more often disappearance) of anonymity, Zhuo draws on a long history that rightly perceives the relationship between mediation, in its most apprehensible form as media, and anonymity.

This is the relationship that *Everywhere and Nowhere* has sought to draw out across the eighteenth century to argue that the divergent forms of agency and representational logics of different media forms variously call attention to or render transparent the absence of the authorial name. Media shifts, as a form of hyperintermediation, emerge as key historical sites where anonymity is made visible and claims are made to its increase or decline.

Virginia Woolf stakes such a claim in one of her last essays, "Anon."[4] In the essay, Woolf traces the shift from orality to print in the figure of the roving minstrel Anon. Both Anon and anonymity, she argues, were relics of an earlier age characterized by unfixed textuality. "It was the printing press," Woolf writes, "that finally was to kill Anon" (384). Still later, she writes, "Caxton's printing press foretold the end of that anonymous world; It is now written down; fixed; nothing will be added" (385). I have shown, of course, how quite the opposite happened. Anonymity did not disappear with the coming of print; rather, it flourished and continued to do so well into the nineteenth century.

Yet, here, as in Zhuo's opinion piece, media shift is the condition under which anonymity, ever present and persistent, comes to the fore. Lucien Febvre and Henri-Jean Martin, in *The Coming of the Book*, similarly draw attention to anonymity (and its supposed decline) in tracing the shift from manuscript to print. They write, "While in the Middle Ages authors had had little interest in attaching their name to a work, printers were led to seek out, or have sought out, the true identity of the works they printed."[5] The anonymous past and the attributed future are in their, as in Woolf's, estimation intrinsically linked to a shift from one dominant media form to another.

These three examples show what I've argued throughout: it is only by attending to processes of mediation—particularly as manifest in discrete forms of media—that we can begin to both theorize and historicize anonymity. Each instance of media shift invites reflection on the medium qua medium and in turn draws attention to the unique forms of agency they exhibit and the manner in which they refract the agency and intention of others. Principally, it is the interaction between author and medium where this refraction is most evident. Like Walter Scott's man set to cross the river who finds himself farther downstream than he intended, the medium pushes back and redirects the action of the human agent. Typically, when we treat media as transparent, these processes are far less evident, and so too is the absence of the author's name. It is in those moments when we are asked to attend the medium—as in instances of hyperintermediation like media shift—when the various forms of agency, both human and medial, come to the fore and we are asked to adjudicate among them.

Everywhere and nowhere, mediation and anonymity were and are intertwined, often unremarkable and unremarked upon. In this study, I've offered an account of how, across the media culture of the British eighteenth century, the typically tacit and invisible phenomenon of anonymity had its presence felt. As I've suggested in this epilogue, this intertwined relationship persists in our own period and is felt even more urgently as new forms of communicative media emerge on an almost constant basis and our quotidian interactions with them become ever increasingly intimate such that we, like eighteenth-century readers of It-Narratives, have very little difficulty imagining that our tablets, watches, phones, and so on, have a lifeness that exceeds the original intentions of their, typically unnamed, creators.

Acknowledgments

One of the biggest pleasures of bringing this book project to a close is the opportunity to recognize all those who helped along the way. I benefited greatly from fellowships and grants from the Folger Shakespeare Library, the Mellon Foundation, the University of Wisconsin–Madison Graduate School, the Center for Cultural Analysis at Rutgers University, the National Endowment for the Humanities, the American Antiquarian Society, and the Center for 21st Century Studies. Without the generous support from these institutions, this book would never have been. I'd also like to extend thanks to the many libraries that provided images seen throughout the book: University of Wisconsin–Madison Special Collections, the British Library, the Victoria and Albert Museum, the Folger Shakespeare Library, McGill University Rare Books and Special Collections, and the John J. Burns Library at Boston College.

My colleagues have, on an almost daily basis, helped me to make this book and my scholarship better. Theresa Kelley read and improved more drafts than I can count. Joshua Calhoun challenged me to think deeply about the materiality of texts and has been a dear friend. Elizabeth Bearden offered mentorship and perspective throughout the course of writing and rewriting. Robin Valenza saw the early potential of the project and shaped much of my approach to data analysis. Monique Allewaert provoked me to think harder than I thought I could about the theoretical stakes of this book. I'm also grateful to my other incredible colleagues whose conversation over the years has helped shaped my thinking: Susan Bernstein, Leslie Bow, Russ Castronovo, Stephanie Elsky, Ramzi Fawaz, Martin Foys, Sara Guyer, Caroline Levine, Christa Olson,

Ellen Samuels, Jonathan Senchyne, Kate Viera, Tim Yu, and Jordan Zweck. A thank-you to my former students Mattie Burkert and Katie Lanning; what a joy it has been to see you both grow and develop as scholars. Many thanks also to Emily Loney for her top-notch checking of the manuscript.

I was supremely fortunate to spend a year as a fellow at the Center for 21st Century Studies at the University of Wisconsin–Milwaukee. That fellowship changed my work and my life for the better. Thank you to my brilliant and generous interlocutors: Ivan Ascher, Joe Austin, Emily Clark, Richard Grusin, Gloria Kim, Elana Levine, Stuart Moulthrop, Tasha Oren, Jason Puskar, and Nigel Rothfels.

Eighteenth-century studies, and literary studies writ large, is filled with generous scholars whose work and conversation continues to enrich and challenge me. Thank you to the many scholars who, in various ways, have helped and shaped my thinking: David Brewer, Lezlie Cross, Darryl Domingo, Robert Griffin, Stephanie Hershinow, Jess Keiser, Kathleen Lubey, Sandra Macpherson, Laura Mandell, James Mulholland, Marcy North, Gillian Paku, Brad Pasanek, and Deborah Payne. Special thanks to the anonymous readers for the University of Minnesota Press who made this book much, much better.

My colleagues and friends in San Antonio played an early and ongoing role in the shape of this book. Thank you to Mark Bayer, Kinitra Brooks, and Joycelyn Moody. Thank you, too, Michael Cepek and Cathryn Merla Watson. One rarely meets such brilliant and dear friends, GSG.

This book began its life as a dissertation at Rutgers University, and I am grateful for all those who helped shepherd it along. Jonathan Kramnick pushed me to turn a few abstract thoughts on anonymity into a developed project. I cannot thank him enough for the trust he put in me as a developing scholar. This project was further challenged, refined, and made better by Michael McKeon, Lynn Festa, and Paula McDowell. My thinking was also indelibly shaped by Meredith McGill and Michael Warner, whose seminars provoked many of the animating questions of this book. I'm also grateful for the incredible cohort who surrounded me and read very early versions of many of my chapters, including Joshua Gang, Michael Gavin, Sarah Ligon, Lizzie Oldfather, Liz Reich, and Natalie

Roxburgh. Special thanks to Cheryl Robinson and Eileen Faherty, who kept it all together.

To my friends in the cycling community in Madison, San Antonio, Highland Park, and beyond: even if we never talked about my work, your help has been invaluable. Thank you especially to Craig Callan, Alec Donahue, Jerry Dryer, Jeff Fitzgerald, Matt Hamlin, Molly Hurford, Michael Jenks, Toby Jones, Kate Konkle, Amber Krueger, Todd Kruger, Alex Martin, Adam Myerson, and Margy Robinson. To my mentors and guides, thank you. Greg Tomso, without you, none of this would have been possible. Masha Raskolnikov, Madhavi Menon, and Gil Harris, your early influence and ongoing scholarship resonate with me daily. Larry Perfetti, thank you. Finally, a thank-you with love and gratitude to my partner, cycling companion, and pressmate, Jenna Loyd.

Appendix

Note: Kewes offers a similar analysis in her appendix to *Authorship and Appropriation*, also based on Burling's *Checklist*. Her numbers are lower than mine because she excludes pantomime and Italian opera. Because my interest is in a view of the entirety of theatrical representation during this period, I have chosen not to exclude these genres. As I suggested earlier, these percentages are based on those plays that have not been retrospectively attributed to an author. If we were to examine only evidence of performance and not the published pieces, it is likely that these percentages would be much higher. Likewise, if we were to take a selection of pieces, both published and not, that were anonymous during the period before being attributed to an author, these percentages would be higher still.

Season	Number of anonymous plays and entertainments	Number of new plays and entertainments	Percentage of new anonymous plays and entertainments
1700-1701	7	26	26.9
1701-1702	2	12	16.6
1702-1703	3	20	15.0
1703-1704	3	17	17.6
1704-1705	1	14	7.1
1705-1706	3	16	18.7
1706-1707	0	8	0.0
1707-1708	0	8	0.0
1708-1709	0	7	0.0
1709-1710	3	14	21.4
1710-1711	1	6	16.6
1711-1712	0	9	0.0
1712-1713	1	14	7.1
1713-1714	1	6	16.6
1714-1715	2	14	14.2
1715-1716	2	23	8.6
1716-1717	4	16	25.0
1717-1718	5	21	23.8
1718-1719	14	48	29.1

Season	Number of anonymous plays and entertainments	Number of new plays and entertainments	Percentage of new anonymous plays and entertainments
1719-1720	14	43	32.5
1720-1721	18	48	37.5
1721-1722	7	58	12.0
1722-1723	3	24	12.5
1723-1724	6	20	30.0
1724-1725	28	50	56.0
1725-1726	10	22	45.4
1726-1727	20	33	60.6
1727-1728	5	16	31.2
1728-1729	6	23	26.0
1729-1730	10	37	27.0
1730-1731	11	41	26.8
1731-1732	14	37	37.8
1732-1733	12	43	27.9
1733-1734	8	33	24.2
1734-1735	15	63	23.8
1735-1736	12	36	33.3
1736-1737	12	42	28.5

Notes

Introduction

1. This position contests that of Gérard Genette, who, while he denaturalizes the notion that named authors are "both necessary and 'natural,'" suggests that anonymity is like the name of the author, a "threshold of interpretation." Genette assumes that anonymity is something that is evident to readers, that it is a threshold over which the reader must pass to enter into the text. Anonymity may be made evident to readers; however, it is not necessarily the case that anonymity is obvious. It is, after all, an absence that can only be noticed when we are expecting the presence of an author's name. See Genette, *Paratexts*, trans. Jane E. Lewin (Cambridge: Cambridge University Press, 1997), 37.

2. Susan S. Lanser, "The Author's Queer Clothes: Anonymity, Sex(uality) and the *Travels and Adventures of Mademoiselle de Richelieu*," in *The Faces of Anonymity: Anonymous and Pseudonymous Publication from the Sixteenth to the Nineteenth Century*, ed. Robert Griffin (New York: Palgrave Macmillan, 2003), 83.

3. This is not to suggest a total absence of scholarship. In the early modern period, Marcy North's *Anonymous Renaissance: Cultures of Discretion in Tudor-Stuart England* (Chicago: University of Chicago Press, 2003) early on served as a model for my study. There also have been article-length studies of anonymity as a general phenomenon, accounts of the anonymity of particular authors, and a collection of essays. See, e.g., Kate E. Tunstall, "'You're Either Anonymous or You're Not!': Variations on Anonymity in Modern and Early Modern Culture," *MLN* 126, no. 4 (2011): 671–88; Pat Rogers, "Nameless Names: Pope, Curll, and the Uses of Anonymity," *New Literary History* 33, no. 2 (2002): 233–45; Anne Ferry, "Anonymity: The Literary History of a Word," *New Literary History* 33, no. 2 (2002): 193–214; Griffin, *Faces of Anonymity*.

4. Such an account follows from the tradition in analytic philosophy that has sought to define and separate out intention and motive as distinct concepts. This is also a distinction that is largely held among bibliographers, many of whom are either directly or indirectly indebted to Anscombe's formulation of intention concepts. See, e.g., James McLaverty, "The Concept of Authorial Intention in Textual Criticism," *The Library* 6, no. 2 (1984): 121–38.

5. Peter Garside, James Raven, and Rainer Schöwerling, *The English Novel, 1770–1829: A Bibliographical Survey of Prose Fiction Published in the British Isles* (Oxford: Oxford University Press, 2000), 1:81.

6. Access to such wildly expensive databases is, of course, limited to those scholars with credentials at institutions that subscribe to them. For a further theoretical account of the relationship between search and research, see Ted Underwood, "Theorizing Research Practices We Forgot to Theorize Twenty Years Ago," *Representations* 127, no. 1 (2014): 64–72. Brad Pasanek paints a picture of ECCO and other online databases as "an uneven and treacherous online archive of remediated page images, dirty OCR, and imperfect transcriptions" Pasanek, *Metaphors of Mind: An Eighteenth-Century Dictionary* (Baltimore: Johns Hopkins University Press, 2015), 14.

7. See Franco Moretti, "The Slaughterhouse of Literature," in *Distant Reading* (London: Verso, 2013), 87.

8. I am grateful to Brian Geiger, Virginia Schilling, and Carl Stahmer for their generous assistance in facilitating access to the ESTC metadata. I am further indebted to Martin Mueller, who assisted in making this connection. I wish to thank Laura Mandell and her team of researchers at Texas A&M for sharing the ECCO metadata with me.

9. This count is based on the metadata available as of March 2016.

10. The ESTC includes titles printed both in Britain and America; an identical analysis of ECCO, whose metadata is derived from ESTC but which skews primarily British in its holdings, yields a count of nearly 211,000 total titles (1700–1799), with 51,605 (24.46 percent) of those remaining anonymous.

11. The highest percentage of anonymous texts in the ESTC data comes in 1750 (38.3 percent). My concern is that this spike may be due to unknown publication dates being rounded to the median of 1750; a similar spike comes at 1800 and has been left out of my analysis for this reason.

12. Michael F. Suarez, "Towards a Bibliometric Analysis of the Surviving Record, 1701–1800," in *1695–1800*, vol. 5 of *The Cambridge History of the Book in Britain*, ed. Suarez and Michael L. Turner (Cambridge: Cambridge University Press, 2009), 37–65.

13. James Raven, "The Anonymous Novel in Britain and Ireland, 1750–1830," in Griffin, *Faces of Anonymity*, 143.

14. Leah Orr, "Genre Labels on the Title Pages of English Fiction, 1660–1800," *Philological Quarterly* 90, no. 1 (2011): 67–95.

15. Robert J. Griffin, introduction to *Faces of Anonymity*; "Fact, Fiction, and Anonymity: Reading Love and Madness: A Story Too True (1780)," *Eighteenth-Century Fiction* 16, no. 4 (2004): 619–37.

16. Griffin, "Anonymity and Authorship," *New Literary History* 30 (1999): 887. Henry VIII's July 8, 1546, proclamation did indeed require the naming of the author, along with the name of the printer and the date of printing; however, as Lyman Ray Patterson notes, Henry died shortly after this proclamation, and with his death, his proclamations "would have ceased to have any legal effect"; additionally, all of Henry's statutes and

proclamations regarding religion and opinions were repealed under Edward VI. See Lyman Ray Patterson, *Copyright in Historical Perspective* (Nashville, Tenn.: Vanderbilt University Press, 1968), 25–26.

17. On the relationship between authorship, property, and liability, see, e.g., Mark Rose, *Authors and Owners: The Invention of Copyright* (Cambridge, Mass.: Harvard University Press, 1993); Jody Greene, *The Trouble with Ownership: Literary Property and Authorial Liability in England, 1660–1730* (Philadelphia: University of Pennsylvania Press, 2005); and James Raven, *The Business of Books: Booksellers and the English Book Trade* (New Haven, Conn.: Yale University Press, 2007),

18. "Anonymous," in *A Dictionary of the.English Language . . . by Samuel Johnson, A.M. in Two Volumes*, vol. 1 (London, 1755).

19. G. E. M. Anscombe, *Intention* (Cambridge, Mass.: Harvard University Press, 2000), 89.

20. Bateson, "The Literary Artifact," *Journal of General Education* 15, no. 2 (1963): 80.

21. While Bateson links the temporal unfolding specifically to the linguistic aspect of texts, a range of scholars have argued for the polychronic and multitemporal aspects of materiality. Michel Serres and Bruno Latour, *Conversations on Science, Culture, and Time* (Ann Arbor: University of Michigan Press, 1995), 60; Christopher Pinney, "Things Happen: or, From Which Moment Does That Object Come?," in *Materiality*, ed. Daniel Miller (Durham, N.C.: Duke University Press, 2005), 256–72; Tim Ingold, "Materials against Materiality," *Archaeological Dialogues* 14, no. 1 (2007): 1–16; Jonathan Gil Harris, *Untimely Matter in the Time of Shakespeare* (Philadelphia: University of Pennsylvania Press, 2011).

22. Richard Grusin, "Radical Mediation," *Critical Inquiry* 42, no. 1 (2015): 129.

23. William Warner and Clifford Siskin, for example, understand mediation "in its broadest sense as shorthand for the work done by tools" and thus raise the possibility of nonhuman agency in mediation. They do, however, hold on to the sense of mediation as "everything that intervenes, enables, supplements, or is simply in between." See their introduction to *This Is Enlightenment* (Chicago: University of Chicago Press, 2010), 5.

24. Sarah Kember and Joanna Zylinska, *Life after New Media: Mediation as a Vital Process* (Cambridge, Mass.: MIT Press, 2012), xvii.

25. John Guillory, "Genesis of the Media Concept," *Critical Inquiry* 36, no. 2 (2010): 321–62.

26. Theodor Adorno, "Theses on the Sociology of Art," in *Working Papers in Cultural Studies* (Birmingham, U.K.: Centre for Contemporary Cultural Studies, 1972), 2:128.

27. Raymond Williams, *Marxism and Literature* (Oxford: Oxford University Press, 1977), 99.

28. Derrida, *Limited Inc.: Supplement to Glyph 2* (Evanston, Ill.: Northwestern University Press, 1977), 8.

29. Chartier, *Frenchness in the History of the Book: From the History of*

Publishing to the History of Reading (Worcester, Mass.: American Antiquarian Society, 1988), 307.

30. D. F. McKenzie, *Bibliography and the Sociology of Texts* (Cambridge: Cambridge University Press, 1999), 12.

31. Robert Darnton, "What Is the History of Books?," *Daedalus* 111, no. 3 (1982): 81.

32. Darnton has revisited and reimagined the scope of his groundbreaking 1982 "What Is the History of Books?" in his 2007 "'What Is the History of Books?' Revisited." In particular, his call to attend to paratextuality and intertextuality begins to open the possibilities for exploring the life of the text beyond its initial moments of production and consumption. Robert Darnton, "'What Is the History of Books?' Revisited," *Modern Intellectual History* 4, no. 3 (2007): 495–508.

33. C. Deidre Phelps posed this problem of the disappearing book in 1996 by asking of McKenzie, Darnton, and Jerome McGann, "Where's the Book?" More recently, work by Leah Price, Jonathan Lamb, and Christina Lupton has variously sought to bring the book back to the center of book history by attending to books as sometimes self-aware, sometimes agential "Things." Phelps, "Where's the Book? The Text in the Development of Literary Sociology," *Text* 9 (1996): 63–92; Leah Price, *How to Do Things with Books in Victorian Britain* (Princeton, N.J.: Princeton University Press, 2012); Jonathan Lamb, *The Things Things Say* (Princeton, N.J.: Princeton University Press, 2011); Christina Lupton, *Knowing Books: The Consciousness of Mediation in Eighteenth-Century Britain* (Philadelphia: University of Pennsylvania Press, 2011).

34. McKenzie, *Bibliography and the Sociology of Texts*, 14; Bruno Latour, *Reassembling the Social: An Introduction to Actor-Network-Theory* (Oxford: Oxford University Press, 2007), 5.

35. Christopher Flint, "Speaking Objects: The Circulation of Stories in Eighteenth-Century Prose Fiction," *PMLA* 113, no. 2 (1998): 212–26; Mark Blackwell, "Extraordinary Narrators: Metafiction and It-Narratives," in *The Cambridge History of the English Novel*, ed. Robert L. Caserio and Clement Hawes, 230–45 (Cambridge: Cambridge University Press, 2012); Blackwell, "Hackwork: It-Narratives and Iteration," in *The Secret Life of Things: Animals, Objects, and It-Narratives in Eighteenth-Century England*, ed. Mark Blackwell, 187–217 (Lewisburg, Pa.: Bucknell University Press, 2007); Blackwell, "The It-Narrative in Eighteenth-Century England: Animals and Objects in Circulation," *Literature Compass* 1, no. 1 (2003); Blackwell, Liz Bellamy, Christina Upton, and Heather Keenleyside, eds., *British It-Narratives, 1750–1830* (London: Pickering and Chatto, 2012); Nicholas Hudson, "It-Narratives: Fictional Point of View and Constructing the Middle Class," in Blackwell, *Secret Life of Things*, 292–306; Sara Landreth, "The Vehicle of the Soul: Motion and Emotion in Vehicular It-Narratives," *Eighteenth-Century Fiction* 26, no. 1 (2013): 93–120; Christina Lupton, "The Knowing Book: Authors, It-Narratives, and Objectification in the Eighteenth Century," *Novel: A Forum on Fiction* 39, no. 3 (2006): 402–20; Julie Park, "The Search for

'It,'" *Eighteenth-Century Life* 34, no. 3 (2010): 114–23; Chloe Wigston Smith, "Clothes without Bodies: Objects, Humans, and the Marketplace in Eighteenth-Century It-Narratives and Trade Cards," *Eighteenth-Century Fiction* 23, no. 2 (2010): 347–80.

36. Jonathan Swift, *A Tale of a Tub. Written for the Universal Improvement of Mankind. To Which Is Added, an Account of a Battel between the Antient and Modern Books in St. James's Library* (London: John Nutt, 1704).

37. Here I draw on Thomas Hobbes's account of "natural" and "artificial" persons, wherein "A PERSON is he 'whose words or actions are considered, either as his own or as representing the words or actions of another man, or of any other thing, to whom they are attributed, whether truly or by fiction.'" While I am less interested than he in adjudicating between natural and artificial persons, this theorization makes thinkable a spectrum of personhood from empirical individuals to fictional characters that may be distinguished from objects and things. Where I obviously depart from Hobbes is in his commitment to the inanimacy of objects. Hobbes, *Leviathan,* chapter XVI. See also Lamb, *Things Things Say,* 156. For a rich account of character, see Deidre Lynch, *The Economy of Character: Novels, Market Culture, and the Business of Inner Meaning* (Chicago: University of Chicago Press, 1998).

38. Harold Love, *Attributing Authorship: An Introduction* (New York: Cambridge University Press, 2002), 4.

39. Donald Foster, "Commentary: In the Name of the Author," *New Literary History* 33, no. 2 (2002): 376.

40. Taylor and Mosher write, "By 1700, modern usage was established: the student of anonyma and pseudonyma was expected to separate them and to disregard plagiaristic writings." Archer Taylor and Fredric J. Mosher, *The Bibliographical History of Anonyma and Pseudonyma* (Chicago: University of Chicago Press, 1951), 129.

41. Susan Stewart, *Crimes of Writing: Problems in the Containment of Representation* (Durham, N.C.: Duke University Press, 1994).

42. Taylor and Mosher, *Bibliographical History,* 81.

43. Leah Orr has offered an account of the history of, and problems with, Halkett and Laing's *Dictionary.* See Orr, "The History, Uses, and Dangers of Halkett and Laing," *Papers of the Bibliographical Society of America* 107, no. 2 (2013): 193–240.

44. Archer Taylor, "Three Epochs in Bibliographical History," *Library Chronicle* 18 (1952): 45–50. See also Thomas R. Adams and Nicolas Barker's account of the progress of bibliography, "A New Model for the Study of the Book," in *A Potencie of Life: Books in Society* (London: British Library, 1993), 6–7.

45. Joshua Calhoun, "Ecosystemic Shakespeare: Vegetable Memorabilia in the Sonnets," *Shakespeare Studies* 39, no. 1 (2011): 64–73, and Jonathan Senchyne, "Paper Nationalism: Material Textuality and Communal Affiliation in Early America," *Book History* 19, no. 1 (2016): 66–85.

46. While Warner focuses primarily on print within the eighteenth-century media culture, I wish to emphasize its intermedial character. See

William B. Warner, *Licensing Entertainment* (Berkeley: University of California Press, 1998), xi.

47. Jonathan Kramnick has offered a thoroughgoing challenge to "print culture" as a coherent or useful concept. See Kramnick, "Response: Some Thoughts on Print Culture and the Emotions," *Eighteenth Century: Theory and Interpretation* 50, no. 2–3 (2009): 263–67.

48. David J. Bolter and Richard Grusin, *Remediation: Understanding New Media* (Cambridge, Mass.: MIT Press, 1999), 21.

49. I. A. Richards, *Practical Criticism: A Study of Literary Judgment* (New York: Harcourt, Brace, 1929), 3.

50. Barthes, "The Death of the Author" (1967), in *Image, Music, Text*, trans. Stephen Heath (New York: Hill and Wang, 1977), 147. Nancy K. Miller has put pressure on the evacuation of the writing subject in Barthes's account: "At issue, however, is not so much the 'Death of the Author' himself—in so many ways, long overdue—but the effect the argument has had of killing off by delegitimating other discussions of the writing (and reading) subject. This suppression is not simply the result of an arbitrary shift in emphasis: when a theory of the text called 'hyphology' chooses the spider's web over the spider, and the concept of textuality called the 'writerly' chooses the threads of lace over the lacemaker, the productive agency of the subject is self-consciously erased by a model of text production which acts to foreclose the question of identity itself." Miller, "Arachnologies: The Woman, the Text, and the Critic," in *The Poetics of Gender*, ed. Nancy K. Miller (New York: Columbia University Press, 1986), 271.

51. Michel Foucault, "What Is an Author?," in *Language, Countermemory, Practice: Selected Essays and Interviews* (Ithaca, N.Y.: Cornell University Press, 1980), 120.

52. The occasion of Foucault's reflection on authorial names comes, we are told, from questions he received about his use of the names "Marx" and "Freud" in his earlier *Order of Things*; see "What Is an Author," 113–15.

53. My argument builds upon Jerome McGann's accounts of social authorship and authorship as a social nexus to expand those functions to the nonhuman aspects of textual production. See McGann, *A Critique of Modern Textual Criticism* (Charlottesville: University of Virginia Press, 1983), 62. I am further influenced by Henry Staten's work on *technē* and intention and the manner in which he locates the impersonality of the intention embodied in the formal aspects of texts such as genre and style. See Staten, "Art as *Techne*; or, The Intentional Fallacy and the Unfinished Project of Formalism," in *A Companion to the Philosophy of Literature*, ed. Garry L. Hagberg, 420–35 (New York: Wiley-Blackwell, 2010).

54. *Reports of Cases Argued and Determined in the High Court of Chancery, in the Time of Lord Chancellor Hardwicke* (London: H. Woodfall and W. Strahan, 1767), 2:507.

55. *Reports*, 501, 507.

56. Robert Searles Walker, *The Constitutional and Legal Development of*

Habeas Corpus as the Writ of Liberty (Stillwater: Oklahoma State University Press, 1960), 5.

57. Walker notes, "The Act of 1679 did crystalize a long history of ideas respecting the legal procedure surrounding personal liberty. Despite its shortcomings, it made the writ of habeas corpus the most efficacious safeguard of personal liberty ever devised" (85).

58. Giorgio Agamben, *Homo Sacer*, trans. Daniel Heller-Roazen (Stanford, Calif.: Stanford University Press, 1998), 123.

59. Sandra Macpherson, *Harm's Way: Tragic Responsibility and the Novel Form* (Baltimore: The Johns Hopkins University Press, 2009), 23.

60. Barthes writes that "as soon as there is a society, it converts every usage into a sign of that usage." Roland Barthes, *Elements of Semiology* (New York: Hill and Wang, 1977), 41.

61. "Meaning," Knapp and Michaels write, "is just another name for expressed intention." Steven Knapp and Walter Benn Michaels, "Against Theory," *Critical Inquiry* 8, no. 4 (1982): 742.

62. W. K. Wimsatt and Monroe Beardsley, "The Intentional Fallacy," in *The Verbal Icon: Studies in the Meaning of Poetry* (Lexington: University Press of Kentucky, 1954), 4. The essay appeared first in *The Sewanee Review* 54, no. 3 (1946): 468–88.

63. Joshua Gang, "Behaviorism and the Beginnings of Close Reading," *ELH* 78, no. 1 (2011): 18.

64. The "design or plan in an author's mind" apart from the text offered by Wimsatt and Beardsley may also meet the definition, offered by Donald Davidson, of "pure intending," that is, intention that is not, or not yet, manifest in action. Davidson, "Intending," in *Essays on Actions and Events* (Oxford: Oxford University Press, 2001), 127.

65. Wimsatt and Beardsley, "Intentional Fallacy," 3.

66. Wimsatt and Beardsley, 4.

67. I question the assumption here of the intentionless nature of objects, machines in particular. As Wimsatt and Beardsley have defined intention as related to a nebulous mental state, it follows that neither puddings nor machines would have intention; however, drawing from a definition of intention that seeks to describe the nature of an action, the actions of an object may be spoken of as having an intentional character. As I will argue throughout, texts, and figures within texts, may very well have intentions and agencies that are not reducible to those of their authors.

68. Stanley Cavell, "A Matter of Meaning It," in *Must We Mean What We Say?* (New York: Cambridge University Press, 2002), 226.

69. Cavell, 230.

70. Anscombe, *Intention*, 8. See also Kramnick, *Actions and Objects from Hobbes to Richardson* (Stanford, Calif.: Stanford University Press, 2010), 25.

71. Anscombe, *Intention*, 86.

72. Anscombe distinguishes between three kinds of motive: forward-looking motive, backward-looking motive, and motive-in-general. Forward-

looking motive is deemed identical to intention insofar as it is attached to action. Backward-looking motive names some reason for action, such as love or revenge. Motive-in-general is interpretive of a given action in that it asks one to "see the action in this light" (21). In the case of literary criticism, we are primarily interested in backward-looking motives and motives-in-general, because the temporal aspect of criticism involves reconstruction of some prior or past state, that is, "What was she thinking before or when she wrote X?" Susan Feagin offers a much fuller account of Anscombe's distinction between forms of motive and their applicability to literary study in "Motives and Literary Criticism," *Philosophical Studies* 38, no. 4 (1980): 403–18.

73. Quentin Skinner, "Motives, Intentions and Interpretation," in *Visions of Politics* (New York: Cambridge University Press, 2002), 1:98. An earlier version of this essay appears as "Motives, Intentions and the Interpretation of Texts," *New Literary History* 3, no. 2 (1972): 393–408.

74. Of the many accounts of the place of intention in literary criticism, it is the strain inaugurated by coauthors Knapp and Michaels, "Against Theory," that offers some of the best summations of the stakes of the debate. See also W. J. T. Mitchell, *Against Theory: Literary Studies and the New Pragmatism* (Chicago: University of Chicago Press, 1985); John R. Searle, "Structure and Intention in Language: A Reply to Knapp and Michaels," *New Literary History* 25, no. 3 (1994): 677–81; Steven Knapp and Walter Benn Michaels, "Reply to John Searle," *New Literary History* 25, no. 3 (1994): 669–75; John R. Searle, "Literary Theory and Its Discontents," *New Literary History* 25, no. 3 (1994): 637–67; Walter Benn Michaels, *The Shape of the Signifier: 1967 to the End of History* (Princeton, N.J.: Princeton University Press, 2006). The July 2012 issue of *nonsite.org*, "Intention and Interpretation," continues the debate in our current critical moment: http://nonsite.org/issue-description/intention-and-interpretation.

75. Among the many branches of the "New Materialism," my work is particularly influenced by those accounts interested in considering the agency of objects and troubling the ontological difference between the material and the immaterial. See, e.g., Tim Ingold, "Materials against Materiality," *Archaeological Dialogues* 14, no. 1 (2007): 1–16; Christopher Tilley, "Materiality in Materials," *Archaeological Dialogues* 14, no. 1 (2007): 16–20; Jane Bennett, *Vibrant Matter: A Political Ecology of Things* (Durham, N.C.: Duke University Press, 2010); Diana Coole and Samantha Frost, "Introducing the New Materialism," in *New Materialisms: Ontology, Agency, and Politics*, ed. Diana Coole and Samantha Frost, 1–43 (Durham, N.C.: Duke University Press, 2010).

76. Latour, "Agency at the Time of the Anthropocene," *New Literary History* 45, no. 1 (2014): 12.

77. Daniel Defoe, *The Life and Strange Surprising Adventures of Robinson Crusoe*, ed. W. R. Owens and P. N. Furbank (London: Pickering and Chatto, 2008–9), 170.

78. Alfred Gell, *Art and Agency: An Anthropological Theory* (New York: Oxford University Press, 1998), 14.

79. Similarly, Latour and others, like John Law, have expanded the sense of semiotics beyond solely the linguistic. Latour writes, "Now the ontological proposition I'd like to make is that what semiotics designates as a common trading zone—that is, morphism—*is a property of the world itself* and not only a feature of the language *about* the world." Latour, "Agency at the Time of the Anthropocene," 12.

80. I draw here on the Arendtian distinction between labor and work. While labor is a unique product of human action, work names that which is done by nonhumans as well. See Hannah Arendt, *The Human Condition* (1958; Chicago: University of Chicago Press, 1998), 85–87.

81. R. S. Crane, *The Languages of Criticism and the Structure of Poetry* (Toronto: University of Toronto Press, 1953), 143.

82. Sandra Macpherson, "A Little Formalism," *ELH* 82, no. 2 (2015): 390.

83. Jonathan Kramnick and Anahid Nersessian, "Form and Explanation," *Critical Inquiry* 43 (2017): 657.

84. My method approaches what Heather Love has dubbed "thin description." Thin description "consider[s] forms of analysis that describe patterns of behavior and visible activity but that do not traffic in speculation about interiority, meaning, or depth. Through its exhaustive, fine-grained attention to phenomena, thin description offers a model for close reading after the decline of the linguistic turn." See Love, "Close Reading and Thin Description," *Public Culture* 25, no. 3 (2013): 404. Love draws upon the primacy given to description by Latour and Stephen Best and Sharon Marcus's account of surface reading. See Latour, "Why Has Critique Run Out of Steam? From Matters of Fact to Matters of Concern," *Critical Inquiry* 30 (2004): 225–48, and Best and Marcus, "Surface Reading: An Introduction," *Representations* 108, no. 1 (2009): 1–21.

85. Pasanek offers an excellent discussion of toggling between close and distant reading in keyword search in the introduction to his *Metaphors of Mind*, esp. 17–18.

1. Anonymous as Author

1. Throughout this chapter, I will capitalize Anonymous to signal its use as a name or noun. Marcy North has distinguished between tacit and explicit anonymity by dubbing them "quiet anonymity" and "conspicuous anonymity." See North, "Ignoto in the Age of Print: The Manipulation of Anonymity in Early Modern England," *Studies in Philology* 91, no. 4 (1994): 390–416.

2. Kate E. Tunstall has also considered the ways in which Anonymous may function as an authorial name in the *Encyclopedie*. See Tunstall, "'You're Either Anonymous or You're Not!': Variations on Anonymity in Modern and Early Modern Culture," *MLN* 126, no. 4 (2011): 671–88.

3. Anne Ferry, *By Design: Intention in Poetry* (Stanford, Calif.: Stanford University Press, 2008), 182.

4. Sir Isaac Newton, *Opticks* (London: Sam. Smith and Benj. Walford, 1704), 116.

5. "Anonymous." John Quincy, *Lexicon Physico-Medicum: or, A New Medicinal Dictionary; Explaining the Difficult Terms Used in the Several Branches of the Profession* (London: E. Bell, 1722), 27.

6. "Anonymous." Nathan Bailey, *An Universal Etymological English Dictionary* (London: E. Bell, J. Darby et al., 1721). Bailey, it seems, misapprehends Robert Boyle, from whom this usage comes. In Boyle, "anonymous" indicates the unknown or nameless "spirit that may be separated from wood." Cf. Peter Shaw, *The Philosophical Works of the Honourable Robert Boyle Esq . . .* (London: W. and J. Innys, 1725), 3:384.

7. Marcy L. North, *The Anonymous Renaissance: Cultures of Discretion in Tudor-Stuart England* (Chicago: University of Chicago Press, 2003), 59.

8. For this study, I searched ECCO in chunks of ten years, beginning with 1700–1709, for anonym* with "fuzzy search" set to low to compensate for OCR issues. The asterisk permitted stemming the search term, which allowed for results including "anonymous," "anonymus," and "Anonymous." I looked at each instance of "anonym*" to confirm whether it was used as an adjective or as a name. This study was begun on February 18, 2015, and was a rerunning of an experiment conducted with ECCO 1 alone in 2007.

9. My study has found fewer than twenty instances of "Anonymous" on literary texts prior to 1770. Many of these instances are found as attributions to epigrams.

10. See, e.g., G. Thomas Tanselle, *Bibliographical Analysis: A Historical Introduction* (New York: Cambridge University Press, 2009).

11. Fredson Bowers, "Some Relations of Bibliography to Editorial Problems," *Studies in Bibliography* 3 (1950): 38.

12. Margreta de Grazia, *Shakespeare Verbatim: The Reproduction of Authenticity and the 1790 Apparatus* (New York: Clarendon Press, 1991), 5.

13. Cf. Philip Gaskell: "the chief purpose of bibliography is to serve the production and distribution of accurate texts. . . . Bibliography's overriding responsibility must be to determine a text in its most accurate form." Gaskell, *A New Introduction to Bibliography* (New Castle, Del.: Oak Knoll Press, 1972), 1.

14. See Tanselle, *Bibliographical Analysis*, 6–9.

15. Martin W. Maner notes, for example, that "[Edmond] Malone wrote that Nichols had collated all of Swift's holograph letters to Mrs. Johnson in the British Museum with the printed texts, and had found those texts to be full of omissions and mutilations" and that, "furthermore, by scrutinizing the letters to Mrs. Johnson, Nichols had shown Swift to be 'the author of many little pieces in the time of Queen Anne, which have not yet been inserted in his works'" (485). Maner, "An Eighteenth-Century Editor at Work: John Nichols and Jonathan Swift," *PBSA* 70 (1976): 481–99. See

also Edward Hart, "The Contributions of John Nichols to Boswell's Life of Johnson," *PMLA* 67, no. 4 (1952): 391–410; Albert H. Smith, "John Nichols, Printer and Publisher," *The Library* 18, no. 3 (1963): 169–90.

16. Cf. Bruno Latour, *We Have Never Been Modern*, trans. Catherine Porter (Cambridge, Mass.: Harvard University Press, 1993).

17. Armand Mattelart offers a similar account of circulation and communication. He writes, "Communication will be understood here from a wider viewpoint, encompassing the multiple circuits of exchange and circulation of goods, people, and messages. This definition simultaneously covers avenues of communication, networks of long distance transmission, and the means of symbolic exchange, such as world fairs, high culture, religion, language, and of course the media." Mattelart, *Invention of Communication*, trans. Susan Emanuel (Minneapolis: University of Minnesota Press, 1996), xiv.

18. Steele, *Poetical Miscellanies, Consisting of Original Poems and Translations* (London: Jacob Tonson, 1714).

19. "To Mr. Congreve, Occasion'd by his Comedy, call'd, *The Way of the World*," by Steele.

20. Brewer, "The Tactility of Authorial Names," *The Eighteenth Century* 54, no. 2 (2013): 195–213.

21. Forty-seven of the eighty-three poems in the collection are anonymous.

22. Barbara Benedict, *Making the Modern Reader: Cultural Mediation in Early Modern Literary Anthologies* (Princeton, N.J.: Princeton University Press, 1996), 13–14.

23. Those miscellanies are *Poetical Miscellanies Consisting of Original Poems and Translations* (1714), *A Collection of Epigrams. To Which Is Prefix'd, a Critical Dissertation on This Species of Poetry* (1727), *Poetical Miscellanies Consisting of Original Poems and Translations* (1727), *Poetical Miscellanies: Consisting of Original Poems and Translations. By the Best Hands. Publish'd by Mr. J. Gay* (1729), *A Collection of Epigrams. To Which Is Prefixed, a Critical Dissertation on This Species of Poetry* (1735), *The Flowers of Parnassus: or, the Lady's Miscellany for the Year M. DCC. XXXV* (1736), *The Sports of the Muses. Or a Minute's Mirth for Any Hour of the Day* (1752), *The Comic Miscellany*, vol. 2 (1756), *The Festoon: A Collection of Epigrams, Ancient and Modern* (1766), *The Festoon: A Collection of Epigrams, Ancient and Modern* (1767), *A Select Collection of Poems with Notes Biographical and Historical* (1780), *The Festoon: A Collection of Epigrams, Ancient and Modern* (1780). ("In church the prayer book and the fan displayed," *Digital Miscellanies Index*, June 4, 2015.)

24. John Nichols, *A Select Collection of Poems: With Notes, Biographical and Historical; and a Complete Poetical Index* (London: J. Nichols, 1780), 4:14.

25. Nichols is particularly noted for his work as a scholar of the book trade: "It is as chronicler of the book trade that Nichols is pre-eminent. His interest in printing history began when he and Bowyer edited the *Origin of*

Printing, in Two Essays by Conyers Middleton and Gerard Meerman (1774); a supplement by A. C. Ducarel was added in 1781. In the same year came *The Biographical Memoirs of William Ged, Including a Particular Account of His Progress in the Art of Block Printing* (1781)." "Nichols family (*per. c.* 1760–1939)," Julian Pooley, in *Oxford Dictionary of National Biography*, ed. H. C. G. Matthew and Brian Harrison (Oxford: Oxford University Press, 2004), http://www.oxforddnb.com/view/article/63494.

26. Maner, "'The Last of the Learned Printers': John Nichols and the Bowyer-Nichols Press," *English Studies* 65, no. 1 (1984): 13.

27. *Bibliotheca: A Poem* (London, 1712).

28. Nichols, *A Select Collection*, 3:19.

29. As Janine Barchas has argued, frontispiece author portraits are "not merely caste labels of authority" whose presence is meant to invoke the author and her authority (21). On frontispieces in collections in particular, Abigail Williams has noted, "Collections of works by various authors, whether in verse, prose, jest book, could not by definition be prefaced by an authoritative image of a single figure. In many cases, the material within them was anonymous, and unattributed, even if the author was known" (92–93). While the example of the Steele frontispiece and the frontispieces of all the volumes of *A Select Collection* suggest that an image of a single figure may in fact preface a collection, Williams does suggest the ways in which these images may be read beyond their purely representational and authoritative function and gesture to the contents and medium of the volume itself. See Barchas, *Graphic Design, Print Culture, and the Eighteenth-Century Novel* (New York: Cambridge University Press, 2003), and Williams, "How to Read a Book: 18th-Century Frontispieces and Popular Collections," *Anglistik* 25, no. 2 (2014): 91–102.

30. This same frontispiece, with the inscription, appears again in the two-volume *The Epistolary Correspondence of Sir Richard Steele* (1787), compiled and edited by Nichols.

31. Brewer, "Tactility," 197.

32. Jane Austen, *Northanger Abbey*, ed. Claire Grogan (New York: Broadview Press, 2002), 38.

33. Charles Lamb, *The Complete Correspondence and Works of Charles Lamb: With an Essay on His Life and Genius*, ed. Thomas Purnell and Barry Cornwall (London: E. Moxon, 1870), 3:435.

34. *The Gentleman's Magazine* LX, pt. II (1790): 971–72.

35. *The Gentleman's Magazine* LXI, pt. II (1791): 852. Tellingly, a footnote to the poem refers to the correspondent from whom the magazine received a copy of the poem.

36. Indeed, it is not until 1851 that the poem is attributed to Moss more often than not.

37. From the handwritten attribution in *Poems on Several Occasions* (Wolverhampton: G. Smart, 1769) held by the British Library.

38. Advertisement in *Poems on Several Occasions*.

39. William Scott, *Stourbridge and Its Vicinity* (Stourbridge: J. Heming, 1832), 155.

40. "The Beggar" by Thomas Moss appears in *The Oxford Book of Eighteenth-Century Verse*, ed. R. Lonsdale (1984) and is explored thematically based on this edition in Sandro Jung, "The 'Beggar' in Augustan and Romantic Poetry: King, Moss, and Wordsworth," *La Questione Romantica; Rivista Interdisciplinare di Studi Romantici* 10 (2001): 121–34.

41. William Enfield is likely responsible for the title change and the following line changes: line 8, *Poems on Several Occasions*, "Has been the Channel to a Stream of Tears" becomes "Has been the channel to a flood of tears"; line 14, "*Here* craving for a Morsel of their Bread" becomes "Here, as I crav'd a morsel of their bread." Similarly, in line 24, "And Tears of Pity could not be represt" becomes "And Tears of Pity would not be represt."

42. Here I adopt Barbara Benedict's broad notion of the anthology. There is, however, considerable disagreement on the terminology surrounding anthologies, miscellanies, and collections. See Laura Mandell, *Misogynous Economies: The Business of Literature in Eighteenth-Century Britain* (Lexington: University Press of Kentucky, 1999); Michael Suarez, "The Production and Consumption of the Eighteenth-Century Poetic Miscellany," in *Books and Their Readers in Eighteenth-Century England: New Essays*, ed. Isabel Rivers, 217–51 (New York: Leicester University Press, 2001); Chantal M. Lavoie, *Collecting Women, Poetry and Lives 1700–1780* (Lewisburg, Pa.: Bucknell University Press, 2009).

43. Jennifer Batt has asserted the particular importance of collections in mediation and circulation: "Mediating the literary culture that 18th-century readers experienced, these collections exerted a significant influence on the poems, and poets, that were in general circulation" (394). Batt, "Eighteenth-Century Verse Miscellanies," *Literature Compass* 9, no. 6 (2012): 394–405.

44. It was also set to music by T. A. Geary (and misattributed to Oliver Goldsmith in *A Collection of New and Favorite Songs* [Philadelphia: Carr, 1793]), printed on handkerchiefs (if Charles Dickens's *Nicholas Nickelby* is to be believed), and, not infrequently, represented visually.

45. Mary E. Phillips, *James Fenimore Cooper* (New York: John Lane, 1913), 26.

46. Anecdotes from America, particularly frontier America, suggest such recitations of the poem as a common practice.

47. *The Speaker* was popular. It was in its third edition by 1779 and was reprinted well into the nineteenth century.

48. Margaret Weedon notes, "Almost all the excerpts from poems mentioned in the first chapter of *Northanger Abbey* were to be found in *The Speaker*" (161). See Weedon, "Jane Austen and William Enfield's *The Speaker*," *Journal for Eighteenth-Century Studies* 11, no. 2 (1988): 159–62.

49. *The Speaker* (London: Joseph Johnson, 1774).

50. "Dr. Enfield, whose taste in selecting has generally been applauded,

gave great offence to Mr. Moss, by introducing material alterations into his poem, and, unfortunately, the innovations became permanent." Scott, *Stourbridge*, 155–56.

51. [Thomas Moss], *Poems on Several Occasions* (Wolverhampton, U.K.: G. Smart, 1769).

52. For a further discussion of the complexities of this difference, see Jacqueline George, "Public Reading and Lyric Pleasure: Eighteenth Century Elocutionary Debates and Poetic Practices," *ELH* 76, no. 2 (2009): 371–97.

53. Horace, *Epistles* II.50–52.

54. Colin Macleod, *Horace, The Epistles: Translated into English Verse with Brief Comment*, vol. 3 (Rome: Ateneo, 1986), II.2.51–53.

55. Cf. Barthes, "Death of the Author," 148.

56. Such guidance follows on Sheridan's *A Course of Lectures on Elocution* (1762) and anticipates Walker's *Elements of Elocution* (1781).

57. Richard Wendorf writes about the mid-century standardization and abandonment of capitalization and italicization in printing practice in "Abandoning the Capital in Eighteenth-Century London" that "this pervasive levelling of the text, with its less visually and intellectually mediated form of presentation, in turn placed much more emphasis on the discriminating power of the individual reader. These fundamental changes in printing conventions, in other words, are not only a result (and reflection) of the development of the reading public but also a cause of increased facility and sophistication as readers were faced with a greater uniformity in the presentation of printed texts. Such a revolutionary development did not go unnoticed, of course, and the most vociferous opposition to these changes was voiced—much too late in the century, as it turned out—by Benjamin Franklin. Writing to his son William in 1773, Franklin complained about the reprinting of one of his anonymous pieces, which had been 'stripped of all the capitalling and italicing, that intimate the allusions and marks [*sic*] the emphasis of written discourses, to bring them as near as possible to those spoken.'" Wendorf, *Reading, Society, and Politics in Early Modern England*, ed. Kevin Sharpe and Steven N. Zwicker (Cambridge: Cambridge University Press, 2003), 88.

58. Michael Shortland, "Moving Speeches: Language and Elocution in Eighteenth-Century Britain," *History of European Ideas* 8, no. 6 (1987): 639.

59. Harrington, "Remembering the Body: Eighteenth-Century Elocution and the Oral Tradition," *Rhetorica* 28, no. 1 (2010): 67–95. As Paul Goring states, "a public speaker is clearly no mere fount of words—an invisible medium of verbal language—but is a far more complex signifying site where verbal language and the language(s) of the body inevitably intermingle." Goring, *The Rhetoric of Sensibility in Eighteenth-Century Culture* (New York: Cambridge University Press, 2005), 34.

60. "For Sheridan, then, language was only truly effective when it emerged from a body—when verbal discourse was animated with non-

verbal, somatic signs which transformed it into a vehicle of the passions."
According to Goring, Sheridan was not prescriptive in modes of bodily expression, as were his predecessors. In effect, he recognized and enabled the
agency of the medium (108).

61. Warren Guthrie notes, "Sheridan, Enfield and [James] Burgh are
among the most popular books in the college and society libraries at Brown
from 1788 through 1800" and that from these libraries Enfield was borrowed slightly more often than Sheridan. Guthrie, "The Development of
Rhetorical Theory in America 1635–1850—V: The Elocution Movement—
England," *Speech Monographs* 18, no. 1 (1951): 21.

62. Albert Nicholson, "Percival, Thomas (1740–1804)," rev. John V. Pick-
stone, in *Oxford Dictionary of National Biography*, http://www.oxforddnb
.com/view/article/21921.

63. Thomas Percival, *A Father's Instructions to His Children: Consisting
of Tales, Fables, and Reflections; Designed to Promote the Love of Virtue, a
Taste for* . . . (London: J. Johnson, 1776), 42. In editions from 1779 on, the
poem continues to appear; however, the title of the poem is dropped, but
the section title, "Compassion to the Poor," is maintained. This leads to the
poem, largely outside of the metropoles, circulating with "Compassion" or
"Compassion to the Poor" as its title.

64. The preface to the 1776 London edition of *A Father's Instructions* is
signed only "The Author."

65. Harrington has pointed to the project of oratory, as shaped by Sheridan and drawing from Shaftesbury (though inspired by Classical models),
being bound to the cultivation of the ethical subject (78–83). The orienta-
tion toward training the body as a starting point for training the mind is,
however, an inversion of the formulation offered by Percival. Harrington,
"Remembering the Body," 94.

66. There are, of course, exceptions. *The Pleasing Instructor* (1795) offers
no attribution for the poem while attributing other anonymous texts to
"Anonymous." Similarly, *A Collection of English Prose* (1781), *Poems on Various Subjects* (1785), and *The Companion* (1790) offer no attribution.

67. Palpable mediation builds on Bolter's and Grusin's notion of
"hypermediacy." It invokes the visceral nature of the embodied medium.
As we will see in the following chapter, this tracks very closely onto the
conditions of theatrical representation. Bolter and Grusin, *Remediation*.

68. There are at least two letters to *Gentleman's Magazine* in the period
between 1785 and 1795 that attribute "The Beggar's Petition" to authors
other than Thomas Moss.

69. *The British Poetical Miscellany* (Huddersfield, U.K.: Sikes, [1799]), 5–7.

70. Cf. Jeffrey Masten, "Beaumont and/or Fletcher: Collaboration and
the Interpretation of Renaissance Drama," in *The Construction of Authorship: Textual Appropriation in Law and Literature*, ed. Martha Woodmansee
and Peter Jaszi (Durham, N.C.: Duke University Press, 1994), 362.

2. "Acting Plays" and "Reading Plays"

1. William J. Burling's *A Checklist of New Plays and Entertainments on the London Stage, 1700–1737* (Rutherford, N.J.: Farleigh Dickinson University Press, 1993) shows that of the thirty new plays and entertainments presented that season, twenty were anonymous, and they remain so.

2. *The Case of Authors by Profession or Trade, Stated. With Regard to Booksellers, the Stage, and the Public. No Matter by Whom* (London: printed for R. Griffiths, 1758), 45.

3. Samuel Johnson, *The Plays of William Shakespeare* (London: Tonson, 1765).

4. I suggest that some of Langbaine's schemas were drawn from earlier Latinate dictionaries of anonyma, pseudonyma, and plagiaries.

5. Jacob, prior to publishing his *Historical Account*, in fact published a dramatic catalog that drew on Langbaine's cataloging method. Thus the cataloging of poetry in *An Historical Account* is indebted to a mode cataloging drama rather intrinsically linked to poets and poetry.

6. Robert D. Hume, "Before the Bard: 'Shakespeare' in Early Eighteenth-Century London," *ELH* 64, no. 1 (1997): 46–47.

7. Paulina Kewes, *Authorship and Appropriation: Writing for the Stage in England, 1660–1710* (Oxford: Clarendon Press, 1998), 30.

8. Allardyce Nicoll, *A History of English Drama, 1700–1750* (Cambridge: Cambridge University Press, 1952–59), 39.

9. The Mears catalogs, for example, maintained the title, then author, format throughout the 1720s and eventually dropped the authors' names entirely.

10. Intermediation "describe[s] the complex relations that media share in determinate historical conjunctures." Ted Striphas proposes that (1) "media shouldn't be isolated analytically from one another" and (2) "the relationships among media are socially produced and historically contingent rather than given and necessary." See Striphas, *The Late Age of Print: Everyday Book Culture from Consumerism to Control* (New York: Columbia University Press, 2011), 15–16. See also Charles R. Acland, *Screen Traffic: Movies, Multiplexes, and Global Culture* (Durham, N.C.: Duke University Press, 2003), x. For recent work on intermediation and eighteenth-century drama, see the special issue of *Eighteenth-Century Fiction* 27, no. 3/4 (2015), on "Georgian Theatre in an Information Age," particularly Joseph Roach's afterword "What Now?"

11. Edward Phillips, *Theatrum Poetarum, or a Compleat Collection of the Poets* (London: printed for Charles Smith, 1675), 4–5.

12. This catalog is appended to Philip Massinger, *The Excellent Comedy Called, The Old Law; or, A New Way to Please You by Phil. Massinger, Tho. Middleton, William Rowley . . . ; Together with an Exact and Perfect Catalogue of All the Playes, with the Authors Names, and What Are Comedies, Tragedies, Histories, Pastoralls, Masks, Interludes, More Exactly Printed Than Ever Before*, ed. William Rowley (London: printed for Edward Archer, 1656).

13. Hume argues that "after 1680 an interested party could buy one of Langbaine's catalogues, but such people were probably a small percentage of the London audience: none of Langbaine's books appears to have been a bestseller." Hume, "Before the Bard," 44.

14. Gerard Langbaine, *A New Catalogue of English Plays* (London: printed for Nicholas Cox, 1688), np.

15. Paulina Kewes, "Gerard Langbaine's 'View of Plagiaries': The Rhetoric of Dramatic Appropriation in the Restoration," *Review of English Studies* 48, no. 189 (1997): 6–7.

16. See Louis B. Wright, "The Reading of Plays during the Puritan Revolution," *Huntington Library Bulletin* 6 (1934): 73–108.

17. *Theatrical Remembrancer* is quickly reprinted in 1788 as *Egerton's Theatrical Remembrancer*. Thomas Egerton and John Egerton, *The Theatrical Remembrancer: Containing a Complete List of All the Dramatic Performances in the English Language; Their Several Editions, Dates, and Sizes, and the Theatres Where They Were Originally Performed: Together with an Account of Those Which Have Been Acted and Are Unpublished, and A Catalogue of Such Latin Plays as Have Been Written by English Authors, from the Earliest Production of the English Drama to the End of the Year MDCCLXXXVII: To Which Are Added Notitia Dramatica, Being a Chronological Account of Events Relating to the English Stage* (London: printed for T. and J. Egerton, 1788).

18. Egerton and Egerton , iii–iv.

19. See, e.g., Joseph Roach, *It* (Ann Arbor: University of Michigan Press, 2007); Felicity Nussbaum, *Rival Queens: Actresses, Performance, and the Eighteenth-Century British Theater* (Philadelphia: University of Pennsylvania Press, 2011); Julia H. Fawcett, "The Overexpressive Celebrity and the Deformed King: Recasting the Spectacle as Subject in Colley Cibber's *Richard III*," *PMLA* 126, no. 4 (2011): 950–65; Stuart Sherman, "Garrick among Media: The 'Now Performer' Navigates the News," *PMLA* 126, no. 4 (2011): 966–82.

20. See Aparna Gollapudi, "Selling Celebrity: Actors' Portraits in Bell's Shakespeare and Bell's British Theatre," *Eighteenth-Century Life* 36, no. 1 (2012): 54–81.

21. See Vincent J. Liesenfeld, *The Stage and the Licensing Act, 1729–1739* (New York: Garland, 1981), and Liesenfeld, *The Licensing Act of 1737* (Madison: University of Wisconsin Press, 1984).

22. See David A. Brewer, "The Tactility of Authorial Names," *The Eighteenth Century: Theory and Interpretation* 54, no. 2 (2013): 195–213.

23. *The London Stage, 1660–1800: A Calendar of Plays, Entertainments and Afterpieces, Together with Casts, Box-Receipts and Contemporary Comment* (Carbondale: Southern Illinois University Press, 1960).

24. Burling, *Checklist*, 131.

25. The ESTC has, however, added a note that this attribution is likely dubious. Bullock died in 1722, seven years prior to the performance and publication of *Love and Revenge*. The attribution appears to be based on a 1781 London edition of the play that includes Bullock's name on the title page.

26. John Dryden, *The Letters of John Dryden*, ed. Charles E. Ward (Durham, N.C.: Duke University Press, 1942), no. 59, 112–13.

27. Robert Hume has shown that "as of 1710 only about one play in twelve was advertised with its author's name attached." Hume, "Before the Bard," 55.

28. I am indebted to Mattie Burkert for her assistance with this analysis. See Vareschi and Burkert, "Archives, Numbers, Meaning: The Eighteenth-Century Playbill at Scale," *Theatre Journal* 68, no. 4 (2016): 607–8.

29. Shirley Strum Kenny, "The Publication of Plays," in *The London Theatre World, 1660–1800*, ed. Robert D. Hume (Carbondale: Southern Illinois University Press, 1980), 314.

30. Kenny, "Publication of Plays," 313.

31. See Nicoll's discussion of the "Hand-list of Plays, 1700–1750," in *History of English Drama*, 2:293.

32. John O'Brien, *Harlequin Britain: Pantomime and Entertainment* (Baltimore: The Johns Hopkins University Press, 2004), xvii–xviii.

33. Darryl Domingo has written brilliantly about the gestural *elocutio* of pantomime in the second chapter of his *The Rhetoric of Diversion in English Literature and Culture, 1690–1760* (Cambridge: Cambridge University Press, 2016), 88–92.

34. Scriblerus Secundus, *The Author's Farce; and the Pleasures of the Town as Acted at the Theatre in the Hay-Market* (London: J. Roberts, 1730). All references are to this edition.

35. Kenny, "Publication of Plays," 314.

36. J. Paul Hunter, *Occasional Form: Henry Fielding and the Chains of Circumstance* (Baltimore: The Johns Hopkins University Press, 1975), 72.

37. Albert Rivero, "Fielding's Artistic Accommodations in *The Author's Farce* (1730)," *Restoration and 18th Century Theatre Research* 1, no. 2 (1986): 22.

38. Anthony Hassall, "The Authorial Dimension in the Plays of Henry Fielding," *Komos* 1 (1967): 4.

39. C. J. Rawson, "Some Considerations on Authorial Intrusion in Fielding's Novels and Plays," *Durham University Journal* 33 (1971): 32–44.

40. Frances Kavenik, *British Drama, 1660–1779: A Critical History* (New York: Twayne, 1995), 136.

41. J. Raithby, ed., *Statutes at Large* (London: Eyre and Strahan, 1811), 5:266–68.

42. Richard Cross, John Brownsmith, and William Hopkins, *Diaries of Drury Lane Theater Performances Kept by Richard Cross and William Hopkins, 1747* (Folger W.a.104): 1–13.

43. Christopher Mosier Rich, "An Account of Plays Acted at Lincoln's Inn Fields and at Drury Lane Theatres," n.d. (Folger W.a.32).

44. It is of course notable that Lavinia Fenton, Polly, was the lover of Bolton.

45. Heather McPherson, "Theatrical Riots and Cultural Politics in Eighteenth-Century London," *The Eighteenth Century* 43, no. 3 (2002): 236–52.

46. Michael Gavin, "James Boswell and the Uses of Criticism," *Studies in English Literature 1500–1900* 50, no. 3 (2010): 665–81.

47. *Case.* All references are to this edition.

48. Gillen D'Arcy Wood, *The Shock of the Real* (New York: Palgrave Macmillan, 2001), 38.

49. *Case*, 45.

3. Attribution, Circulation, and "Defoe"

1. Rogers writes, "Throughout the eighteenth century, only a handful of his enormous range of books enjoyed any kind of esteem. Apart from *Crusoe*, there were *The Family Instructor*; the widely popular ghost story, *The Apparition of Mrs. Veal*; in some quarters, *The Complete English Tradesman*; and the *Tour thro' Great Britain*, which reached a ninth edition in 1779." Pat Rogers, *Defoe: The Critical Heritage* (Boston: Routledge and Kegan Paul, 1972), 1.

2. Charles Lamb, *Detached Thoughts on Books and Reading* (Boston: Herbert Copeland and F. H. Day, 1894), 8.

3. In discussing Defoe's learning and its application to his writing, Scott writes, "Exclusive of politics, De Foe's studies led chiefly to those popular narratives." Sir Walter Scott, *The Miscellaneous Works of Sir Walter Scott* (Edinburgh: Robert Cadell, 1847), 1:401.

4. P. N. Furbank and W. R. Owens, *The Canonisation of Daniel Defoe* (New Haven, Conn.: Yale University Press, 1988), 29.

5. See Ashley Marshall, "Did Defoe Write *Moll Flanders* and *Roxana*?," *Philological Quarterly* 89 (2010): 209–41; P. N. Furbank and W. R. Owens, "On the Attribution of Novels to Daniel Defoe," *Philological Quarterly* 89 (2010): 243–53; and Robert J. Griffin, "Did Defoe Write *Roxana*? Does It Matter?," *Philological Quarterly* 89 (2010): 255–62.

6. Love writes, for example, "To identify authorship as a form of human work is to validate individual agency" and "attribution studies demands that we attend to the notion of individual agency in a way that cannot be fully satisfied by structuralist and poststructuralist epistemologies because it raises questions which they have no capacity to address." Love, *Attributing Authorship*, 32, 7.

7. J. R. Moore, introduction to *An Essay on the Regulation of the Press* (Oxford: Basil Blackwell, 1948), xi–xii.

8. Furbank and Owens, *Canonisation*, 29.

9. See, e.g., Peter Jaszi, "Toward a Theory of Copyright: The Metamorphoses of 'Authorship,'" *Duke Law Journal* 2 (1991): 455–502, and Mark Rose, *Authors and Owners: The Invention of Copyright* (Cambridge, Mass.: Harvard University Press, 1993).

10. Jody Greene, *The Trouble with Ownership* (Philadelphia: University of Pennsylvania Press, 2005), 124–25.

11. See the exchanges between Furbank and Owens and Maximillian Novak: Furbank and Owens, "*A Vindication of the Press* (1718): Not

by Defoe," *Papers of the Bibliographical Society of America* 78, no. 3 (1984): 355–60; Novak, "A Vindication of the Press and the Defoe Canon," *Studies in English Literature, 1500–1900* 27, no. 3 (1987): 399–411; and Furbank and Owens, "The Defoe Canon Again," *Papers of the Bibliographical Society of America* 82, no. 1 (1988): 95–98. Additionally, Laura A. Curtis, "The Attribution of *A Vindication of the Press* to Daniel Defoe," *Studies in Eighteenth-Century Culture* 18 (1988): 433–44. Stephen Bernard has argued that Giles Jacobs may actually be the author of this pamphlet. See Bernard, "After Defoe, before the *Dunciad*: Giles Jacobs and 'A Vindication of the Press,'" *Review of English Studies* 59 (2008): 487–507.

12. Otho Clinton Williams, introduction to *A Vindication of the Press* (Los Angeles: University of California Press, 1951), i.

13. Paula Backscheider echoes the first strain in Williams's claim about Defoe as individual author: "*A Vindication of the Press* (1718) give[s] the reader important insights into how Defoe saw his writing, how the publishing world worked, and how he functioned in it" (64). Such a reading contributes to Backscheider's larger discussion of Defoe's pamphlet writing as a kind of juvenilia. She writes, for example, "They are . . . important apprentice pieces for Defoe's novels, and familiarity with them allows us to see the developing artist and the full range of his technical craftsmanship" (46). Backscheider, *Daniel Defoe: Ambition and Innovation* (Lexington: University Press of Kentucky, 1986).

14. Foster, "Commentary," 376.

15. Moore, Introduction, viii.

16. Among the many examples, see Ian Watt, *The Rise of the Novel: Studies in Defoe, Richardson, and Fielding* (Berkeley: University of California Press, 1957), and Michael McKeon, *The Origins of the English Novel, 1600–1740* (Baltimore: The Johns Hopkins University Press, 1987). For the "invention" story, see, e.g., Homer Brown, "The Institution of the English Novel: Defoe's Contribution," *Novel* 29 (1996): 299–331, and Richard C. Taylor, "James Harrison, the Novelist's Magazine, and the Early Canonizing of the English Novel," *Studies in English Literature, 1500–1900* 33, no. 3 (1993): 629–43.

17. George Chalmers writes, "Robinson Crusoe had scarcely drawn his canoe ashore, when he was attacked by his old enemies, *the savages*. He was assailed first by *The Life and Strange Adventures of Mr. D—De F—, of London, Hosier, who has lived above Fifty Years by himself in the Kingdoms of North and South Britain*." Charles Gildon's anonymous print attack on Defoe and *Robinson Crusoe* serves as external evidence of Defoe's authorship and the immediate popular acceptance of that attribution. Chalmers, *The Life of Daniel De Foe* (London: John Stockdale, 1790), 53.

18. Furbank and Owens have detailed the logic and role of internal evidence (relating to style, word choice, ideas, etc.) and external evidence (relating to attributions made by contemporaries, or near-contemporaries, of the author) in the attribution of works to Defoe in *Canonisation*, 32–34. See also Love, *Attributing Authorship*.

19. Archer Taylor and Frederic Mosher have suggested a clear progres-

sion from the study of pseudoepigrapha in the sixteenth and seventeenth centuries to the secular study of anonyms and pseudonyms in *The Bibliographical History of Anonyma and Pseudonyma*, 149. Martin Muslow has traced this link more fully in the work of Vincent Placcius. See Muslow, "Practices of Unmasking: Polyhistors, Correspondence, and the Birth of Dictionaries of Pseudonymity in Seventeenth-Century Germany," *Journal of the History of Ideas* 67 (2006): 219–50.

20. P. N. Furbank and W. R. Owens, *Defoe De-attributions: A Critique of J. R. Moore's Checklist* (Rio Grande, Ohio: Hambledon Press, 1994).

21. P. N. Furbank and W. R. Owens, "Defoe and Francis Noble," *Eighteenth-Century Fiction* 4 (1992): 301.

22. James Raven, "The Noble Brothers and Popular Publishing, 1737–89," *Library* 12 (1990): 314–15.

23. While the Nobles were publishers, booksellers, and library proprietors, it must be noted that most of their published novels went to supply other circulating libraries and that the circulating libraries were the most profitable aspect of the Nobles' business. Raven, 314. Furthermore, owing to the prohibitively high cost of novels throughout the period, circulating libraries were the central source of new novels for most readers. See William St. Clair, *The Reading Nation in the Romantic Period* (New York: Cambridge University Press, 2004), 237–44.

24. I am drawing on Michael McKeon's articulation of the relationship between the virtual and the actual in the domain of the public sphere: "The emergent public sphere was understood by contemporaries as a virtual collectivity, a metaphorical place of assembly constituted principally by publication and its readership. But it was also associated (unlike 'the public domain') with actual spaces" (75). For more on the relationship between the virtual and the concrete particularities of the actual, see McKeon, *The Secret History of Domesticity* (Baltimore: The Johns Hopkins University Press, 2005), 108–9.

25. A March 7–10, 1778, Noble advertisement in *St. James's Chronicle* lists "The Fortunate Mistress, by Daniel DeFoe" and "Moll Flanders, by Daniel DeFoe" for sale at both John and Francis Noble's establishments.

26. Here I am working from James Raven's excellent list of the Nobles' publications, which is found in "Noble Brothers and Popular Publishing," 320–21.

27. See Spiro Peterson, "Defoe's *Roxana* and Its Eighteenth-Century Sequels: A Critical and Bibliographical Study" (PhD diss., Harvard University, 1953).

28. Introduction to *Roxana*, by Daniel Defoe (New York: Oxford University Press, 1998), vii–xxvii.

29. Robert J. Griffin, "The Text in Motion: Eighteenth-Century Roxanas," *ELH* 72 (2005): 387–406.

30. These revisions, Furbank and Owens have suggested, "fit the work for a polite circulating-library readership of the 1770s." Furbank and Owens, "Defoe and Francis Noble," 304.

31. The ambiguity in the phrase "Where may be had, by the same Author, Roxana; or, The Fortunate Mistress" invites speculation that the unknown hand responsible for the reworking of *Roxana* was also responsible for the reworking of *Moll Flanders*.

32. Edward Jacobs, "Anonymous Signatures: Circulating Libraries, Conventionality, and the Production of Gothic Romances," *ELH* 62 (1995): 603–29, and Jacobs, "Eighteenth-Century Circulating Libraries and Cultural Book History," *Book History* 6 (2003): 1–22.

33. *A New Catalogue of the Large and Valuable Collection of Books (Both English and French) in John Noble's Circulating Library. Consisting of Several Thousand Volumes . . . Which Are Lent to Read* ([London]: J. Noble, [1761]), 41.

34. *T. Lowndes's Catalogue for 1778. Consisting of Books Collected in Different Parts of England . . . and Now Selling . . . by T. Lowndes, Bookseller* ([London]: Thomas Lowndes, [1778]), 102–4.

35. I have surveyed thirty booksellers, library, and estate catalogs from 1777 to 1800 and found no consistent pattern of attribution. There seem to be equal numbers of 1775 *Roxana* and 1776 *Moll Flanders* editions that bear no attribution as those that do.

36. *Daniel De Foe's Voyage Round the World, by a Course Never Sailed Before. To Which Is Prefixed the Life of the Author, by William Shiells, Esq.*, vol. 3 (London: F. Noble, 1787).

37. Furbank and Owens, "Defoe and Francis Noble," 309.

38. I draw from Barthes the notion of the text as a "methodological field" rather than a concrete entity that "can be held in the hand." Where I depart from Barthes is in my insistence that the work, too, must be separated from the concrete entity of the book. The work, I argue, is as much a virtual entity as the text and is itself contingent on factors like authorial attribution to demarcate itself from the text. See Roland Barthes, "From Work to Text," in *Image, Music, Text*, ed. and trans. Stephen Heath (New York: Hill and Wang, 1977), 157.

39. Here I understand the commodity to function in the Marxist sense that once turned into a commodity, the object is valued not for its material and qualitative use value but for the abstract quantity of exchange value it is assigned in circulating on the market. Karl Marx, "Capital," in *The Marx-Engels Reader*, ed. Robert C. Tucker, 215–24 (New York: W. W. Norton, 1972).

40. It is the case that in holiday towns, the circulating library tended to be a social center, whereas in London, the circulating library tended to be a literary center. See K. A. Manley, "Booksellers, Peruke-Makers, and Rabbit-Merchants: The Growth of Circulating Libraries in the Eighteenth Century," in *Libraries and the Book Trade*, ed. Robin Myers (New Castle, Del.: Oak Knoll, 2000), 30.

41. Raven writes that such sociability at libraries, particularly in spa towns, was "fed by texts and London connection, but . . . supported and encouraged by the institution of the library itself" (260). James Raven, "Libraries for Sociability: The Advance of the Subscription Library," in *The*

Cambridge History of Libraries in Britain and Ireland, ed. Giles Mandelbrote and K. A. Manley (New York: Cambridge University Press, 2006), 2:260.

42. She writes, "Whereas subscription libraries were in a sense owned by the subscribers who appointed officials to run the library, circulating libraries were commercial enterprises run for profit in a world of mobile readers with no necessary connection to one another or to the proprietors of the library." Barbara M. Benedict, "Jane Austen and the Culture of Circulating Libraries: The Construction of Female Literacy," in *Revising Women: Eighteenth-Century "Women's Fiction" and Social Engagement,* ed. Paula R. Backscheider (Baltimore: The Johns Hopkins University Press, 2000), 164.

43. Raven, "Libraries for Sociability," 258.

44. "The availability of novels and popular anthologies in the circulating libraries was influential in stimulating the growth of a new popular culture. For the first time, the subscribers to the libraries—the well-to-do, the middle-class professionals, working-men, merchants, shopkeepers, domestic servants, and their families, shared a common literary interest and began to develop a similar set of social values. This common culture and lessening of the literary class lines have been considered by some scholars to have had a significant effect on the social and political unity of the country." Charlotte Stewart-Murphy, *A History of British Circulating Libraries* (Newtown: Bird and Bull Press, 1992), 49.

45. Paul Kaufman has further suggested that the relationship between the social imaginary and the circulating library was forged from the very outset with the emergence of circulating library practices in the ur-locales of sociability—the London coffeehouses and newsrooms. Kaufman writes that "these two kinds of center stimulated the development of booksellers' rental facilities we can hardly doubt." Kaufman, *The Community Library: A Chapter in English Social History* (Philadelphia: American Philosophical Society, 1967), 9.

46. Furbank and Owens, "Defoe and Francis Noble," 304.

47. Jan Fergus, *Provincial Readers in Eighteenth-Century England* (New York: Oxford University Press, 2006), 80.

48. Hilda M. Hamlyn has suggested that "books, in the eighteenth century, were often published 'sewn' or 'half-bound.' Their life, in circulation, cannot have been very long. . . . With novels, popular for a short time only, a more expensive and durable binding was unnecessary" (217). Hamlyn, "Eighteenth-Century Circulating Libraries," *Library,* 5th series 1 (1947): 197–222. Edward Jacobs has since contested the commonplace assumption that circulating library books were cheaply bound and thus their lives were short. See Jacobs, "Eighteenth-Century British Circulating Libraries and Cultural Book History," *Book History* 6 (2003): 1–22.

49. There are approximately nineteen extant copies of the 1775 *New Roxana* and ten extant copies of the 1776 *The History of Laetitia Atkins Vulgarly Called Moll Flanders* (ESTC). This speaks broadly to the popularity and wide circulation of the texts and the weight given to their attribution

to Defoe. However, these texts are not the versions edited and available in modern editions. Even in the case of the preservation of the physical text because of the name attached, they exist only as material variants or continuations of essential and originary works—*Roxana* and *Moll Flanders*.

50. Lamb, *Detached Thoughts*, 7–8.

51. Furbank and Owens write, "As the reviewers never wearied of pointing out, there was a quintessentially 'Noble' style of novel, manufactured according to a strict formula; and this, presumably, must have implied a team of hired authors to supply them." Furbank and Owens, "Defoe and Francis Noble," 308.

52. *London Magazine*, December 1772, 543.

53. *An Appeal to the Public (by F. and J. Noble, Booksellers) from the Aspersions Cast on Them by the Anonymous Editor of the "London Magazine"* ([London]: F. and J. Noble, 1772), 2.

54. From the imprint of *The Way to Please Him; or The History of Lady Sedley: By the Author of the Way to Lose Him* ([London]: F. and J. Noble, 1773).

55. See K. A. Manley, "London Circulating Library Catalogues of the 1740s," *Library History* 8 (1989): 75.

56. James Raven, "From Promotion to Proscription: Arrangements for Reading and Eighteenth-Century Libraries," in *The Practice and Representation of Reading*, ed. James Raven, Helen Small, and Naomi Taylor (Cambridge: Cambridge University Press, 1996), 182.

57. More recently, Manley has argued "that many pictorial representations [of library interiors] are idealized rather than naturalistic and may not tell the truth. They represent another form of advertising, and advertisements have to be taken with a pinch of salt. They convey the message of 'books' and 'readers,' but the two together do not necessarily mean that the two literally came together in a circulating library." Manley, "Booksellers, Peruke-Makers, and Rabbit-Merchants," 42.

58. Unprinted stockbooks seem to follow this convention of organization. For example, an unknown London bookseller's stockbook listing titles through 1730 lists the stock by size and then alphabetically by title so that "Gulliver's Travels 3 vols. 80 1726 13/6" is listed under "Books in 80 G." "Booksellers Stockbook to 1730," Folger MSADD 923.

59. I am indebted to Michael McKeon for his insightful discussion of my readings of these images.

60. Charles Lamb and Mary Lamb, *The Works of Charles and Mary Lamb*, ed. E. V. Lucas (London: Methuen, 1906), 7:600.

4. Motive, Intention, Anonymity

1. For a full account of the issues arising in the attribution practices in the *Dictionary*, see Leah Orr, "The History, Uses, and Dangers of Halkett and Laing," *Papers of the Bibliographic Society of America* 107, no. 2 (2013): 193–240.

2. Samuel Halkett and John Laing, *Dictionary of Anonymous and Pseudonymous English Literature* (London: Oliver and Boyd, 1926), xi.

3. Halkett and Laing, xii.

4. Halkett and Laing, xii.

5. Halkett and Laing, xii.

6. See Catherine Gallagher, *Nobody's Story: The Vanishing Acts of Women Writers in the Marketplace* (Berkeley: University of California Press, 1994). For more on anonymity and signing, see Samuel Choi, "Signing Evelina: Female Self-Inscription in the Discourse of Letters," *Studies in the Novel* 31, no. 3 (1999): 259–78.

7. For this line of criticism, see also Gina Campbell, "How to Read Like a Gentleman: Burney's Instructions to Her Critics in *Evelina*," *ELH* 57, no. 3 (1990): 557–84. For a thoughtful account of anonymity and its relation to gender and the novel's reception, see Helen Thompson, "Evelina's Two Publics," *The Eighteenth Century: Theory and Interpretation* 39, no. 2 (1998): 147–67.

8. Those fourteen new anonymous novels were *The Example: or, The History of Lucy Cleveland* by a Young Lady; *Greenwood Farm*, written by a warrant officer belonging to the navy; *The History of Eliza Warwick*; *The Offspring of Fancy, A Novel* by a Lady; *The Sentimental Connoisseur: or, Pleasing and Entertaining Novelist*; *Sketches from Nature: or, The History of Henry and Emma, and of Fanny and Lucy Stanley*; *The Travels of Hildebrand Bowman, Esquire . . .* ; *A Trip to Melasge: or, Concise Instructions to a Young Gentleman . . .* ; *The Unfortunate Union: or, The Test of Virtue*; *Evelina: or, A Young Lady's Entrance into the World*; *Friendship in a Nunnery: or, The American Fugitive*; *Munster Village: A Novel*; *Memoirs of the Countess D'Anois: Written by Herself before Her Retirement*; and *Learning at a Loss; or, The Amours of Mr. Pedant and Miss Hartley: A Novel*. Listed in Peter Garside, James Raven, and Rainer Shöwerling, *The English Novel* (New York: Oxford University Press, 2000).

9. David Brewer has argued convincingly for distinguishing *Evelina* from the other anonymous novels published in 1778 based on its "footprint" and "resonance" over time. Brewer, "Counting, Resonance, and Form: A Speculative Manifesto (with Notes)," *Eighteenth-Century Fiction* 24, no. 2 (2012): 163, 166. However, my argument is less interested in the novel's impact over time, which is indisputable, than with its similarity to other novels published simultaneously and how it might have come to have such resonance.

10. In his analysis of the holdings of Samuel Clay's circulating library, Edward Jacobs finds that "circulating-library publishers were 5.7 times more likely to publish works by anonymous authors, 1.8 times more likely to publish works by female authors, and .7 times less likely to publish works by men." While Jacobs is tentative about the conclusions that may be extrapolated about gender and authorship from Clay's holdings, he is confident to assert that "proportionally, circulating-library publishers dominated the production of anonymous fiction." Jacobs, "Anonymous

Signatures: Circulating Libraries, Conventionality, and the Production of Gothic Romances," *ELH* 62, no. 3 (1995): 607. What Jacobs, along with Raven, suggests is that the new novel of the late eighteenth century was by default anonymous and that circulating libraries "dominated" the production of these anonymous novels.

11. Frances Burney, *Evelina*, ed. Edward A. Bloom (New York: Oxford University Press, 1968), 7. Hereafter cited parenthetically by page number.

12. See Margaret Anne Doody, "Beyond Evelina: The Individual Novel and the Community of Literature," *Eighteenth-Century Fiction* 3, no. 4 (1991): 364.

13. The first edition in 1778 signs the letter "*** ****," and it is unclear if the space between the third and fourth asterisk is intended or an artifact of the typesetting.

14. Cf. St. Clair, *Reading Nation*, 175, and McKeon, *Origins of the English Novel, 1600–1740* (Baltimore: The Johns Hopkins University Press, 1987), 120–23, respectively.

15. Gallagher, of course, is careful to attend to this context and its implications for Burney and the novel (see 217–23).

16. Doody, "Beyond Evelina," 364.

17. Burney, *The Early Journals and Letters of Fanny Burney: The Streatham Years, Part 1, 1778–1779* (Buffalo, N.Y.: McGill-Queen's University Press, 1994), 32.

18. Betty A. Schellenberg, *The Professionalization of Women Writers in Eighteenth-Century Britain* (New York: Cambridge University Press, 2005), 148.

19. Burney, *Early Journals and Letters of Fanny Burney*, 180–81.

20. Burney, *Diary and Letters of Madame d'Arblay* (Philadelphia: Carey and Hart, 1842), 9.

21. Schellenberg, *Professionalization*, 148.

22. George Justice, "Burney and the Literary Marketplace," in *The Cambridge Companion to Frances Burney*, ed. Peter Sabor (New York: Cambridge University Press, 2007), 150.

23. Justice, 149.

24. Gallagher, *Nobody's Story*, 223.

25. I follow Gallagher's notion that women are "representatives of the condition of the author in the eighteenth century" rather than belonging to a separate tradition; as such, we may imagine some particularly gendered motivations for anonymous authorship on the part of the biographical person, but the effect or function of anonymity within the text in the literary marketplace itself may not be all that different for male and female authors (xv).

26. Such an articulation of persona as a second self calls to mind Wayne Booth's notion of the "implied author" and Alexander Nehamas's "postulated author." Booth, *The Rhetoric of Fiction* (Chicago: University of Chicago Press, 1961), 71–76; Nehamas, "The Postulated Author: Critical Monism as a Regulative Ideal," *Critical Inquiry* 8, no. 1 (1981): 145. Both Booth and Nehamas construct the author as part of the process of textual interpreta-

tion, but neither of them looks to understand how authorship, anonymity, genre, medium, and so forth, may work in a mutually dependent fashion as equally products of agential action to mediate between text and world. Persona, in my account, is not bounded by a single text. To that end, it may more closely align with Susan Lanser's account in "(Im)plying the Author," where she argues that the implied author is produced through reader practices and contests the singularity of the implied author as operating in a single text. Her choice of genre fiction in this essay, however, may actually demonstrate more about the agency of genre than that implied to authorial personae. See Lanser, "(Im)plying the Author," *Narrative* 9, no. 2 (2001): 153–60. In my account, the editorial persona of *Evelina* gains traction only because it is connected to both *Evelina* as a discrete novel and the broader literary world in which it operates, both connected to and beyond the particularities of genre.

27. Garside continues, "Of the 2,256 titles in this volume [covering 1800–1829], almost a half were anonymous when first published, with only some 970 carrying the author's name on the title-page (or a description full enough to point to the identity of the true author), and a further 190 titles being issued pseudonymously." Garside et al., *English Novel*, 2:66. St. Clair, too, notes, "Most novels of the period were still published, as had been a custom in the eighteenth century, without the author even being named." St. Clair, *Reading Nation*, 173.

28. Feldman writes, "Walter Scott, too, applied a double standard. . . . He had no such scruples about his earlier books of poetry, which had all been published under his own name. Poetry was a legitimate and highly respected literary form, while the novel, a more recent genre, was not" (283). Paula Feldman, "Women Poets and Anonymity in the Romantic Era," *New Literary History* 33, no. 2 (2002): 279–89.

29. Mullan notes, for example, "Literary history exhibits few more obstinate practitioners of anonymity than the author of the so-called 'Waverley novels.'" John Mullan, *Anonymity: A Secret History of English Literature* (Princeton, N.J.: Princeton University Press, 2008), 20.

30. Scott, *Chronicles of the Canongate* (Edinburgh: printed for Cadell and Co., 1827), 1:iv.

31. Seamus Cooney, "Scott's Anonymity—Its Motives and Consequences," *Studies in Scottish Literature* 10, no. 4 (1973): 207–19; Thomas R. Dale, "One Word More on Scott's Anonymity," *Studies in Scottish Literature* 14, no. 1 (1979): 143.

32. Cooney, "Scott's Anonymity," 215.

33. Lamont, "Walter Scott: Anonymity and the Unmasking of Harlequin," in *Authorship, Commerce, and the Public*, ed. E. J. Clery, Caroline Franklin, and Peter Garside (New York: Palgrave Macmillan, 2002), 54. Jane Austen, for example, in a letter to Anna Austen in September 1814, expresses her knowledge of Scott's authorship.

34. Sir Walter Scott, *Waverley*, ed. Peter Garside (1814; repr., Edinburgh: Edinburgh University Press, 2008), 6. Hereinafter cited parenthetically.

35. Georg Lukács, *The Historical Novel*, trans. Hannah Mitchell and Stanley Mitchell (Lincoln: University of Nebraska Press, 1983), 58; James Chandler, *England in 1819: The Politics of Literary Culture and the Case of Romantic Historicism* (Chicago: University of Chicago Press, 1999), 213.

36. Cooney, "Scott's Anonymity," 217.

37. Walter Scott, "Letter of 28 July 1814," in *The Letters of Sir Walter Scott*, ed. H. J. C. Grierson (London: Constable, 1932–37), 3:479–81.

38. Cooney, "Scott's Anonymity," 209.

39. "*Waverley*, supposed by W. Scott," *The British Critic* 2 (1814): 189.

40. Sir Walter Scott, *Introductions and Notes from "The Magnum Opus*," ed. J. H. Alexander (Edinburgh: Edinburgh University Press, 2012), 62.

41. Sir Walter Scott, *Chronicles of the Canongate* (Edinburgh: printed for Cadell, 1827), 1:xxii.

42. Anscombe, *Intention*, 21.

43. Sir Walter Scott, *The Prefaces to the Waverley Novels*, ed. Mark A. Weinstein (Lincoln: University of Nebraska Press, 1978), 93.

44. Frank Jordan, "Scott, Chatterton, Byron, and the Wearing of Masks," in *Scott and His Influence: The Papers of the Aberdeen Scott Conference*, ed. J. H. Alexander and David Hewitt (Aberdeen: Association for Scottish Literary Studies, 1983), 283.

45. Staten, "Art as *Techne*," 422.

Epilogue

1. Julie Zhuo, "Where Anonymity Breeds Contempt," *New York Times*, November 29, 2010, http://www.nytimes.com/2010/11/30/opinion/30zhuo .html.

2. Anne Ferry, *By Design: Intention in Poetry* (Stanford, Calif.: Stanford University Press, 2008), 203; Rita Raley, "Dataveillance and Countervailance," in *Raw Data Is an Oxymoron*, ed. Lisa Gitelman and Virginia Jackson, 121–46 (Cambridge, Mass.: MIT Press, 2013); John Naughton, "Attempts to Stay Anonymous on the Web Will Only Put the NSA on Your Trail, " *Guardian*, May 10, 2014, http://www.theguardian.com/world/2014/ may/11/anonymous-web-nsa-trail-janet-vertesi.

3. Paula McDowell, "Defoe's Essay upon Literature and Eighteenth-Century Histories of Mediation," *PMLA* 130, no. 3 (2015): 573.

4. Brenda R. Silver, "'Anon' and 'The Reader': Virginia Woolf's Last Essays," *Twentieth Century Literature* 25, no. 3/4 (1979): 356–441.

5. Lucien Febvre and Henri-Jean Martin, *The Coming of the Book*, trans. David Gerard, ed. Geoffrey Nowell-Smith (New York: Verso, 2010), 261.

Index

Page numbers in italics refer to figures

Mark Vareschi is associate professor of English at the University of Wisconsin–Madison.